Praise for
The Positive Leader

▐▐ *The Positive Leader* . . . is the perfect guide that can help unlock greatness in any leader who wishes to be a catalyst for change and transformation.

DEEPAK CHOPRA, AUTHOR, *THE SOUL OF LEADERSHIP*

▐▐ Inspired, thought-provoking and easy to apply. Based on Jan's own authentic approach, this book shows leaders how to plug into the power of positivity to bring out the very best in themselves and others. Learn valuable lessons about strengths, purpose, energy management and, of course, happiness. Classic Jan!! He is the real deal, and so is this book!

ORLANDO AYALA, CORPORATE VICE PRESIDENT, CHAIRMAN OF EMERGING MARKETS, MICROSOFT CORPORATION

▐▐ The impact of positivity and authenticity in leadership. Jan Mühlfeit has put his finger on a real game changer here.

FRANK BROWN, CHIEF OPERATION OFFICER, GENERAL ATLANTIC

▐▐ The cornerstone of world-class success and happiness is self-awareness. This book addresses the most important decisions you ever will make: to uncover who you are and offer your best to the world.

DAVID SVOBODA, ATHELETE, 2012 OLYMPIC CHAMPION IN MODERN PENTATHALON

▐▐ Jan's guide to achieving sustained success and happiness is an inspirational reminder of the true qualities of modern leadership. *The Positive Leader* is both a practical handbook and a thoughtful reflection on what it takes to helm organisations in an increasingly complex world.

JEAN-PHILIPE COURTOIS, EVP AND PRESIDENT, MICROSOFT GLOBAL SALES, MARKETING AND OPERATIONS, MICROSOFT

II Full of wisdom garnered over a long and distinguished career and building on the best positive psychology, this book shows you how to be the person who inspires others to new heights. A great guide to becoming an authentic leader and an inspiration for a happier and more meaningful life.

PROFESSOR STEPHEN JOSEPH, AUTHOR, *AUTHENTIC: HOW TO BE YOURSELF AND WHY IT MATTERS*

II This is a book that champions the value of people over profit with a wisdom that profits will be the by-product of happy and positive people.

TIM GALLWEY, AUTHOR, *THE INNER GAME OF TENNIS*

II In an era in which good leadership is scarce, this book, a product of years of experience by its author in leadership positions, is an excellent guide to young aspiring new leaders.

ANDROULLA VASSILIOU, FORMER EU COMMISSIONER FOR EDUCATION, CULTURE, MULTILINGUALISM AND YOUTH

II Leadership gets much easier when you have great talent that works well together in a strong culture. Jan provides a powerful and enlightened approach for you to achieve your potential as a leader.

JEFF RAIKES, CO-FOUNDER, RAIKES FOUNDATION, AND FORMER CEO, BILL & MELINDA GATES FOUNDATION

II A clear and compelling roadmap for energising your leadership! The book is a fantastic source of practical insights grounded in positive psychology.

PETER ZEMSKY, DEPUTY DEAN OF EXECUTIVE EDUCATION, INSEAD

II A totally new perspective on leadership. Scrap the old belief that happiness follows success. Instead, think that success follows happiness. A true paradigm shift.

PATRICIA FALCO BECCALI, FOUNDER AND CEO, PRINCIPLE AG, FORMER ANCHOR OF CNBC

II Jan Mühlfeit proposes a very human-centered and emotionally literate management approach. This book is a must read for managers navigating today's complex and fragmented environment.

JENNIFER BLANKE, CHIEF ECONOMOST, WORLD ECONOMIC FORUM

The Positive Leader

The Positive Leader

How energy and happiness
fuel top-performing teams

Jan Mühlfeit

Melina Costi

PEARSON

Harlow, England • London • New York • Boston • San Francisco • Toronto • Sydney
Auckland • Singapore • Hong Kong • Tokyo • Seoul • Taipei • New Delhi
Cape Town • São Paulo • Mexico City • Madrid • Amsterdam • Munich • Paris • Milan

EDINBURGH GATE
HARLOW CM20 2JE
UNITED KINGDOM
TEL: +44 (0)1279 623623
WEB: WWW.PEARSON.COM/UK

First edition published 2017 (print and electronic)

ISBN: 978-1-292-16615-5 (print)
          978-1-292-16616-2 (PDF)
          978-1-292-16617-9 (ePub)

British Library Cataloguing-in-Publication Data
A catalogue record for the print edition is available from the British Library

Library of Congress Cataloging-in-Publication Data
Names: Mühlfeit, Jan, author. | Costi, Melina, author.
Title: The positive leader : how energy and happiness fuel top-performing
   teams / Jan Mühlfeit, Melina Costi.
Description: 1 Edition. | New York : Pearson Education, 2017. | Includes
   index.
Identifiers: LCCN 2016033815 (print) | LCCN 2016035646 (ebook) | ISBN
   9781292166155 (pbk.) | ISBN 9781292166179
Subjects: LCSH: Leadership. | Teams in the workplace. | Attitude (Psychology)
Classification: LCC HD57.7 .M836 2017 (print) | LCC HD57.7 (ebook) | DDC
   658.4/092—dc23
LC record available at https://lccn.loc.gov/2016033815

10 9 8 7 6 5 4 3 2 1
20 19 18 17 16

Cover design by Rob Day
Cover image: Maria Toutoudaki/Getty Images

Print edition typeset in Frutiger LT Com and 9.25/14 by Aptara

Printed by Ashford Colour Press Ltd, Gosport

NOTE THAT ANY PAGE CROSS REFERENCES REFER TO THE PRINT EDITION

Contents

Acknowledgements

I'd like to acknowledge all those that have inspired and championed me on my mission to unlock human potential around the world.

I will be forever grateful to my co-author, Melina Costi, whose devoted work helped to manifest this book. Her belief in the project and her tireless commitment in researching, clarifying and editing the text have been invaluable. Mel was a fantastic co-pilot at all stages in bringing our book to life.

Special thanks to my good friends at OpenGenius, particularly Chris Griffiths (CEO) and Liz Oseland (Head of Training), who were monumental pillars of support in the early stages of writing this book. I'm deeply grateful for their sound advice and enthusiastic input. Additional thanks go to researcher Dino Costi for his superb assistance with the material.

It goes without saying that I owe a huge debt of gratitude to my wonderful wife and daughter for their unstinting patience, encouragement and understanding throughout this project, and to my loving parents who inspired me to be who I am.

I must pay tribute to all the bosses at Microsoft who granted me the freedom and autonomy to play to my strengths and set my own standards of excellence. Without their exceptional mentoring and wisdom, I dare say I wouldn't have been anywhere near as successful as I was in leading my teams towards our shared goals. Major credit goes to my ultimate role model Bill Gates for being a shining example of positive leadership in making the world a better place to live. And, of course, I'm profoundly grateful to all my colleagues and teammates (past and present) for their eager adoption of my crazy ideas during a long and enjoyable executive career.

I extend my sincerest thanks to the pioneering work being done by so many extraordinary individuals in the field of positive psychology, especially to Dr Martin Seligman, Tal Ben-Shahar, Shawn Achor and Sonja Lyubomirsky. They are true ambassadors of happiness and this book would not have been possible without their illuminating insights and empirical expertise.

Thank you to the publishing team at Pearson for the chance to share my message. Particular acknowledgements go to Eloise Cook (Senior Commissioning Editor), Melanie Carter (Senior Content Producer) and Antonia Maxwell (Copy-Editor), whose utter dedication and editorial wizardry helped to ensure the quality of this book.

My heartfelt thanks to the following individuals for their stirring endorsements: Deepak Chopra, Tim Gallwey, Peter Zemsky, Jeff Raikes, Stephen Joseph, Orlando Ayala, Androulla Vassiliou, Frank Brown, Jennifer Blanke, David Svoboda, Jean-Philippe Courtois and Patricia Falco Beccalli.

And, finally, thank you to all my friends, fellow leaders and supporters who have been following my journey with interest. I hope this book reflects your best hopes in creating a positive future for mankind, one filled with success and happiness.

Publisher's acknowledgments

We are grateful to the following for permission to reproduce copyright material:

Table on p 8 copyright © 2013 Gallup, Inc. All rights reserved. The content is used with permission; however, Gallup retains all rights of publication; figure on p 11 from Towers Perrin, Global Workforce Study 2007/8; figure on p 27 courtesy of Ready to Manage; figure on p 85 from van Gorp, T. and Adams, E., *Design for Emotion* (Morgan Kaufman, 2012); reproduced with permission of Trevor van Gorp; figure on p 126 used with permission from Bain & Company (www.bain.com). figure on p 217 from Covey, S., *The 7 Habits of Highly Effective People* (Simon & Schuster, 2004); reprinted with permission of FranklinCovey; figure on p 193 from Schwartz, T. and Porath, C., 'The power of meeting your employee's needs'; reproduced with permission of Harvard Business Publishing; logo and screenshot on p 306 reproduced courtesy of DropTask.

About the authors

Jan Mühlfeit is a global strategist, executive coach and mentor. He is the former Chairman of Microsoft Europe and a seasoned ICT industry veteran, having served 22 years at the high-tech giant. Jan specialises in leadership coaching, helping prominent individuals and organisations from business, academic, political and sports backgrounds tap into their strengths to deliver exceptional performance. He is currently an 'entrepreneur in residence' at INSEAD and a coach for Executive MBA students at Cambridge University, as well as a member of the Business Advisory Board at Imperial College London.

Jan's impassioned approach to life and his accomplishments as a leader and coach have made him a popular speaker. He is a well-regarded presenter at WEF, OECD, EC, EP, Harvard, INSEAD, Cambridge and *Economist* events. He has also been interviewed by CNN, CNBC, Bloomberg, *Financial Times*, *New York Times* and *The Wall Street Journal*, amongst others.

Born in 1962, Jan Mühlfeit grew up in Czechoslovakia. Before joining Microsoft he worked in both the public and private sectors. Jan rose up from humble circumstances to succeed in the global economy 'premier league'. Central to Jan's success has been his ability to inspire people and teams to achieve more than they imagined possible. His personal mission: 'I help individuals, organisations and countries around the world to unlock their human potential.'

Keep up with Jan at: http://janmühlfeit.com/en

Melina Costi is a professional business writer with a background in marketing management. She is co-author (with Chris Griffiths) of the Amazon bestseller *GRASP the Solution* and works closely with global training and software provider OpenGenius. Melina holds a first-class BSc (Hons) degree in Business Studies from City University, London. Besides her writing work, she provides academic support services for adult students with learning difficulties and disabilities.

Introduction:

SETTING THE SCENE FOR POSITIVE LEADERSHIP

'Average leaders are viewed as business executives, the best leaders are viewed as great human beings.'
MIKE MYATT, *FORBES* LEADERSHIP COLUMNIST AND CEO COACH

You were born an original; don't live as a copy. These days, the world is obsessed with *weaknesses*. Individuals, organisations and even countries think that fixing faults and flaws is the only way to climb 'Mount Everest' and reach the pinnacle of success. In the business arena especially, we're caught up with the idea of changing ourselves to fit the ideal profile of a first-class leader. In my view, this preoccupation with weaknesses is the biggest illusion of our time and a huge waste of the most valuable resources we have as human beings – our unique *strengths*.

The route to victory as a leader doesn't lie in correcting what's *wrong* with us, but building on what's *right*. For decades – centuries even – we've been looking at leadership the wrong way. Leadership as a subject has been broken down, packaged up and re-engineered over and over. It's been revered as an art and it's been subjected to the rigours of hard science. We have the 7 golden rules, the 21 laws and the 50 effective habits (amongst others) to tell us what leadership is about and how to make ourselves worthy of it. There are even as many as 850 definitions of the term according to US business school professors Warren Bennis and Burt Nanus![1] I won't repeat any of them here, I'll let you Google them. All these years, experts have been trying to confine leadership to one box, when in reality it comes in all flavours, shapes and sizes. Instead of striving to transform ourselves to become what society tells us we should be, we should focus on

[1] Bennis, W. and Nanus, B. (1997). *Leaders: Strategies for Taking Charge*. New York: Harper Business.

becoming *more of who we are*. For leaders and teams alike, sustained success and happiness comes from unlocking the full potential of our talents and doing what we love, not slogging away on the areas where we can, at best, only be average.

With more than 24 years in business behind me (22 of those at high-tech giant Microsoft), I've observed that happiness is often massively overlooked in the corporate world. Usually when we think of leadership, we think of performance, productivity and profits. But these are the *results* of excellent leadership, not the causes of it. Happiness is the real game changer. Success comes much more easily when we're passionately engaged and positively inspired by what we're doing and where we're going. That's the magic of *positive leadership* – it offers another, better way to reach the top of the mountain, while still enjoying the climb. Through endeavouring to become a positive leader we can create *both* happy and successful lives for ourselves and for our teams. Positivity lifts us from mediocrity to excellence by giving us vision, confidence, authenticity, energy, passion, charisma, creativity and added meaning in everything we do.

In this book, I've done my best to create a friendly and accessible model of leadership that isolates, cultivates and celebrates what's most important about being a positive leader – the *4Ps of Positive Leadership*. The tools, processes and techniques are designed to empower *any* kind of leader at *any* stage of their career, from wannabes and novices to seasoned old hands. Don't think you have to be running a FTSE 100 company to be reading this book – the same principles apply whether you're the head honcho of a huge conglomerate or a small business owner. You could be a spiritual leader, a technological leader, a sports leader, or simply looking to lead yourself to personal excellence, it makes no difference. Through the 4Ps model, you'll awaken to your greater potential as a leader by fully getting to know and be your best self while also bringing out the best in others. You'll learn the 4Ps that form the prime dimensions of positive leadership so you can rise to the challenge of leadership in any situation. And most vitally, you'll find out how to apply them to catapult you, your colleagues and your entire organisation to new heights of success and happiness. Clue: *Performance* isn't one of them!

P is NOT for 'performance'

It's an innovation-crazed, moving-at-the-speed-of-now world out there. Most leaders are just trying to do the best they can while shouldering mammoth responsibilities in an economy overwhelmed with disruptive change. There are so many urgent things to do, so many important people to meet and so many momentous decisions to make. I know what you're up against, and I know how easy it is to get caught up in securing the quick wins that build your equity as a high achiever.

Looking back at the early years of my career at Microsoft, I had a serious addiction to Performance with a capital 'P'. I had been fortunate to learn from some of the greatest business minds and thinkers across the globe, including Mike Kami (strategy), Philip Kotler (marketing), Edward de Bono (creativity) and Tony Buzan (thinking skills). I'd attended development programmes at top executive schools such as Harvard, Wharton and the London School of Economics – and I was eager to put my newfound knowledge into practice in a BIG way. Oh and let's not forget, I had a fantastic role model in the form of Microsoft's inspirational founder Bill Gates, one of the most successful human beings on the planet. He taught me to always see opportunities where others saw problems, and he marshalled my natural strengths in strategy, vision and communication to help target new growth. While heading up the Central and Eastern Europe (CEE) division, my hunger for success led me on an ambitious path to overthrow the existing management system and instigate a new strengths-based formula to crank up team performance and boost motivation levels in the shifting European marketplace. It was pretty risky . . . but it worked. And so with increased confidence and a dramatically enhanced team at my disposal, I threw my energy into meeting goal after goal and experienced some tremendous triumphs as a result. Not least was transforming the CEE into Microsoft's best performing region worldwide for four years in a row, during a time when the company was the biggest on the stock exchange. Soon I was lecturing at prestigious universities and speaking at business events across the world, totting up 42 countries across four different continents.

But success is, as ever, a moving target, and I was running myself and my team into the ground with the pressure to produce. Like many leaders before me, I believed that round-the-clock stress and hassle was 'part of the package' of being a leader and that success always came with a price – by that I mean the huge personal cost to my health and my family. It took years of extreme fast flying before I inevitably crashed and burned, even winding up in a mental hospital for a short time. Maybe you're at that breaking point right now? A life-changing breakthrough came when I snapped out of performance 'tunnel vision' and refocused my sight on the wider view. Performance isn't the whole picture. It's much bigger than that. Being a hotshot leader isn't just about winning in terms of business results, but also about winning in life. Through a journey of self-discovery and consolidation of my experience, I began to understand that being an exemplary leader is essentially about one thing:

. . . MAKING LIVES BETTER

Doing what it takes to win and succeed for the business is important. After all, US leading authority on personal and business success Brian Tracy made it clear that 'the number one job of a leader is to get results'.[2] But you don't have to turn yourself and your team into slaves of success in the process. Chasing the next victory doesn't have to be a recipe for burnout. 'Performance' is of course a big part of the job, but there's also the 'People' side to think about. If anything, it's the human aspect of leadership that should be receiving first-line attention.

It's no secret that a huge chunk of people leave their jobs because of their bosses. A 2015 Gallup study of 7272 US workers found that 50 per cent had left a job to get away from their boss so they could improve their overall life.[3] Ineffective leaders are leading people out of the door by overloading them with responsibilities, micro-managing, being out of touch with what's going on, not caring about them, communicating poorly and failing to inspire. Incredibly, bosses account for as much as 70 per cent of variance in employee engagement scores. Accomplished employees don't just want any old j-o-b, they want meaning, purpose and satisfaction; and this comes via leaders who can provide vision, set a positive example and value them enough to help them be bigger and better than they already are. What's even more enlightening is that, according to the same Gallup report, employees who have highly engaged managers are also 59 per cent more likely to be engaged. So your happiness is important too!

[2] Gell, Anthony (2014). *The Book of Leadership: How to Get Yourself, Your Team and Your Organisation Further Than You Ever Thought Possible*. London: Piatkus.
[3] Gallup (2015). 'State of the American manager: Analytics and advice for leaders', April. [Online] Available from: http://www.gallup.com/services/182138/state-american-manager.aspx

WHERE LEADERS GO WRONG

Here's where I think leaders frequently go off beam, both in how they manage themselves and manage their teams:

1. **They target weaknesses, not strengths.** Misguided leaders waste vital time, money and energy grappling with faults and failures rather than recognising and leveraging people's natural talents. The result? Disengaged and dissatisfied teams. Positive leaders do things differently. They succeed by building on their 'signature strengths', and they work around their weaknesses by letting other people in their team fill in the gaps. What's more, they encourage their teams and organisations to do the same.

2. **They fail to 'have a dream'.** Leaders must love what they do, and they must do it with *purpose* . . . otherwise they may as well call it quits and go home. A leader who is in touch with their personal 'why' is able to *inspire* others and create an emotional connection with their team that rallies everyone in a unified direction. Leadership is about leading people to lives that matter. Exceptional leaders dream up a glittering *vision* of the future that energises people and fills their work with added meaning.

3. **They manage time, not energy.** Facing non-stop demands in the workplace, leaders cram their diaries to the brim believing that they're skilfully maximising their time. Instead, they're recklessly abusing their energy, diluting their focus and heading straight for a burnout. While time is a finite resource, energy is not. It's renewable. Leaders need to set the right example by eradicating energy-depleting behaviour and establishing strategies to recharge their batteries physically, mentally, emotionally and spiritually.

4. **They put *success* before *happiness*.** When leaders focus on just the material trappings and tangible accomplishments of life, such as money and metrics, they ignore the deeper connections and meaningful activities that produce both long-lasting success *and* happiness. Profits and prestige are all well and good, but one of the greatest privileges of leadership is the chance to make a difference in the world. The best leaders are driven by a genuine desire to help others – their customers, the team they lead, their community and society as a whole. If a boss is all 'gimme gimme' and they never give back, they'll undoubtedly lose the respect and love of their followers.

Positive psychology at work

Positive psychology is a huge part of positive leadership and nurturing goodwill between you and your team. Before you roll your eyes and snigger, I'm not talking about the proliferation of pseudoscience and 'happy-go-lucky' self-help advice that's been making the rounds. Positive psychology is not plastering a cheesy smile on your face and making half-attempts to look on the bright side and be nice to people in the office. It's about fostering a mindset and workplace culture that's been empirically proven to fuel greater success and achievement.

In 1998, Martin Seligman, on becoming the new president of the American Psychological Association, declared that it was finally time to usher in a new era of psychology that would look at the sunnier side of life. He flung the door wide open to investigating what makes people happy and fulfilled, not just what makes them unhappy, stressed or depressed. And on that turning point, *positive psychology* came into being. Shockingly, at the time of Seligman's announcement, there was a 17-to-1 negative-to-positive ratio of research in the field of psychology. In other words, for every one study about happiness and thriving, there were 17 studies on depression and disorder.[4] Positive psychology is defined as 'the scientific study of human flourishing, and an applied approach to optimal human functioning'.[5] It shifts the focus from weaknesses to 'uncovering people's *strengths* and promoting their positive functioning', enabling them to flourish and excel.[6] Positive psychology goes above and beyond the naively simple 'pink and fluffy' advice expounded by positive thinking gurus to offer precise and rigorously tested interventions for creating a fulfilling and engaging life. It is a science after all.

Due to the burgeoning efforts of research in this spine-tingling new field, we now know that we can become more successful and generate better results when we put happiness first. Until recently, the common belief was that if we grafted hard enough and focused on making oodles of money, we would then

---

[4] Achor, Shawn (2010). *The Happiness Advantage: The Seven Principles that Fuel Success and Performance at Work*. New York: Crown Business.

[5] Positive Psychology Institute (2012). 'What is positive psychology?' [Online] Available from: http://www.positivepsychologyinstitute.com.au/what_is_positive_psychology.html

[6] Pennock, Seph Fontane (2015). 'What is Positive Psychology: 7 definitions + PDF'. *Positive Psychology Program*, 3 April. [Online] Available from: http://positivepsychologyprogram.com/what-is-positive-psychology/

be successful – and only if we are successful will we become happy. But if that was the case then every ambitious soul that landed a well-paid job, flashy car and glamorous lifestyle would be happy and stay happy. What happens instead is that, with each major win (windfall, qualification, pay rise), the finish line gets pushed further back and happiness disappears from sight. People spend their time pursuing financial success as a central goal in life only to find that it fails to provide them with an experience of sustained wellbeing. A 2005 study review put this whole 'happiness follows success' notion to bed. Based on three types of studies (cross-sectional, longitudinal and experimental), researchers Sonja Lyubomirsky, Laura King and Ed Diener found that people who were successful were happy *before* their successes.[7] So, the formula actually works the other way around – happiness breeds success. Being successful in the external world won't necessarily make you happy inside, but having an optimistic perspective from the outset makes you both happy and successful in whatever you're doing. Happiness and performance go hand in hand.

TURNING LEADERSHIP UPSIDE DOWN

Leadership is changing. Groundbreaking new research on happiness and optimism in the workplace is beginning to flip the business realm upside down and inside out. As with the introduction of collaborative, participative and transformational leadership models, bosses who ignore these new developments lose out on an amazing opportunity to accelerate their organisations forward. For open-minded CEOs, managers, supervisors and entrepreneurs, these new approaches are a welcome change to the old form of command-and-control, where leaders were all-imperious in their ivory towers and employees were expected to perform their roles with machine-like obedience. In this autocratic 'leader knows best' style of leadership, the man at the top would resort to using the power of his position to get the job done, and succeeded by provoking fear, or at best a cold respect, in his people. But nowadays, fear tactics won't get you very far. In a business world characterised by extreme change and ambiguity, stress and negativity abounds and there's a loud call to help people maximise their wellbeing, manage their energy levels and drive their productivity when and where it's needed most. As you can

---

[7] Lyubomirsky, Sonja, King, Laura and Diener, Ed. (2005). 'The benefits of frequent positive affect: Does happiness lead to success?' *Psychological Bulletin*, *131*(6), pp. 803–855. [Online] Available from: http://www.apa.org/pubs/journals/releases/bul-1316803.pdf

guess, a lot of it is about making people *happy*. When teams are happy, success and improved organisational performance comes naturally, you don't have to 'command' it. By embracing positive practices that value self-awareness, strengths, enjoyment, meaning, purpose and kindness, leaders can get the 'hard' financial results they need through 'soft' support and collaboration.

IT PAYS TO BE HAPPY

Happier employees are linked directly to a stronger bottom line. Fact! This *positivity–performance nexus* has been confirmed in study after study. In their meta-analysis of 225 academic studies, researchers Sonja Lyubomirsky, Laura King and Ed Diener found that life satisfaction leads to successful business outcomes.[8] A positive mindset results in:

- 23 per cent greater energy when under stress
- 31 per cent higher productivity
- 37 per cent higher levels of sales
- 40 per cent higher likelihood to be promoted
- three times higher creativity.

Fresh stats from a 2014 study by economists at the University of Warwick reveal that happiness leads to a 12 per cent spike in productivity, while unhappy workers prove to be 10 per cent less productive.[9] The Institute of Leadership & Management (ILM) also found that happiness flows up and down through an organisation, from leaders to their teams and back again.[10] Being happy gives leaders a level of independence and wellbeing that spurs them on and prolongs their winning streak. And by encouraging and safeguarding the happiness of their teams, leaders can fuel performance and productivity on a company-wide scale.

[8] Achor, Shawn (2012). 'Positive intelligence'. *Harvard Business Review*, January–February. [Online] Available from: https://hbr.org/2012/01/positive-intelligence

[9] Revesencio, Jonha (2015). 'Why happy employees are 12 per cent more productive'. *Fast Company*, 22 July. [Online] Available from: http://www.fastcompany.com/3048751/the-future-of-work/happy-employees-are-12-more-productive-at-work

[10] Institute of Leadership & Management, ILM (2013). 'The pursuit of happiness: Positivity and performance among UK managers'. [Online] Available from: https://www.i-l-m.com/~/media/ILM_per_cent20Website/Downloads/Insight/Reports_from_ILM_website/research_positivity_and_performance_per_cent20pdf.ashx

Some heavyweight employers have cottoned on to the 'happiness factor' pretty swiftly. For instance, Microsoft has made significant shifts to create an environment where employees feel supported and rewarded to do their best work, offering opportunities for remote working, creative project labs, family events, celebrations, mentoring programmes, volunteer schemes, on-campus doctors and salons, personalised development plans and a host of other enviable perks. Microsoft and other like-minded companies (e.g. Google, Cisco, FedEx Corporation) know what many others don't – that if they keep employees happy, they'll get results in the marketplace.

However, being a great place to work isn't just about providing free gym memberships, ping pong tables, telecommuting and laundry facilities; it's about having a 'heart and soul' which makes work exciting and energising for everyone involved.[11] The best companies invest in training and developing people's strengths so they can grow. They believe in the value of empowerment, altruism and coaching. And they have a vision that goes beyond 'making lots of money' to bring meaning and purpose to the whole business. This potent combination is what makes an organisation great to work for *AND* with. And it's your job as a leader to provide it.

THE 'NEW' COMPETITIVE ADVANTAGE: HUMAN POTENTIAL

We're all operating amidst a backdrop of supersonic developments in technology that are bringing dynamic innovations to every aspect of our lives and business. *Moore's Law* predicts an evolution pattern where computer processing power doubles every two years. The crushing load of data available to us and the breakneck speed it is added to means that everything needs to be done in rapid-fire time. A decision that might have taken two months to make 20 years ago now has to be made within just two minutes. So with 100 per cent more information comes 100 per cent more stress, and workers in every industry need to find new ways to cope with it, or risk burning out.

---

[11] Bersin, Josh (2014). 'Why companies fail to engage today's workforce: The overwhelmed employee'. *Forbes*, 15 March. [Online] Available from: http://www.forbes.com/sites/joshbersin/2014/03/15/why-companies-fail-to-engage-todays-workforce-the-overwhelmed-employee/

As technology evolves and becomes ubiquitous in society and the economy, the more we will see it turn into a commodity. And in the process of this happening, human capital will emerge as being more critical than ever before. I call this the *digital paradox*. In the not-too-distant future, human beings will be the primary source of differentiation in any and every industry or playing field. It's obvious then, that individuals, companies and even countries will gain their competitive advantage predominantly through the ability to *unlock human potential*. How leaders adapt their long-term strategies, organisations and business processes to make the best use of the extraordinary people resources at their disposal will be what separates the winners from the losers. Novel ideas, emotional intelligence, visionary thinking and mastery of personal strengths are the new keys to fast-tracking leadership and prosperity. Are you preparing your people so they can develop their full potential? Are you and your team applying your respective strengths to their best advantage? Are you inspiring your team to achieve more than they ever imagined possible? One thing's for sure, those who are in a position to play to their strengths, serve a meaningful purpose, and work with their hearts as well as their minds will escape commoditisation.

Being the best *you*!

We can all recognise a brilliant leader when we see one; they have fire in their bellies for achieving remarkable results and a knack for getting the best out of people. And we all have those legendary leaders we admire and take inspiration from, whether Alan Sugar, Winston Churchill, Steve Jobs or Mother Teresa. Not all successful leaders, CEOs and entrepreneurs glitter with charisma and regal presence, however. Not all frontrunners are super smart or have Zen-like wisdom. In fact, no leader that's 'made it big' seems to conform to a single pattern. They're all unique in their own way and they all play to that uniqueness while pursuing a clear vision and implementing solid strategies.

This may not sound helpful to aspiring leaders who want to know exactly what it takes to become a celebrity CEO right NOW. But, it's actually a blessing that after thousands of studies, there's still no clear 'cookie-cutter' profile of the ideal leader. For you, it means that becoming a positive leader isn't about being perfect or getting ticks in all the right boxes. You don't have to transform yourself into Virgin's Richard Branson or Google's Larry Page, or sacrifice your personality to appear 'leader like'. You don't have to be right brained or left brained, extrovert or introvert, telegenic or photogenic. However, you do have to be one important thing . . . You have to be AUTHENTIC.

WHO YOU ARE = HOW YOU LEAD

These days there's a greater premium on authenticity, as employees (the younger generations especially) are less willing to tolerate superficial and insincere leaders. They want someone genuine to follow. Being authentic means throwing your title out of the door and unleashing your 'real' self. People's desire to follow someone comes from any multitude of reasons, whether it's their courage, integrity, technical savvy, people-focus or whatever, so there's no need to jump on a pedestal or embark on crazy antics to advertise your position. On the other hand, breezing along and hoping everyone will recognise your supreme excellence won't work either. It's no use saying 'what you see is what you get' and leaving it at that. You must lead yourself and take responsibility for your own development. Authenticity starts with *self-awareness*. Self-aware leaders aim to understand their strengths and weaknesses, and they go to great lengths to maximise the former and play down the latter. They also reflect on their character strengths, core values and the impact they have on others, and work hard to cultivate the range of positive qualities and behaviours that enable them to lead by example. So, through self-awareness, being an authentic leader becomes a matter of *substance*, *style* and *service*:

- **Substance:** Your practical strengths and competencies – the *Doing* of leadership. *For example*: leading people through change, being proactive, empowering others, analytical thinking, strategy execution, problem solving, collaborative working, public speaking, financial management, effective influencing, future thinking, commitment to excellence.

- **Style:** Your character strengths and moral code – the *Being* of leadership. *For example*: integrity, values, vision, humour, warmth, humility, consistency, empathy, confidence, optimism, honesty, fairness, courage and communication.

- **Service:** Your ability to care for others and build strong connections – the *Giving* of leadership. *For example*: valuing and appreciating others, caring for and about your team, seeking win–win arrangements in all dealings, developing people to be all they can be, seeing the good in people, establishing social support networks, helping others accomplish tasks.

The 4Ps of Positive Leadership

Introducing the 4Ps of Positive Leadership Model

PURPOSE
Mission/Vision:
The 'WHY'

PLACE
Success vs Happiness:
The 'WHERE'

PEOPLE
Strengths:
The 'WHO'

PROCESS
Energy
management:
The 'HOW'

The 4Ps pyramid doesn't just look pretty; it helps leaders prepare for a new set of positive leadership rules that will help them thrive at the top. *Each dimension of the 4Ps model targets the Who, Why, How and Where of Positive Leadership.*

1. POSITIVE PEOPLE: BUILDING STRENGTHS – THE 'WHO'

Understand who you are. Identify and play to your strengths to release your full leadership potential. Nurture talent and build top teams by showing you care and paying attention to what people are good at, not their shortcomings. Be authentic!

2. POSITIVE PURPOSE: PERSONAL MISSION AND ULTIMATE VISION – THE 'WHY'

Your purpose is to add value to the world and be happy in the process. Strike out on your own meaningful mission by leveraging your unique strengths, values and passions. Inspire and be inspired by setting your sights on the highest vision for you and your team . . . and perhaps even achieve the impossible.

3. POSITIVE PROCESS: ENERGY MANAGEMENT –
THE 'HOW'

Manage energy (yours and other people's) to achieve outstanding feats without running out of steam. Become a Chief Energy Officer (CEO) and set the right example to marshal the collective energy of those you lead. Avoid classic burnout by taking care of your physical, mental, emotional and spiritual resources.

4. POSITIVE PLACE: SUCCESS VS HAPPINESS –
THE 'WHERE'

Follow your heart instead of the rat race to the place where success and happiness are in balance. Happiness breeds success. By putting happiness first, you can learn strategies for positive living that bring meaningful rewards to you and your team, while also delivering bottom-line results. Help others and use your position of authority to make a difference in the world.

Notice what's missing here? That's right. *Performance.*

Why doesn't it have its own rightful place in the pyramid? Aren't all leaders performance obsessed as a rule? Usually they are, but performance isn't a separate dimension in itself. This is because performance isn't a cause or strategy of excellent leadership, but rather a *result* – a successful side-effect of following a positive approach. As you incorporate the ideas in this book, you'll sharpen your competitive edge and drive your performance skyward.

You'll notice that the book is split into four parts. Each part will give you a more detailed picture of what lies behind each of the 4Ps, converting the pyramid into 3D – something concrete that you can use to develop these vital leadership practices in yourself and with your colleagues. The specific chapters are bursting with priceless nuggets of information: research summaries, leadership frameworks, personal anecdotes, positive ideas, business examples and real can-use-now tools to learn from and apply.

Now go ahead and get positive!

part one

**Building strengths –
positive people
(the 'WHO')**

Who am I? (self-awareness, strengths and the EQ factor)

'Leadership – it is an extension of personality. It is the most personal thing in the world for the simple reason that it is just plain you.'
FIELD MARSHALL VISCOUNT SLIM, BRITISH MILITARY COMMANDER

What if I told you that there was one killer leadership competency that, if cultivated, would help you be a better, more positive leader in every way? And what if I said that this cool meta-skill would stand the test of time and see you through any leadership challenge?

Well, there is, and it's called *self-awareness*.

As a leadership topic, self-awareness usually gets a bum rap, particularly in the Western world where macho, testosterone-pumped leaders often sneer at it. Yet it's the most valuable element of leadership for the simple reason that it props up all the others. It's the catalyst for vision, determination, adaptability, strategic thinking, charisma and all the rest of the traditional bevy of skills and qualities that makes someone a great leader.

Self-awareness: the reality check

First of all, self-awareness is NOT naval-gazing or excessive self-absorption. Self-awareness means having a realistic assessment of your own abilities, such as:

- what you're good at
- your deficiencies
- your successes
- your mistakes
- your motivations
- your preferences
- your attitudes
- your effect on others
- the learning gaps you need to fill.

This whole idea of being self-aware and introspective may sound a bit egotistical to you. Shouldn't you be focusing on leading your team rather than reflecting on yourself? Well, yes of course. But the beauty of having undergone a full reality check on yourself is that you'll be able to relate better to other people. It's only through self-awareness that you can discover and reveal your true *authenticity*, and this is the secret ingredient that will gain the trust and respect of others. If people around you know you better than you know yourself and have a keener sense of your strengths and vulnerabilities, you lose credibility. By knowing who you are and understanding the impact you have on others, you'll naturally become more open, empathetic and influential, and you can skilfully interact with your colleagues without compromising your core principles or character. Tapping into self-awareness means being able to lead yourself to your highest potential, and that can only be a good thing. This may all sound very soft and fuzzy-wuzzy so far, but believe me the results are hardcore!

A SOFT SKILL WITH HARD RESULTS

An online assessment of more than 2750 executives by The Korn Ferry Institute found that self-awareness measurably contributes to superior performance and is an indicator of long-term career success.[1] Furthermore, in attempting to discover why certain business leaders succeed, a study by consultancy firm Green Peak Partners and Cornell's School of Industrial and Labor Relations discovered that a 'high self-awareness score was the strongest predictor of overall success'.[2] Leaders who were self-aware were better at:

- working with clients and business partners
- grasping and executing strategy
- delivering bottom-line results.

These leaders weren't pushovers; they could still demand strong performance and make tough decisions, but they did it in an inspiring and respectful manner. By being aware of their weaknesses, these leaders were also wise enough to hire subordinates who performed well in categories where they lacked acumen. And they were open to admitting that someone on their team might have a better idea than their own.

The reward for self-awareness is pretty spectacular, but the lack of self-awareness bears a hefty price too – and shows its face right across the organisation. The Korn Ferry Institute researchers David Zes and Dana Landis analysed 6977 self-assessments at 486 publicly traded companies.[3] They found that professionals in poor performing companies were 79 per cent more likely to have low overall self-awareness than people in companies with a robust rate of return (ROR). The Korn Ferry Institute also revealed that:

'80 per cent of leaders have blind spots about their skills and another 40 per cent have under-used hidden strengths.'

[1] Orr, Evelyn J. (2012). 'Survival of the most self-aware: Nearly 80 percent of leaders have blind spots about their skills'. *The Korn Ferry Institute*.

[2] Flaum, J.P. (2010). 'When it comes to business leadership, nice guys finish first'. *Green Peak Partners*.

[3] Zes, David and Landis, Dana (2013). 'A better return on self-awareness'. *The Korn Ferry Institute*, August [Online] Available from: http://www.kornferryinstitute.com/sites/all/files//documents/briefings-magazine-download/KFI-SelfAwareness-ProofPoint-6.pdf

And next to this, employees at poor performing companies had 20 per cent more blind spots than those working at financially strong companies. To quote Dana Landis:

'Self-awareness is not a soft skill, a nice-to-have. It's playing out in your bottom line. This is about leadership effectiveness.'

DELVING DEEPER INTO OURSELVES

I find it really ironic that leaders are in an ultra-powerful position, but most of them have never taken the time to look within themselves to discover who they truly are. There are lots of smart leaders out there with profuse *external* knowledge – industry expertise, market know-how, in-depth technical learning, facts, figures and the like – but not enough *intrinsic* knowledge. External awareness is an essential requisite for any leader to have a sound understanding of how their business works, but without self-awareness it's easy to get overwhelmed and lose your way. It's why you often see the most quick-minded and intelligent people do some of the most stupid things! With all the hard evidence around, it would be foolish to continue fobbing self-awareness off as being 'unbusiness-like' and not worth the bother.

Exercise 1.1: Self-awareness

Here are a couple of handy tips for keeping watch on yourself:

- Keep a journal to note down your key decisions and actions, how they were made and the motivations behind them. Look back every so often to re-examine those decisions/actions and reflect on their outcomes. Were your initial assumptions correct? Do you need to make any tweaks or adjustments in your approach?

- You can also jot down your extreme attitudes or feelings to situations or people. This will help you make sense of what your emotions are telling you. Why does that one particular person always rub you up the wrong way? Why do you always throw a tantrum in that particular scenario? Do you notice any recurring themes? Use this awareness to rewire your brain to choose a better response next time.

The super-successful know their strengths

One of the most worrisome aspects in the workplace today is our obsession with fixing weaknesses. Leaders will spend whopping amounts of energy and untold hours, days, weeks and months trying to address the legion of discernible flaws in themselves, their teams and their organisations. In a way, this is understandable. It's human nature to look for problems to solve, weak spots to erase, wrongs to right and gaps to fill. And for a leader especially, people hold a mighty batch of expectations in connection to your role, so the stakes are through-the-roof. It's common to feel pressure to meet these sweeping expectations so you don't let yourself or the entire side down. But I can tell you for sure that it's not the optimal way to achieve greatness or get the best out of others. People aren't machines – they're not cars or computer devices. We can't just fix or replace their faulty parts and expect everything to be working perfectly afterwards. Still, that hasn't stopped many a leader trying to fine-tune them.

While we're kept busy on our mission to 'fix' or 'improve' ourselves and our colleagues by working on our weaknesses, we often completely overlook the things that make us great – our *strengths*. Strengths come from our inherent gifts and talents; the things we do well naturally and which we enjoy. These talents are enduring and unique, and everyone should work at identifying them, crafting them and channelling them into strengths. People can't be 'fixed' but they can be motivated, engaged, energised and supported. And focusing on their strengths is the principal way to do it. If I had to single out the best leadership decision I ever made during my entire career at Microsoft, the one momentous action that made the biggest difference, it would have to be – hands down – the decision to start working on my own and my team's strengths. I truly believe that the only way to make spectacular progress in any industry, any career or any project is to harness people's natural talents and turn them into powerful assets.

FITTING SQUARE PEGS INTO ROUND HOLES

What I find really disheartening is that most organisational hierarchies and procedures unknowingly set people up to fail in their roles. Take the standard performance appraisal scenario as an example. A leader will typically sit down with a member of their team, let's call him Adam, and discuss which 'areas of improvement' (the fancy, dressed-up term for 'weaknesses') are needed for the upcoming period. Let's say Adam is an expert software developer who's incredibly skilled at creating glitch-free tools that satisfy user specifications, and he's adept at a multitude of intricate programming tasks. Because Adam's so amazing at what he does and he knows the products inside out, you (as his boss) believe that he should be making presentations to potential clients and to the board to show off his work. The only snag is his presentation skills are dire to say the least and he gets extra-nervous in public speaking situations. So you both 'agree' that Adam needs to go away and do some kind of training on making presentations and public speaking skills so that this so-called defect can be fixed.

Despite Adam showing little enthusiasm or natural aptitude for this task, you believe that you're empowering him and helping him to develop. And Adam genuinely wants to do well at this new challenge and receive recognition for his work. So he goes and gets all the necessary training and puts in X^2 amount of effort until he manages to become 'adequate' at giving presentations. Adam then starts spending more time in client and management meetings giving presentations that are, in truth, mediocre. All the while, he's spending less and less time doing the things he's exceptional at and actually enjoys! Do you see what's wrong with this picture? By focusing on overcoming this person's weaknesses, you're basically neglecting their most valuable gifts and turning them into someone they're not. You're trying to ram a square peg into a round hole.

It's a similar story with job promotions. When someone shows brilliant technical or creative competence in their field and wants to make headway in the company, they get bumped up into a completely different role to the one they succeeded in. Take this situation where Laura, who's talented at producing imaginative marketing campaigns and has a gift for customer insight, gets promoted to manage the marketing department. She's overjoyed with her promotion but soon realises that it calls for a whole different set of skills than she's used to applying. Perhaps she discovers that she's not so great at things like compiling reports, budgeting or tracking projects, which are important requirements in her new position. Sure enough, Laura starts spending her days working primarily on these 'weaknesses' so she can perform better and keep on top of her workload; and her remarkable creative strengths and customer awareness barely get a look in. Her natural strengths have no opportunity to thrive in this context. This is typical for the lot of us – we throw all of our attention and energy into our weaknesses and take our strengths for granted. A much better approach for someone like Laura would be to allow for an entire career of progression within a specific role that fits her talents and that she can excel in, rather than trying to mould her into someone else. After all, a screwdriver will never be good at being a hammer and a hammer will never be good at being a screwdriver. We all need to figure out what tools we have in our toolbox and learn to use them in the right way.

THE ENGAGEMENT CRISIS

When people are forced to ignore their talents to struggle with their weak spots, all sorts of productivity and performance problems crop up. In 2013, Gallup reported on its latest worldwide study on the topic of employee engagement (how positive and productive people are at work).[4] Spanning 142 countries, this research revealed that a staggering *87 per cent of employees are not engaged in their workplace*. The table below shows the full results of engaged, not engaged ('tuned out') and actively disengaged employees:

Worldwide, actively disengaged employees outnumber engaged employees by nearly 2–1

2011–2012 results among employed residents, aged 18 and older, in 142 countries and areas

	2009–2010	2011–2012
Actively disengaged	27%	24%
Not engaged	62%	63%
Engaged	11%	13%

Source: Copyright © 2013 Gallup, Inc. All rights reserved. The content is used with permission; however, Gallup retains all rights of republication.

What this tells us is that across the world and in every industry, the majority of people are just 'showing up' to work. They aren't interested in customers,

---

[4] Gallup (2013). 'The state of the global workplace: Employee engagement insights for business leaders worldwide'. [Online] Available from: http://www.gallup.com/services/178517/state-global-workplace.aspx

productivity, profitability, safety, mission and purpose or anything. Most of them are simply killing time until lunch or their next break. Those who are actively disengaged are more or less out to cause destruction in their company. They monopolise managers' time, have more accidents, account for more quality defects, miss more days and generally just p*ss people off. They go from crisis to crisis and consequently underperform. Some actively disengaged employees may even go as far as to undo the good work of engaged employees, perhaps by sabotaging innovation initiatives, damaging new customer relations or ruining hard-won solutions to problems – a scary thing to behold for any top-level leader. This all boils down to the fact that disengaged and actively disengaged employees are usually in jobs that are mismatched to their inherent skills. People will always resist what they don't like doing.

People who don't use their strengths at work:[5]

- dread going to work
- have more negative than positive interactions with colleagues
- treat their customers poorly
- tell their friends what a miserable company they work for
- achieve less on a daily basis
- have fewer positive and creative moments.

Decades of Gallup research has shown that there's a powerful connection between level of engagement/job satisfaction and the degree to which people are maximising their strengths on the job. Researchers found that people who have the chance to focus on their strengths are:[6]

- *six times* as likely to be engaged in their jobs
- *three times* as likely to report having an excellent quality of life.

[5] Rath, Tom (2007). *StrengthsFinder 2.0*. New York: Gallup Press.
[6] Sorenson, Susan (2014). 'How employees' strengths make your company stronger'. *Gallup*. 20 February. [Online] Available from: http://www.gallup.com/businessjournal/167462/employees-strengths-company-stronger.aspx

> ## People who work in their strengths zone:[7]
>
> - look forward to going to work
> - have more positive than negative interactions with co-workers
> - treat customers better
> - tell their friends they work for a great company
> - achieve more on a daily basis
> - have more positive, creative and innovative moments.

Leaders need to take stock of this. When someone shows a natural predisposition for a certain task, it's usually something that they really like to do. This means that they'll enjoy the process of getting better at it. The upshot is that they tend to be more involved in and enthusiastic about their work; they make the effort to understand the full scope of their jobs and look for new and better ways to achieve outcomes. They also show 100 per cent commitment and have fewer performance issues.

BE STRENGTHS-DRIVEN, NOT PROFIT-DRIVEN

So what's the impact on the bottom line?

A 2009 study of 115 companies by consulting firm Watson Wyatt concluded that companies with highly engaged employees achieve a financial performance four times greater than companies with poor engagement.[8] In terms of individual performance, the highly engaged were more than twice as likely to be top performers. Almost 60 per cent of them exceeded or far exceeded expectations for performance. In a similar vein, a study of 50 multinational companies by Towers Perrin-ISR found that over a 12-month period, companies

[7] Rath, Tom (2007). *StrengthsFinder 2.0*. New York: Gallup Press.
[8] Watson Wyatt (2009). 'Continuous engagement: The key to unlocking the value of your people during tough times'. *Work Europe Survey Report* 2008–2009. London: Watson Wyatt.

with high levels of engagement outperformed those with less engaged employees in three key financial measures:[9]

- operating income
- net income growth
- earnings per share.

Impact of employee engagement on financial performance

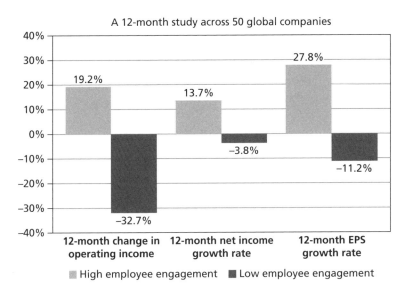

A 12-month study across 50 global companies

Source: Towers Perrin, Global Workforce Study 2007/8 (http://engageforsuccess.org/wp-content/uploads/2015/10/Closing-the-engagement-gap-TowersPerrin.pdf)

It doesn't stop there. Kenexa studied 64 organisations and found those in the top quartile for engagement achieved twice the annual net income of those in the bottom quartile, even after controlling for organisation size.[10] These high engagement organisations also returned seven times more to shareholders over a five-year period than organisations whose employees were less engaged.

We can see from these amazing facts that building strengths makes good business sense. As a leader, you should work hard at liberating the human

[9] Towers Perrin-ISR (2008). 'Employee engagement underpins business transformation'. July. [Online] Available from: http://www.ifcaonline.com/wordpress2/wp-content/uploads/2013/10/Employee-Engagement-Underpins-Business-Transformation.pdf
[10] Kenexa Research Institute (2009). 'The impact of employee engagement'. White Paper.

talent in your organisation, not limiting it. If you treat people as individuals and aim to uncover the energy, ability and genius that lies within them, they'll respond with a burst of productivity. Some people are brilliant at analysis; others are good at dealing with people; some are fabulous at selling; and yet others are great at organisation. Help them find out and free them up to look for a better fit for their talents either within their job or elsewhere in the workplace. Let them do what they're great at. This is exceptionally motivating for them. Comprehensive surveys have shown that the more people use their 'signature strengths' in life, the *happier* they become. When 577 participants were encouraged to pick one of their 'signature strengths' and use it in a new and different way each day for one week, they became considerably happier and had less depressive symptoms than participants in a placebo control group.[11] What's more, these benefits lasted. Even six months after the experiment, levels of happiness remained high.

With all that happiness comes a powerful *health* boost. Gallup's studies show that focusing on people's talents leads to tremendous health and wellness outcomes. The more hours people spend using their strengths to do what they do best, the less likely they are to report experiencing worry, stress, anger, sadness or physical pain, and the more likely they are to report having ample energy to get things done, feeling well-rested, being happy, smiling or laughing a lot, learning something interesting and being treated with respect.[12]

> People who have the opportunity to use their strengths at work are not only more materially successful in terms of *productivity and performance*; they're *happier and healthier* too.

What can you take from all this as a leader?

Well, first off you should make it a priority to help the people around you develop their strengths. By dignifying and honouring their potential, you'll

---

[11] Seligman, Martin E. P., Steen, Tracy A., Park, N. and Peterson, Christopher (2005). 'Positive psychology progress: Empirical validation of interventions'. *American Psychologist*. July-August, *60*(5), pp. 410–421. [Online] Available from: http://www.ppc.sas.upenn.edu/articleseligman.pdf

[12] Sorenson, Susan (2014). 'How employees' strengths make your company stronger'. *Gallup*. 20 February. [Online] Available from: http://www.gallup.com/businessjournal/167462/employees-strengths-company-stronger.aspx

reap results in the form of a loyal, happy and imaginative workforce. I'm not saying you have to put aside decisions on productivity, customer satisfaction and quality, or any of the myriad other business issues you have to contend with. This isn't an either/or situation. When you put the development and enhancement of your people first, you don't disregard the bottom line, you enrich it. Big household-name companies like Facebook, Microsoft, 3M and Google are all embracing strengths-based leadership and aligning people's strengths and passions with the projects and ideas they are passionate about.[13] They understand that great work comes out of allowing people to spend time using their strengths in creative and enjoyable ways. It's more important than any fancy title or bonus you can give them. When your people are able to live and work at their highest levels, profits and success are certain to come.

BECOMING A WORLD-CLASS LEADER

Who said you need to be heroic and all-powerful to be a great leader? The best leaders don't pretend to know it all and they don't try to be the best at everything. They know they have weaknesses but they don't dwell on them. They understand that it's far better to become a world-class authority on one or two of their signature strength areas than to be average across the board. Weaknesses are hard or impossible to develop. It takes huge quantities of effort to transform them into assets – a whole lot more than it does to take your natural gifts to the next level. Both are upgrades that will increase your value to the world, but the pay-offs are completely different. Targeting your deficiencies can improve them to the point where they're no longer obstacles, but it's doubtful that you'll be able to reach megastar excellence when you're always in 'self-improvement' mode. It's a hit and miss process. On the other hand, you have greater room for exponential growth when you target your power areas. Smart leaders know that instead of balancing their deficits, they should be focusing on increasing their personal GDP instead. A bit of 'damage control' and improvement is to be expected if a weakness is particularly fatal to your leadership, but it shouldn't divert your energy from the real development of your strengths.

---

[13] Walter, Ekaterina (2013). 'Four essentials of strengths-based leadership'. *Forbes*, 27 August. [Online] Available from: http://www.forbes.com/sites/ekaterinawalter/2013/08/27/four-essentials-of-strength-based-leadership/

The EQ Factor: emotional intelligence

Take a moment to think about the leaders you admire. I'll wager that, talented though they are, they probably aren't the most highly intelligent or technically skilled executive in their area. Yet they're credited as star performers for their special flair in working with people and being able to accomplish amazing things. This is revealing. Daniel Goleman, author of the groundbreaking book *Emotional Intelligence*, found that, though the personal styles of brilliant leaders vary dramatically – some are loud, some are subdued, some are forceful, some are eccentric – they are all alike in one crucial way. According to Goleman, the elusive quality that sets these leaders apart isn't their IQ (Intelligence Quotient), it's their EQ (Emotional Quotient), or simply – their emotional intelligence.[14]

GIVE ME EMOTIONAL STRENGTH

For a long time, IQ has been the pre-eminent standard of excellence in life. This measures general intelligence purely in terms of logical ability – the standard stuff like reasoning, attention, memory, maths and spatial awareness. But, after painstakingly examining a bunch of academic studies, Goleman made the enlightening discovery that IQ only accounts for between *4 and 10 per cent* of factors that determine career success. That's it! IQ can influence the profession you embark on as an 'entry-level requirement', but after a criterion level of 115 it hardly matters and has no added benefit. So if your IQ is hitting super-genius levels at 170+, sorry to disappoint you but it's just not enough. Features that are more important in showing how you're likely to perform are aspects of personality, emotion and behaviour, such as:

- imagination
- self-esteem
- conscientiousness
- intuitive reasoning
- playfulness
- curiosity
- adaptability

[14] Goleman, Daniel (1996). *Emotional Intelligence: Why It Can Matter More Than IQ*. London: Bloomsbury Publishing.

- empathy
- joyfulness
- big picture thinking
- social dexterity.

Being able to think and act logically is still an asset but it won't do you any great favours as a leadership differentiator. Let's face it, we're living in the 21st century and anything that can be automated has either already been or will be automated soon. New disruptive technologies and algorithms have taken over most of our analytical 'thinking' and procedural tasks, and have helped us make leaps and bounds in our efficiency to boot. However, it's inconceivable that they'll ever be able to replace our humanistic and 'feeling' capabilities – things like caring, creativity, culture, relationship building, social adeptness and empathy – to any major degree. Or that they'll be able to mimic the unique mix of strengths that differentiate each of us as human beings. In the words of business author Daniel Pink, what will distinguish leaders in the coming years is their capacity to 'understand what makes their fellow woman or man tick, to forge relationships and to care for others.'[15] This comes down to – that's right, emotional intelligence. It's tough to copy. You'll be pleasantly surprised at how liberating your emotional intelligence feeds into all kinds of leadership activities, even those thought to be strictly 'logical' – from problem solving and decision making, to reasoning and analysis. When ripened, it can spearhead you to the top 10 per cent of your field and results in great wins for you, your people and your entire organisation. There are five components to take on board:

- Self-awareness: knowing and understanding your own emotions and their effect on others, e.g. having confidence, a sense of humour, being aware of your impression on others.

- Self-regulation: controlling your own emotions, e.g. being conscientious, taking responsibility for your own deeds, adapting to change, thinking before reacting rashly.

- Motivation: understanding how to motivate yourself in particular ways, e.g. initiative, commitment to complete a task, perseverance when things get tough.

---

[15] Pink, Daniel H. (2008). *A Whole New Mind: Why Right-Brainers Will Rule the Future*. London: Marshall Cavendish.

- Empathy: perceiving and understanding other people's emotions, e.g. being perceptive of another's feelings, taking an interest in someone's concerns, anticipating and responding to people's needs, not being phased by office politics.

- Social skill: knowing how to manage relationships and influence the emotions of others productively, e.g. effective listening and communication, the ability to guide and inspire others, being adept at diffusing difficult situations using persuasion and negotiation.

If you're looking at this and thinking about all the times you flew off the handle at people, let events get the better of you or showed zero tolerance, then don't despair just yet. There is hope. Emotional intelligence isn't static. Unlike IQ, it's not fixed for life; it can be worked on to help you become a better leader. Positive leadership requires an ability to read people, accurately understand and manage emotions, and communicate and adapt effectively. Gaining mastery over your thinking and habits is a crucial part of it, as is having a clear understanding of where your strengths lie in each of the five components. The good news is that the strategies in this book are heavily geared towards unleashing your EQ strengths as part of an integrated positive leadership approach.

Exercise 1.2: Emotional intelligence

If you're wondering how emotionally intelligent you are, try asking yourself these questions:

- How well do you manage yourself?
  - Are you able to read your own emotions?
  - Do you stay focused?
  - Are you adaptable?
  - Do you have an honest handle on your strengths and weaknesses?
  - Are you aware when your emotions hijack or enhance your thinking?
  - Can you control your reactions to events?
  - Can you keep a sense of optimism when others are down?

- How well do you manage your relationships?
  - Do you know how to get along well with others?
  - Do you provide feedback and guidance to people?

- Can you read other people?
- Do you inspire trust in others?
- Do you share a vision that people can see and want to be part of?
- Do you build bonds with people?
- Are you a team player?

If you answered 'Yes' to the greater number of these questions, then it's fair to say you have a high EQ factor. People with high emotional intelligence tend to cope well with their own emotions and show maturity in the workplace. They also take notice and respond appropriately to the emotions of other people, making it easier to leverage people's talent, and ultimately to unlock the potential of the entire business.

Testing EQ

The questions here don't constitute a full assessment of your EQ. They're merely designed to provoke self-reflection about your general level of emotional intelligence. But if all this emotional talk has whetted your appetite and you're interested in getting the full measure of your EQ, I recommend the following well-researched and validated tools:

- Mayer-Solovey-Caruso EI Test (MSCEIT)
- Emotional and Social Competence Inventory (ESCI)
- EQ Map by Essi System.

Strengths audit (unlocking strengths and getting authentic)

'Great leaders are not defined by the absence of weakness but by the presence of clear strengths.'
JOHN ZENGER, GERMAN-AMERICAN PUBLISHER AND JOURNALIST

Knowledge is power, so they say; and knowing your strengths is a must for any positive leader. Finding out what you're good at is the starting point to creating a happy and successful life and organisation. Your strengths are a vital source of your get-up-and-go and good feeling, fuelling your drive to lead in ways that make a striking difference. Knowing the strengths of your team is also a no-brainer. Every human being has natural talents and passions that are just waiting to be uncovered and put to action. Your ultimate job as a leader is to crack open the truth about people's potential and free them up to manifest it through the work they do.

Work out your strengths profile

Before you can leverage your strengths, you have to *find* them. Not all strengths are visible at first sight, but if you focus on seeking them out through self-assessment and thorough examination, they're bound to reveal themselves.

SELF-ASSESSMENT TOOLS

There are plenty of tools, psychometric tests and commercial models available that give reliable results without too much effort on your part. Here's a brief rundown of the ones that I believe are most valuable, starting with my personal go-to assessment tool, the StrengthsFinder 2.0.

Tool 1: StrengthsFinder 2.0

The StrengthsFinder 2.0 by Gallup helps you figure out your top five talent themes. By definition, talents are people's naturally recurring patterns of thought, feeling or behaviour that can be productively applied.[1] Our talents help us understand who we are. They:

- describe us
- influence our choices
- direct our actions
- explain why we're better at some things than others
- help us filter our work
- hold great potential for us.

The notion behind StrengthsFinder 2.0 is that your biggest room for growth lies with your dominant talents, and you should work on maturing and polishing them up into strengths through applied knowledge, skill and

---

[1] Gallup. 'What is the difference between a talent and a strength?' [Online] Available from: http://strengths.gallup.com/help/general/125543/difference-talent-strength.aspx

practice. I'm a big fan of this tool, so I genuinely recommend you give it a go to expand your awareness of your own brilliant talents. The insights are revealing to say the least. I bet you're dying to know my top five talents, aren't you? Well, here they are:

1. **Maximiser:** an emphasis on excellence; fascinated by strengths; capitalising on gifts; transforming something strong into something superb.

2. **Strategic:** spotting patterns and issues; able to sort through clutter and find the best route; asking 'what if?'; making selections.

3. **Communication:** bringing ideas to life; words that engage and motivate people to act; good conversationalist and presenter.

4. **Futuristic:** dreamer; 'wouldn't it be great if. . .?'; energised by what the future may hold; inspires others with visions of the future.

5. **Activator:** emphasis on action; 'when can we start?'; getting things done; often impatient.

Find more info at: www.strengthsfinder.com

StrengthsFinder in action

One of the best speeches I ever gave happened as a result of playing three of my top talents in a systematic way. This took place at the European Association for International Education (EAIE) conference in 2014, which was attended by more than 5000 delegates. In delivering my keynote speech, I pulled in my three key strengths of strategy, communication and futuristic (vision), essentially gearing my whole presentation around them. I talked about the nature of our current educational and business systems using humorous stories, gripping research and refreshing examples (communication). I talked about the bright possibilities for the future if we focus on our strengths and have the courage to aim high, and the importance of leadership in inspiring people with a clear, compelling vision (futuristic). And I discussed important strategies for getting there by embracing the widespread use of technology in education, such as enabling individual learning, global connectivity and greater teamwork (strategic). At the end of the speech, I was thrilled to receive a standing ovation from the audience. Just the reaction I was hoping for – and it was all down to playing to my strengths.

Tool 2: VIA (Values in Action) survey

Another good one to try is VIA survey – a free online tool that focuses on your signature character strengths as opposed to your skills or interests. In other words, the core personality characteristics that spark your engagement and shape the way you think, feel and behave.

Find more info at: www.viacharacter.org

Tool 3: Myers-Briggs Type Indicator (MBTI)

Though this isn't a tool specifically developed for finding your strengths, the Myers-Briggs Type Indicator (MBTI) can be a powerful aid for learning more about yourself and valuing your unique differences. Used by companies all over the world, it measures behavioural preferences across four different areas:

- Extroversion or Introversion (E or I): how you give/receive energy or focus your attention. Are you more comfortable being with people, or would you rather be alone?

- Sensing or Intuition (S or N): how you prefer to gather/use information. Do you mainly trust your five senses, or do you place greater trust in your intuition?

- Thinking or Feeling (T or F): how you make decisions (head or heart). Do you rely more on logic or feelings (your own or others) in making decisions?

- Judging or Perceiving (J or P): how you like to order your life and handle the outer world. Are you naturally organised with everything planned out? Or do you enjoy being flexible and open ended with your options?

On completing the test, your main preferences are combined to give you your personality type, which is expressed in the form of a funky four-letter acronym like ENTP or ISFJ.[2] Each character type in MBTI has strengths and weaknesses. It's well worth getting to know both sides so you can be aware of anything that gets in the way of your performance as well as what strengthens it.

Find more info at: www.myersbriggs.org

---

[2] The Myers & Briggs Foundation. 'MBTI basics'. [Online] Available from: http://www.myersbriggs.org/my-mbti-personality-type/mbti-basics/

Tool 4: The DISC model

The DISC model is yet another personality profiling system which is fast growing in popularity as a tool for strengthening workplace skills. It scores you on the basis of four behavioural styles: Dominance (D); Influence (I), Steadiness (S) and Conscientiousness (C) – no points for figuring out that's where the name 'DISC' comes from!

More info at: www.discprofile.com

Tool 5: Realise2

Realise2 is a strengths assessment tool by CAPP (Centre for Applied Positive Psychology) designed to help you identify four distinct categories of your profile: your realised strengths, unrealised strengths, learned behaviours and weaknesses. Through the 4M model, it offers recommendations and advice for:

- marshalling realised strengths
- maximising unrealised strengths
- moderating learned behaviours
- minimising weaknesses.

More info at: www.cappeu.com

Ask others to hold up a mirror

Self-assessments like Gallup's StrengthsFinder 2.0 are excellent tools for helping you work out your strengths from an internal perspective, but they can't give you all the answers. As fallible human beings, we're not always able to grasp our own personalities, and some psychologists have cast doubt on the reliability of our own judgement when it comes to determining what we're good at or what our weaknesses are.[3] If you want a really objective view of your strengths, you need other people to hold up a mirror. When you gaze upon your reflection and see yourself as others see you, it can be a real eye-opener in lighting the way to your most special talents. More often than not, what you learn from others can provide external validation of your own self-assessments, helping to reinforce the strengths that seem to get the best results.

[3] Lebon, Tim (2014). *Achieve Your Potential with Positive Psychology*. Teach Yourself. London: Hachette UK.

How can you harness other people's insight to help you identify your strengths? Here are a couple of straightforward methods that can help:

METHOD 1: 360° FEEDBACK

A 360° feedback assessment is a formal process for getting input on your skills and behaviours from a broad range of sources – your colleagues, superiors, reports, customers, suppliers and clients. If you want a more all-round perspective, you can even get people outside of work to chip in, like your friends and family. Used wisely, this can be one of the most constructive tools for leadership development because it's rich in information and offers views from all angles. The results are meaningful and you should be able to spot fairly quickly the areas that people feel you are best at, and whether there are any blatant weaknesses for you to be aware of. I used it heavily at Microsoft, as a manager, a peer and as a director, and it helped me and my team immensely.

A lot of companies have their own 360° feedback systems in place, and you can implement one of those if they're available to you. Sometimes these are anonymous. The idea behind anonymity is that it's meant to encourage openness and protect your relationship with the participants. But judging from the horror stories around, it often has the opposite effect. Anonymity can lead to people second guessing 'who said what' and creates an air of suspicion around the feedback. Under the safety blanket of anonymity, some people use it as an opportunity to vent their frustration or let loose with the criticism, often unjustly so, while others may be afraid to speak the truth because they fear retaliation on the entire team.

In view of all this, I would certainly think twice about going down the anonymous route! If anything, the feedback works better when it comes from credible, known sources who understand that this whole process is about building strengths, not backstabbing. By being brave enough to ask for the transparent, 'no holds barred' truth, you're demonstrating your authenticity and encouraging others to do the same. It's this open and courageous approach that does a much better job of creating an atmosphere of trust than any anonymous survey possibly could.

Here's how to go about it.

Step 1: Target your sources

First select a range of people (say five to ten) and check if they're willing to take part in this feedback activity. The best sources are a mix of personal and professional contacts. Choose people who you interact with in different ways and who can offer diverse perspectives, for example, your boss, colleague, client, business partner, friend, mentor, spouse, and so on. Let them know you're seeking candid, critical and objective perspectives, and ask them to be as honest and open as possible.

Step 2: Seek feedback

Prepare a simple survey to send out to the willing parties and ask them to return it to you by a given date. The questions could be focused on specific leadership criteria (e.g. self-leadership, sense of purpose, risk-taking, networking, facilitation, use of power) or they can be more general. It's up to you. Mike Roarty and Kathy Toogood, authors of *The Strengths-Focused Guide to Leadership*,[4] suggest the following set of simply-worded questions:

- What strengths do you feel I possess?
- Which of them am I making best use of in your opinion? (Please give examples of concrete situations to back these up.)
- Are there any key strengths I could make more of, in order to make a more powerful contribution?
- Are there any significant weaknesses from your point of view that are creating a big performance risk? (Please give examples of specific situations.) What can I do about them?
- Do you have any suggestions for how to make the most of my strengths?
- Are any strengths being overplayed (being used too much or in an inappropriate context to the point that they have a negative impact)? Do you have any suggestions on what I could do?

You might want to hand over lists of generic strengths and weaknesses to help people clarify their thinking, like the ones available at http://positiveleaderbook. com/strengthsweaknesses. For specific leadership strengths, refer to the task-based examples in the table below. If you prefer a more quantitative approach, you could ask people to rate your capability on various leadership challenges and tasks using a scale of 1–5 (low skill to high skill).

[4] Roarty, Mike and Toogood, Kathy (2014). *The Strengths-Focused Guide to Leadership: Identify Your Talents and Get the Most From Your People*. Harlow: Pearson.

Task-based strengths for leaders[5]

COMMUNICATION:	PROVIDING DIRECTION:
• Able to summarise and clarify. • Actively listen to workers' ideas, views and emotions. • Verbalise ideas in a convincing and concise manner. • Interviewing skills. • Allow effective communication within teams. • Courteous in email communication. • Give constructive criticism to staff. • Take time to make a personal connection. • Handle bad news sensitively. • Good quality report writing. • Presentation skills. • Ability to network. • Persuasive negotiation.	• Provide vision. • Make objectives and outcomes specific. • Clearly communicate objectives and outcomes. • Able to fully explain tasks and delegate them. • Create and provide clear standards and expectations. • Develop checks and controls. • Oversee team to keep people on task. • Maintain focus on the result required and stay headed in that direction.
SUPPORTING TEAMS:	**DECISION MAKING AND JUDGEMENT:**
• Know talents of workers in order to allocate tasks effectively. • Set goals and expectations. • Provide training and development. • Empower people by delegating some of the responsibilities. • Motivate team for highest level of performance. • Give informal performance feedback to teams on a regular basis. • Evaluate people's performance with a formal assessment. • Recognise efforts of workers. • Create harmony and positive feelings in teams. • Support teams to increase efficiency. • Treat every individual fairly. • Collaborate well with others in joint projects.	• Clearly define and communicate issues. • Gather important information. • Make decisions on the best action to take. • Take a decision promptly when needed. • Implement the course of action and get on with what is needed. • Communicate and explain decision to the team. • Follow up on progress of action. • Learn from previous mistakes.

▶

[5] Adapted from: 'Examples of strengths'. YourDictionary. [Online] Available from: http://examples.yourdictionary.com/examples-of-strengths.html

ORGANISING AND PLANNING:	PROBLEM SOLVING:
• Define concrete goals. • Explain goals in detail. • Create a workable plan to achieve goals. • Skilful management of projects. • Gather and assign resources. • Support and motivate team on projects. • Evaluate progress and provide feedback. • Effective meeting management. • Change plans quickly when needed to achieve results. • Organise practicalities in complex situations.	• Recognise the problem. • Analyse the relevant information. • Understand cause and effect relationships. • Develop possible solutions. • Choose the best solution and implement it. • Manage and resolve conflict within teams. • Effective crisis management.

What about task weaknesses? Simply flip any of the above strengths around to pinpoint any weak areas. For example:

- Not setting clear goals.
- Playing favourites with people.
- Not admitting mistakes or being unforgiving of the mistakes of others.
- Critical and condescending communication with workers.
- Not listening to new ideas and suggestions.
- Butting into people's responsibilities and questioning their every decision.
- Not providing people with the appropriate training to succeed.
- Being overly indecisive when solving problems – 'analysis paralysis'.
- Not recognising people for the achievements they've made.
- Being a poor example of execution and follow-up.
- Ignoring people's natural talents.

Step 3: Analyse your data

Once the feedback arrives, review your data and try to spot any patterns or common themes that appear. You might be pleasantly taken aback to hear about strengths you didn't even know you had, and the feedback may illuminate blind spots, i.e. less positive aspects about yourself that you weren't aware of. Pool together the similarities to create a consolidated mind map or list of your strengths and weaknesses, the key examples that support them and any useful suggestions. Compare these with your own thoughts, lists and ratings.

Step 4: Create your profile

Use the insights gained from Step 3 to produce a brief, actionable profile of who you are when you're performing at your best.

METHOD 2: THE JOHARI WINDOW

The Johari Window is one of the most thought-provoking models for helping people learn more about themselves and for getting to grips with human interactions as a whole. It's intuitive and can be easily used to create those 'aha!' moments, helping to reveal your hidden self and bringing to light what others know about you. The model is depicted as a four-paned window, which divides personal awareness into four different quadrants:

Johari Window

	Known to self	*Unknown to self*
Known to others	**Open** (Public knowledge; what I show to you)	**Blind** (Feedback; your gift to me)
Unknown to others	**Hidden** (Private; mine to share if I trust you)	**Unconscious** (Unknown; new awareness can emerge)

Source: Ready to Manage (http://store.readytomanage.com/Shared/products/MiscBooks/360_degree_feedback_booklet-final.pdf)

- Open: *What I know about myself and like to reveal to others.* This quadrant describes characteristics, behaviour, knowledge, skills, attitudes and 'public' experiences that we are aware of ourselves and that we like to tell others (or brag!) about.
- Blind: *What I don't know about myself but others do know.* This quadrant represents things about us that we aren't aware of but that are blatantly obvious to the people around us (our blind spots). Perhaps we think we're expressing things clearly, but others interpret them in a completely different way; or maybe there's some basic information that we're missing.

- Hidden: *What I know about myself but conceal from others.* This 'hidden' quadrant describes things that we know about ourselves but opt not to reveal to the people around us. For instance, we may be well aware that we have certain skills or abilities, but prefer not to show them. Or we might hide the fact that we're uncomfortable in group conditions for fear that it might undermine our authority. Over time and as we get to know people better, we usually start to relax and disclose more about our hidden self in small doses, and so we expand the open quadrant while shrinking this one. Naturally, the more we build up a trusting relationship with others, the more self-disclosure is liable to take place.

- Unconscious: *What I don't know about myself and others also don't know.* There are aspects of us that exist but that are, in this moment, unknown to ourselves and others. We are a lot more complex and multifaceted than we think. Let's suppose we have an awesome talent for mentoring that we haven't caught on to yet. Given the right conditions, we might discover this truth about ourselves at some point (maybe through self-reflection or practice), or we might not. Others may spot this talent in us and make us aware of it through feedback, or they may not.[6] So in effect, this 'unconscious' quadrant represents our potentiality, which from time to time can bubble up to the surface.

With the help of feedback from others (friends, colleagues, bosses, coaches), you can learn about yourself and come to terms with who you are on every level. Start with the Open area and be frank about what you know about yourself already. What are your strengths and weaknesses? What are you comfortable with and willing to share with others? Choose adjectives or verbs (e.g. inspiring, coaching, unreliable, superficial, troubleshooting) that you think best describe you and your abilities. You can use the lists of strengths and weaknesses from the previous exercise to help you. Then ask others to give their input by choosing their own terms to describe you. Work through all of the quadrants in this way, entering all the characteristics into the appropriate panes of the window.[7] In the end, you should have a comprehensive 'portrait' of yourself, your character traits and your behaviours.

[6] Worldwide Center for Organizational Development (WCOD) and Ready To Manage (2009). '360-degree feedback debriefing guide'. [Online] Available from: http://store.readytomanage.com/Shared/products/MiscBooks/360_degree_feedback_booklet-final.pdf
[7] Krogerus, Mikael and Tschäppeler, Roman (2011). *The Decision Book: Fifty Models for Strategic Thinking.* London: Profile Books.

Tell your life stories

When we come into this world, we naturally develop certain strengths over the course of our life through our personal and professional encounters. I would say that about 75 per cent of our strengths come from the inherent talent we are born with, while 25 per cent come from our experiences – that's still a hefty chunk. Take a walk down memory lane to learn what's contributed to making you the person you are today. Think back to your schooldays, your old community and previous workplaces for valuable hints of what you're good at:

1. CHILDHOOD RECOLLECTIONS

Strengths often have deep connections to our early lives. Go back in time to your childhood roots or high school years to find out what they have to tell you. What do you remember doing as a child or teenager that you were great at and probably still do now? What positive skills did you learn from parents, coaches, teachers or mentors? List the things that you did really well in school or enjoyed as a hobby. Perhaps you got a kick out of carrying out science experiments in high school, or loved delving into the literary classics. Maybe you always looked forward to chess club on Tuesday nights or singing in the choir. Or perhaps, you were athletic and played a sport to a professional or competitive level.

2. YOUR WORK IN THE PAST AND PREVIOUS SUCCESSES

Look back to other jobs or roles you've had and consider how they've helped to bring out your strengths:

- Are there any specific work situations that spring to mind where you can recall achieving something you were proud of?
- What activities do your performance records show good results in?
- What specific tasks have you received recognition or reward for?
- What work-related experiences or environmental factors in your past have influenced the development of your strengths?
- What kinds of activities did you seem to pick up quickly?
- What tasks have you previously been drawn to or volunteered for?

Make notes about what skills you used and what you did to get great results. Really zero in on your strengths.

3. YOUR MISTAKES AND BLIND SPOTS

Think about times when you screwed up or something you were involved in went wrong. Reflect on what you might have done better. Maybe you overplayed your strengths and went too far? Or maybe this area represents a source of weakness to you? What lessons have you learned from your mistakes? It's important to be aware of the tasks or situations that have been problematic for you in the past so you can at least be clear on how best to respond to similar situations in future.

Your likes and dislikes

Your strengths are not just defined by what you're good at and get the best results in. For a true strengths-based outlook, you also need to take into account what makes you tick – as well as what doesn't.

1. PERSONAL INTEREST AND ENJOYMENT

Being talented at something doesn't necessarily mean that you'll love doing it. You can be extremely good at jobs you hate. Perhaps you're a whiz at detailed tasks like error-checking, statistical work or using formulas in Excel, but you find them mind-numbingly boring. Yawn. When you're really interested in something, however, you'll go out of your way and put in quadruple the effort to get better and better at it. Your passion encourages you to reach further and follow your own star. Think about the activities, hobbies or projects that get your juices flowing – those you love doing and that excite and motivate you:

- What activities give you an energetic buzz when you're doing them?
- What things do you enjoy learning about?
- What tasks come naturally to you that you love doing?
- Do you ever feel that time flies when you're doing a specific activity?
- What would you fill your 'ideal' workday doing?
- What things do you look forward to doing?
- What hobbies or 'pet projects' do you have?

- What tasks make you feel good or satisfied?
- What things are you doing when you feel like the 'real you'?
- When are you most happy and fulfilled in your work?

All these activities are very likely calling on your strengths. It could well be that you excel at them without even trying.

2. YOUR DISLIKES AND ANXIETIES

As well as looking at your mistakes and blind spots, there are other indicators of your weaknesses based on the tasks you tend to struggle with, that drain you or that provoke anxiety. Strengths proponent and bestselling author Marcus Buckingham defines a weakness as any 'activity that weakens you'.[8] Simple enough. Consider the following questions in relation to your past work and present position:

- What things do you dread doing?
- What activities don't you perform well at?
- What tasks drain your energy?
- What activities rarely get any easier?
- What things do you put off or look for excuses to avoid?
- What makes you feel anxious when you're doing it?
- What tasks make you feel inadequate?

These activities take more of an effort. Whether you do them well or not is irrelevant, what matters is that you wouldn't choose to do them because they make you feel frustrated and slow you down.

Exercise 2.1: Strengths chart template

If you've opted to use a number of these methods for sourcing your strengths, you'll be looking for somewhere to keep track of everything you've uncovered. Create a strengths chart to capture and 'map out' your strengths. To get started, download the following template from http://positiveleaderbook.com/strengthschart

---

[8] Buckingham, Marcus (2007). *Go Put Your Strengths to Work: Six Powerful Steps to Achieve Outstanding Performance*. New York: Free Press.

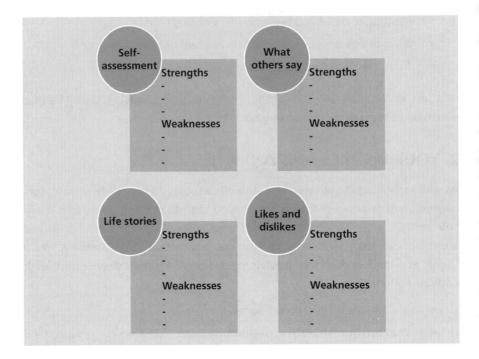

Playing to your strengths: an action plan

Compiling your strengths profile marks the start of your strengths journey, not the end. Like a flight taking off, once the plane's in the air, your journey has begun and the moment has arrived to start soaring with your strengths. This is not a linear journey, but one of infinite possibilities and directions for living and activating your strengths in everyday life. How can you use your strengths more intentionally, starting from now?

You have to name them and aim them.

First, ask yourself these questions:

- Which strengths are most important for accomplishing my leadership or work goals?
- Which of my strengths am I most passionate about?
- What strengths will help me become the leader/person I hope to be?
- Which strengths matter most to the organisation?

Pick the *top three to five* strengths that you feel will make the most difference overall and look at developing each one in turn. Put the spotlight on the strengths where your top skills, passions, work goals and the organisation's needs converge.

Next, get ready for action. Here are some strengths-building and weakness-minimising techniques for you to put to good use:

ACTION 1: SEEK OPPORTUNITIES TO STRETCH YOUR STRENGTHS

Look for opportunities to utilise and flex your strengths right away. This may be as simple as using them more often in situations where you're already getting good results, or volunteering for extra activities in which you can use them. For example, if you have a signature talent for innovative, futuristic thinking, find more ways to readily encourage, share and action your ideas:

- Read articles about the latest technology, science and research to gain knowledge that will fuel your imagination.
- Seek open audiences that will appreciate your ideas for the future and harness their energy to catapult your vision into motion.
- Set aside time to work with colleagues with similar strengths so you can push each other to greater heights of creativity.
- Provide logical support for your exciting visions to make them more concrete – the chances are they'll be better received when rooted in real possibility.
- Produce sketches, step-by-step actions plans or mock-up models to articulate your ideas and make them easier for others to comprehend.

If you're already actioning this special strength to the max and there isn't much scope for further improvement, then try to find ways to exploit it in different contexts. Touching on the same example, why not use your interest in innovative thinking to help others in your team explore and develop their ideas instead? If you catch a vision of what someone is capable of, act as a guide or coach to inspire them to unlock their potential in creative ways. You could even go as far as to choose new roles in which your strength can play a bigger part. For instance, you might excel in entrepreneurial or start-up situations where you can feel free to contribute greater and grander ideas about the future.

ACTION 2: OUTLINE DEVELOPMENT GOALS AND STRATEGIES

So many first-time leaders fail – but not because they don't work hard. Actually, they usually work ridiculously hard. They fail because they spend too much time and effort on improving the skills relevant for their old job or the wrong new ones, rather than developing the solid strengths that will propel them forward. Explore how your greatest natural talents interact with your current skills, knowledge and experience, then set development goals and strategies that will help you maximise your best strengths over a specified period of time. Consider how you can invest in your dominant talents and build them into strengths by gaining additional *knowledge*, getting trained up in new *skills* or by taking on new *tasks*. Need an example? If your aim is to build on an existing raw skill in communication, then look for opportunities, both inside and outside of your organisation, to further enrich your use of the spoken and written word. If you enjoy writing, you could take a course in business writing and set goals to publish your work. If you're an effective public speaker, join a local Toastmasters club to practise your speech-giving skills and receive feedback, or volunteer for opportunities to present at professional meetings or conventions. Think about taking your communication to an even higher standard by developing your knowledge in certain areas, thereby setting yourself up as an expert.

In some cases, you might even want to redefine your entire role and future career options based on your strengths. A great communicator will always prosper in positions that require capturing people's attention, such as in media, marketing or ministry. If this particular signature strength isn't going to make a huge difference at work, then think about ways you could develop it outside of work for a better work–life balance. For instance, set up a personal blog to share your messages with like-minded people and practise your written voice, or offer to give speeches on behalf of your local charity or community.

ACTION 3: AVOID OR DELEGATE YOUR WEAK AREAS

Highlight tasks where you can make a positive difference and look to avoid or delegate those areas and activities which fall into your weak zone. You might be a great strategic leader, but a poor operator when it comes to measuring the details. You could, if you're brave enough, just point blank refuse to do any detail-oriented work at all. Why do something you're bad at if you don't have to? You would just be setting yourself up to be second-rate at it, or worse, a failure. It's possible no one will even notice or care that you've stopped doing it. Of course, most of us don't have the luxury to stop doing necessary tasks just because they involve our weaknesses, so the next option – and the better one at that – is to delegate or outsource these tasks to someone who can do them far better, whether it's a team member, an external consultant or even a fellow boss in your organisation.

Many leaders shy away from delegating because they hate the loss of personal control and the time 'wasted' in explaining, coaching and correcting someone else. But failure to delegate traps you into doing jobs you hate and has you working yourself into an early grave. As a self-aware leader, you need to accept that you can't do everything, be everywhere and make all decisions. Effective delegation frees your time to focus on where you add the most value, such as goal setting, strategic planning, problem solving and communicating with core clients; and it helps broaden the skills of your team. But this only works if you delegate meaningful, visible projects, not just the administrative trivia that you can't be bothered with. If you're no good at accounting or budgeting, rest assured there are bound to be proficient bean counters in your team who can help. Similarly, if you have a poor eye for design, there's probably an abundance of creative talent you can call on to fill the gap, freelance or otherwise. In fact, you can take things further by creating an entire team that compensates for your weaknesses (more on this in **Chapter 3**). You get to hand over the unpleasant tasks and your people get a chance to develop while working on things they enjoy. And together, you all get more done.

ACTION 4: GET CROSS-TRAINING TO MAGNIFY YOUR STRENGTHS

Most of us are used to improving our skills and getting steady, measurable results through a 'linear' route to development, like finding ways to apply a strength more often. However, Dr Jack Zenger and Dr Joseph Folkman (of leadership development firm Zenger Folkman) propose that adopting a 'cross-training' approach can have a more powerful impact on the development of your strengths.[9] This is a non-linear line of attack in that, to draw more

---

[9] Zenger, John H., Folkman, Joseph R., Sherwin, Robert H. and Steel, Barbara A. (2012). *How to Be Exceptional: Drive Leadership Success by Magnifying Your Strengths*. New York: McGraw-Hill.

productivity out of a distinctive strength, you have to work on skills that are *complementary* to it. Cross-training is not some brand-spanking new theory. It's long been employed by athletes and sportspeople of all kinds. A marathon runner doesn't increase his stamina and mileage just by practising running ever longer distances. Although it's the most obvious training option available to him, it won't necessarily make him significantly faster or fitter. To reach the next level, he needs to supplement his running regime with compatible activities that develop complementary skills. For instance, swimming to build stamina and ease his joints, weight training to build muscle, bicycling to gain aerobic capacity, yoga for flexibility and to prevent injury, and so on. The combined influence and interaction of these skills is what will transform him into a truly remarkable runner.

Likewise with your leadership, running a few more miles each day can only take a single strength so far. Let's say one of your top five StrengthsFinder 2.0 talents is that you're a Maximiser, and you're a dab hand at taking things (projects, people, documents or anything) from strong to superb. From a linear perspective, there are some key things you can do to utilise this strength more. To give you one example, you could take on a coaching role in your team to help others work towards mastering their own strengths. But, you can only go so far with this. Increasing your time spent coaching others would be counterproductive eventually, and would pull you away from other crucial leadership tasks. This is where cross-training comes in, allowing you to adopt a correlated strength to make you an even better Maximiser. Perhaps you're good at Connectedness, which means you have a natural ability to build bridges between groups and people, and can connect the dots from the past, present and future to give others perspective, guidance and hope. Cross-training opens up options to apply your Connectedness strength to your Maximiser strength to assist the people around you in coping with the unpredictable events wrought by new change. Through a coaching capacity, you can bring a sense of stability to each individual by showing them how growing their strengths can help secure their position in the team and build their resilience in handling the unexpected. Now do you see how this works? With a cross-training approach, you can usually expect to see concrete evidence of improvement within about 30 to 60 days.[10]

---

[10] Zenger, John H., Folkman, Joseph and Edinger, Scott (2011). 'Making yourself indispensable'. *Harvard Business Review*, October. [Online] Available from: https://hbr.org/2011/10/making-yourself-indispensable/ar/1

ACTION 5: APPROACH UNAVOIDABLE TASKS FROM A STRENGTHS ANGLE

As leaders, we can't always wangle our way out of every disagreeable task or decision. Sometimes there are certain things that we just have to do. So, for challenging but unavoidable tasks that you're particularly weak in, pick one of your signature strengths that you can harness to see you through what needs to be done.[11] For instance, if you have a major presentation coming up and you're frantically worried because you've got a terrible memory and aren't great at gathering facts to back up your points, focus instead on the fact that you're a great story teller and have superb comic timing. No matter what you fail to recall, you can at least make sure your audience is entertained! Think about what crappy tasks you have coming up and give them a strengths-based makeover. Focus on the outcome, not the process. You'll find that they suddenly seem far more appealing.

If you're saddled with a number of tasks that fall under your 'non-talents', you can find a better balance by organising your workload into *'strengths sandwiches'*, i.e. sandwiching the activities that drain you in between the activities that play to your strengths.

ACTION 6: WEAKEN YOUR WEAKNESSES

Though the approach in this book is all about making the most of your strengths, I'm not advocating that you should snub your weaknesses completely. If there's a significant weakness that's undermining your performance as a leader, by all means do something about it! You can't afford to let it develop into a derailer. But, remember that you will only succeed in fixing your weaknesses while you are predominantly building your strengths. Your weaknesses are still going to be your weaknesses whatever you do, so don't divert your energy from your strengths; just manage your weaknesses as best as you can to limit them to the bare minimum. Establish systems to keep things under control, elicit suggestions from the people you work with, find a role model to observe or seek outside help if you need to. There are some basic things like listening, communicating and organisation that we all need to have a minimal level of ability in just to get by. Whatever your issue is, practise to make it 'good enough' until the behaviour

---

[11] Achor, Shawn (2010). *The Happiness Advantage: The Seven Principles that Fuel Success and Performance at Work*. New York: Crown Business.

becomes a habit, not a problem – but then stop! Don't concern yourself with perfecting it. It's illogical to spend too much time on something you're weak in.

FOLLOW UP: TAKE TIME TO REVIEW AND REFLECT

As you work through maximising your strengths and negating your weaknesses, take time at regular intervals to evaluate how you're getting on. Did you get the results you expected? What's been going particularly well? What have you learned along the way? What can you do differently?

Exercise 2.2: Strengths action plan

Ready to put your strengths into action? Use the following action plan template to prepare your strengths-building opportunities and monitor your progress. Download it at http://positiveleaderbook.com/strengthsactionplan

MY TOP STRENGTHS

- Which strengths are most important for accomplishing my leadership or work goals?
- Which of my strengths am I most passionate about?
- What strengths will help me become the leader/person I hope to be?
- Which strengths matter most to the organisation?

List the top three to five strengths where your greatest skills, passions, work goals and the organisation's needs unite.

ACTION 1: STRETCH YOUR STRENGTHS

- Identify ways to use them more.
- Identify new contexts for your strengths.

ACTION 2: DEVELOPMENT GOALS AND STRATEGIES

- List your key goals for developing your strengths, including target dates for achievement.

- List your development strategies for gaining additional knowledge, skills and practice (e.g. reading books, e-learning courses, attending a workshop, mentoring, job rotation, or taking on new tasks and special assignments).
- What support and resource do you need to develop (e.g. equipment, feedback, rewards, etc.)?

ACTION 3: TASKS TO AVOID OR DELEGATE

- Identify tasks that can be avoided.
- Identify tasks that can be delegated.

ACTION 4: CROSS-TRAINING TO MAGNIFY STRENGTHS

1. Core strength:_____
   What complementary activities or behaviours can you work on?
2. Core strength:_____
   What complementary activities or behaviours can you work on?
3. Core strength:_____
   What complementary activities or behaviours can you work on?

ACTION 5: APPLYING A STRENGTHS FOCUS TO UNAVOIDABLE TASKS

1. Unavoidable task:_____
   Identify a strengths angle from which to approach it.
2. Unavoidable task:_____
   Identify a strengths angle from which to approach it.
3. Unavoidable task:_____
   Identify a strengths angle from which to approach it.

ACTION 6: WEAKEN YOUR WEAKNESSES

1. Weak area:_____
   Identify strategies for managing or limiting it.

2. Weak area:_____

   Identify strategies for managing or limiting it.

3. Weak area:_____

   Identify strategies for managing or limiting it.

FOLLOW UP: REVIEW AND REFLECT

How did you get on? What lessons have you learned? What's next?

Using your strengths is not just about turbo-charging your performance as a leader and building competitive advantage, they lead to something even more fulfilling – your *authenticity*.

Authentic leadership: keeping it real

I've come across countless gifted individuals, entrepreneurs and sportspeople in their early careers who are racing so hard to establish themselves in the external world – by focusing on money, fame, power, status, performance, etc. – that they leave little time to take stock of who they really want to be. That was me when I first got started, and I wish I had known better. Your drive and energy is enough to make you successful for a while, perhaps even a champion leader in your field, but it's difficult to keep it up. That's because something is missing, the key ingredient that helps you accept yourself and be confident in who you are – I mean your authenticity of course.

Authentic leadership blows away the mad pressure to conform to some airbrushed, fantasy leader stereotype and reduces great leadership to something that normal people can aspire to. You don't have to be some larger-than-life dynamo to be a leader, like the kind that strews the pages of trendy business magazines. And you don't need to dilute your 'real' personality to fit in with the corporate mould. It's exhausting pretending to be someone else all day. You simply need to be the best of who you are. And how do you become the best of who you are? . . . You guessed it – by being able to deliver on your unique *strengths*. This is number 1. When you can master your innate qualities and abilities, you gain a genuine self-assurance and can be a leader on your own terms. What's more, people will like you for it.

CAPABILITY YIELDS CREDIBILITY

It's important to recognise the value you bring as a leader and celebrate your strengths, whatever they are. This isn't about being self-centred and wanting to be hero-worshipped by your team. Every leader should have at least one or two superior abilities that they've perfected and that are clearly evident to the people around them, whether it's innovative change, public speaking, motivating people or action-oriented judgement. This is far better than trying to be good at everything and ending up with a dozen poorly-developed competencies. Whether they're hard or soft skills, it doesn't matter, just being aware of them will help you create your own brand of personal uniqueness. Your supreme competence in these areas is what will give you respect and credibility. People want to be proud of their leaders, but leaders without obvious skills will lack clout and may even be a source of embarrassment to their team. The great news is that by leveraging your own strengths, you become a natural inspirer and motivator to others. Most workers lack a clear sense of what peak performance is; when you free your own strengths you provide them with a successful model to emulate.

Being authentic as a leader invites something important: RESPECT. Respect is crucial. After all, you can only consistently deliver results through others if you have their respect. But you can't command or demand respect just because of your position in the hierarchy, you have to earn it through your character and example.

Winning respect through tennis

I believe that I showed the makings of a leader at a young age as a result of achieving my ambition to play tennis professionally in the junior league. At first, everyone laughed at me because I was a bit chubby; the Chairman of the tennis club even suggested that I become a sumo wrestler instead! But brimming with the conviction of youth, I was determined not to give up on my dream and worked hard to build my strengths, both physically and mentally. In becoming the top player at my tennis club at only 12 years old, I demonstrated that it was possible to achieve a seemingly impossible goal by trusting my instincts and pursuing my passion for it wholeheartedly. That was the turning point

▶

in my popularity. Other kids admired and respected me for pulling it off and accomplishing exactly what I set out to do. After a while they started to follow my example – even when I was being naughty and getting up to all sorts of shenanigans at school!

The authentic power of charisma

Being positive and authentic can help you get a piece of that star quality that all leaders want . . . even if they won't admit it – yes, I'm talking about *charisma*. Every leader wants to exude that powerful magnetism that allows them to command a room, rouse people's passions and be listened to, respected, followed and, best of all, liked. It's a commonly held myth that charisma is some innate 'X-factor' trait that people are either born with or they're not; an alluring charm that oozes naturally from the chosen few – like Princess Diana, Bill Clinton or Dr Martin Luther King. Happily, this is not the case. Charisma can be taught and every leader can learn how to wield its 'magic' by cultivating specific behaviours. And the good news is that you don't have to be a social dynamite or great speaker to start with.

Please don't think that learning to emulate charismatic behaviours means that you aren't being genuine or real – that it makes you shallow or fake in any way. Positive charisma isn't about manipulating people; getting them to like you so you can make them do whatever you want them to do. It's about controlling your own mind and behaviour, not the other person. In fact, true charisma is essentially the *authenticity* that's derived through someone being comfortable in their own skin. Nothing ruins charisma faster than appearing inauthentic.

Executive coach and charisma expert Olivia Fox Cabane has devised three simple, concrete steps to help people develop the amazing 'It' factor and become more memorable.[12] These are based upon three largely non-verbal categories of behaviour that are critical to achieve charisma: *presence, power and warmth*. By deftly balancing the three elements and practising them until they become natural, you can produce incredible personal magnetism.

[12] Cabane, Olivia Fox (2013). *The Charisma Myth: How Anyone Can Master the Art and Science of Personal Magnetism*. New York: Portfolio.

1. PRESENCE

Have you ever been in a conversation with someone and felt like you didn't have their full attention? It's annoying and quite crushing isn't it? Being completely engaged with the people you're interacting with can be a tough act to pull off, but it can make all the difference in your appeal to others. Pros like Bill Clinton have got this down to a tee. He gives you the feeling that he's entirely with you and intensely 'into' the conversation, like you're the centre of the universe. And that's the real secret to charisma – making the other person feel good about him- or herself, not trying to impress them with your electric personality. Presence can't be faked or feigned. If you're not fully present when you interact with someone, there's a good chance that your facial reaction will be a split-second delayed or that your eyes will glaze over. The human mind can read facial expressions in as little as 17 milliseconds, so it's likely that the other person will notice your lack of presence and get the distinct impression that you're being inauthentic. This leads them to feel undervalued and unappreciated, and makes it difficult to generate trust and good rapport with them. Not exactly the result you bargained for! The good news is that there are techniques you can use to focus your mental and emotional energy during interactions and create that feeling of importance and acknowledgement.

- **Focus on your toes.** If you feel like your mind is wandering while you're in the middle of a conversation, simply bring your attention to your body; and specifically to the physical sensation in your toes. Really feel their contact with the ground. Forcing your brain to sweep your body from head to toe brings you back to the here and now. In just a second or two, you're physically present in the moment again.

- **Deep gazing.** Look the other person in the eye during your exchange. Notice the colour of their eyes or their blink rate. Pay attention. This is extremely powerful in giving you that deep soul-searching eye contact that makes you more mesmerising and creates a sense of connection with the person you're interacting with. Obviously, don't overdo it! A little eye contact goes a long way. You don't want to scare people off.

- **Ask questions.** Don't be a conversational narcissist. Show someone that you're completely with them by focusing on asking the most interesting questions. Body language expert Vanessa Van Edwards suggests thinking, 'How can I get this person to tell me their story?'

to encourage you to make this mentality shift. Asking follow-up questions after they've spoken will also prove that you're really listening, for example, 'What was your favourite part of that?' or 'Am I understanding you correctly?' Not only will you learn more about the person, you'll also increase the bond between you.

2. POWER

Power in a charismatic sense is not necessarily the power of commanding an army or directing a multinational corporation. Your charismatic power is the perception of your ability to affect the world around you, whether through influence, money, expertise, intelligence, raw physical strength or social status. Powerful people give the impression that they can make things happen and they have an irresistible aura that draws people into their orbit like a magnetic force. It's a primal attraction that stems from our caveman heritage. Like it or not, we're still hardwired to flock towards the people who have the resources to help us survive out in the wild. In seeking out those people, we look for clues of power mainly in their demeanour and body language.

- **Strike a 'power pose'.** To increase your power, act like you've already got it. An alpha gorilla will beat his chest when claiming his territory because it makes him look bigger. Similarly, you can be the 'big gorilla' by adopting expansive poses and taking up more space to create the impression of power. While sitting, casually drape your arms over the back of your chair, or lean back with your hands on your head. Alternatively, sit sideways to take up extra room, put your feet up on your desk or even sit on top of it. While walking, inflate your chest slightly and keep your back erect as you saunter along. When standing, try to keep your arms akimbo with hands resting on your waist, like a superhero. In meetings, stand up, lean forward and rest your hands on the table in front of you to convey your point. Stay poised and be still, don't fidget. Like the alpha gorilla, take control of your environment and keep your body language open. When you assume a physically confident, powerful posture in these ways, you actually begin to feel it.

- **Confidence power-boosters.** The most fatal inhibitor to anyone's power is lack of self-confidence or self-doubt, which is usually related to 'Imposter Syndrome' – that feeling that you're a fraud in your job and you're going to be found out any minute. This syndrome is estimated to hit 70–80 per cent of the population. Power begins first in the mind. Think and act like you've already got it together, even if you're still finding your way. If you feel self-assured and confident, others will feel and respond to it too. Confidence is an enticing quality that broadcasts power, makes people want to get to know you and demonstrates that you can affect the world around you. At the very root of developing self-confidence is *mastery*.[13] Attaining mastery over something – a strength, skill, knowledge or resource – will fundamentally change the way you feel about and conduct yourself. I don't think I need to say much more on this. If there's one thing you've learned in this chapter, it's how to go about mastering your strengths!

But how do you handle heavy self-doubt in the meantime?

- One effective way is *destigmatisation*, lifting the stigma off the experience. One of the worst emotions you can feel is shame; it's a real performance killer. Recognise that imposter syndrome is a normal, natural feeling linked to our survival instincts, and that we all experience it from time to time. It's nothing to be ashamed about and it has no bearing on your actual worth or competence. Think of others who've gone through similar uncomfortable feelings, especially people you admire, and see yourself as part of a community of human beings experiencing the same thing at the same moment. As a leader, you are by definition the alpha gorilla of your pack and so you're in an excellent position to help people destigmatise and dedramatise their own uncertain emotions.

- *Detaching* is another step. The key to detaching is recognising that your thoughts (especially the self-critical ones) are not necessarily accurate. As humans, we have a limited capacity for conscious attention which constrains how much we can be aware of at any given moment. Our brain constantly filters for relevant information through the millions of visual inputs our eyes take in at every moment, usually highlighting the negative in our environment. This means that we have an incomplete, sometimes distorted, view of reality. Just because

[13] McKay, Brett and McKay, Kate (2013). 'The 3 elements of charisma: Power'. *The Art of Manliness*, 12 November. [Online] Available from: http://www.artofmanliness.com/2013/11/12/the-3-elements-of-charisma-power/

our mind thinks a certain negative thought, it doesn't mean it has any validity whatsoever. To deal with persistent unhelpful thoughts, make an effort to depersonalise and neutralise the experience. Treat these unproductive reflections as graffiti on a wall that you catch a glimpse of but don't necessarily pay any attention to as you're passing by. Or imagine your annoying mental chatter as coming from a radio; turn down the volume, switch the radio off or put it to the side.

3. WARMTH

The last, but far from least, element of charisma is the warmth that makes people feel comfortable and at ease around you. When you radiate warmth, your charisma quotient soars and people see you as being approachable, caring and full of goodwill. Warmth tells us whether someone would be willing to use the power they have in our favour. It's nigh on impossible to fake. There's far too much going on in our bodies for us to control consciously. What's in our mind always shows up in our body language and even the briefest of micro-expressions will give things away. People will catch these on a gut level and know if you're being inauthentic. If they sense that you're only after something from them, they'll recoil from you, just as they would from a greasy salesman who jacks up the fake warmth with a view to closing the deal. For warmth to pass off as genuine, it must originate in your mind and be grounded in something deeper than a selfish motive – a genuinely good heart. When you have real empathy for folks and are truly interested in their wellbeing, it shows in your face and behaviour, and people perceive you as being caring and warm-hearted. There are techniques that will help you put your best foot forward to display the outward behaviours that match your inner warmth:

- **Rewrite reality.** One of the single biggest obstacles to warmth is negative mental criticism. If you're in the grip of self-disapproval (e.g. feelings of shame, stress or embarrassment) while talking to someone, it puts you in an aggravated state which often shows on your expression and demeanour. The person you're interacting with isn't aware of what's going on in your mind, and so naturally assumes that the tension or criticism on your face is about them. To deal with this negative internal state, don't try to control the output (your body language), go straight to the input (your mind). The brain cannot tell the difference between imagination and reality, so work on creating an alternative reality in order to regain a calm mental outlook and manifest the desired body language. Choose a better, more charisma-enhancing response to the situation. Ask yourself, 'What if this experience is actually a good thing for me?' Watch and marvel at how creative your mind can get with its answers. And see how quickly your current perspective changes to a more helpful one. For maximum effect, write down your new realities on paper and describe them in vivid detail, ideally in the past tense, e.g. 'The project was a complete success because . . . .'

- **Develop your 'fellow-feeling'.** An important factor in developing warmth is empathy. It's one thing *having* a good heart but others need to be able to see and feel it. Empathy is a highly effective way of communicating your kindness and goodwill to others in what's fast becoming a cynical world, enabling them to feel understood, acknowledged and cared for. A key tip is to pick three things about the other person that you can approve of. When you start searching for positive elements, your mental state changes accordingly and the warmth and goodwill it generates will sweep through your body language, softening your eyes and relaxing your facial countenance and form. Putting yourself in another's shoes is also a great approach for dealing with a difficult or annoying person. Imagine a different story about them. Be compassionate and consider possible reasons why they might be rude or annoying. What happened to them yesterday or this morning? What about their past or their childhood? Everyone has hard stuff in their life that they're grappling with. Perhaps you had a similar upsetting experience in the past. Practising this kind of empathy and wishing someone well can generate a miraculously positive response in only the briefest of interactions.

Creating super-talented teams

'If you treat people as they are, they will stay as they are. But if you treat them as they ought to be, they will become bigger and better persons.'

JOHANN WOLFGANG VON GOETHE, GERMAN WRITER AND STATESMAN

Before you 'made it' as a leader, your chief responsibility was for your own performance. Now things are different. You've suddenly picked up a whole bunch of other responsibilities, the main one being to elicit a sparkling performance from your team. One thing you should never forget as a leader is that your people's success is your success.[1] Obviously, your individual

---

[1] Morris, Michael (2005). *The First-time Manager: The First Steps to a Brilliant Management Career.* Third edition. London: Kogan Page.

productivity is still important (that's why you need to play to your strengths!), but there's only one way you can nail your leadership goals and create competitive advantage, and that's through your team. Make no mistake; you'll be judged on how well your people deliver, no matter what you're doing.

Nowadays, the stock of the team concept is at an all-time high. Though we may still admire the heroic 'lone ranger' leader who comes up with all the fancy ideas, carries the load and arrives just in time to save the day, in reality leadership is more of a collective and cohesive process in which people work together to accomplish shared goals. It's not a solo game, it's a team sport. In this chapter, we'll be looking at how to inject a strengths-based concept into your teamwork and performance management processes, from training and development, to coaching and even performance problems.

Strengths-based teams[2]

- Teams that focus on strengths every day have 12.5 per cent greater productivity.
- Teams that receive strengths feedback have 8.9 per cent greater profitability.
- In high-performance teams, people say they call upon their strengths more than 75 per cent of the time.
- Teams with high employee engagement levels experience 37 per cent lower absenteeism.
- Highly engaged teams have 12 per cent higher customer service scores.
- Employees who receive strengths feedback have turnover rates that are 14.9 per cent lower than those who don't.

Building a balanced team

Like their leaders, teams these days come in all shapes, sizes and colours.

---

[2] Buckingham, Marcus (2007). *Go Put Your Strengths to Work: Six Powerful Steps to Achieve Outstanding Performance*. New York: Free Press.

So what makes a box-solid, red-hot team?

The answer lies in bringing together people who have complementary strengths and structuring their roles in ways that play to their unique styles, skills and perspectives. Strong teams are *interdependent*. Like a football team, members need to play and closely interact with one another to score goals and keep springing up the league. They rely on each other to get the work done. Strong teams are also *diverse*. A football team with 11 strikers would be at a serious drawback; you also need mid-fielders, defenders and a heavy-duty goalie to cover every position, balance out skills and maximise the team's collective performance. The *modus operandi* is to position members so that each can do what he or she does best. You could have a team made up of superstar players, each with amazing individual strengths, but together they won't necessarily make a superstar team. On the other hand, you could take great individuals who aren't superstars but who can contribute complementary skills, and put them together to make a superstar team, just like the winners of the 2014 FIFA World Cup, Germany, a team renowned for its unity and efficiency rather than its distinct players. This is what *team synergy* is all about – exploiting the strengths of each individual to increase the performance, balance and capabilities of the whole team, making the sum of the team greater than its individual parts. In top-functioning teams, two plus two equals five, not four.

How do you go about building your dream team? It's a simple matter of putting all the blocks in the right place. Consider these steps:

STEP 1: POOL TEAM MEMBERS' STRENGTHS

Firstly, every 'leader of the pack' should make time to get to know each of their team members' strengths and understand what they all bring to the table. By pooling the individual data from everyone's assessments and profiles, you get an overview of the whole team's collective strengths and weaknesses.

There are various ways you can do this. I like to use the StrengthsFinder 2.0 team grid based on people's top five talents (there's a handy Excel template available on completing the assessment at www.strengthsfinder.com). Alternatively, you can create your own team matrix, map or chart to visualise people's collective talents in a snapshot view.

One option is to start by bundling strengths into different categories or groupings, such as:[3]

- broad expertise (e.g. industry experience, market knowledge or competitor insight)
- specific functions (e.g. technical, finance, marketing, administration, etc.)
- soft/people skills (coaching, negotiating, relationship building)
- overall approach/inclination (e.g. strategic, action-oriented, structured, hands-on).

You can then tick off people's top three to five strengths or allocate ratings based on their level of development or expertise in certain areas. Here's an example of a generic 'tick off' strengths matrix for a fictional team of five members (although you could build a similar matrix for any kind of company, functional department or project team):

Team strengths matrix

STRENGTH	TEAM MEMBERS				
	Lucy	Paul	Ravi	Abigail	Larry
BROAD EXPERTISE					
Industry/segment experience					✓
Competitor insight		✓			
Market knowledge				✓	
FUNCTIONS					
Financial/accounting skills		✓			
Presentation skills	✓				
Writing/documentation				✓	
Use of processes and systems			✓		
Administration			✓		
Marketing campaigns					
Creative and design skills	✓				

▶

[3] Ashman, Joann Warcholic and Shelly, Susan (2011). *Play to Your Team's Strengths: The Manager's Guide to Boosting Innovation, Productivity and Profitability*. Avon, MA: F+W Media Business Now.

STRENGTH	TEAM MEMBERS				
	Lucy	Paul	Ravi	Abigail	Larry
Research/analysis		✓			
Meeting management	✓				
IT/technical skills			✓		
Customer service					
Project management				✓	
PEOPLE SKILLS					
Negotiation	✓				
Managing change					
Coaching others					✓
Teamworking				✓	
Leading					✓
Conflict resolution		✓			
APPROACH					
Strategic/long-term thinker	✓				✓
Planner/goal-oriented					
Hands-on				✓	
Perfectionist			✓		
Action-oriented					✓
Deadline-driven (structured)		✓			
Data-driven (investigator)			✓		
Fire fighting					

The idea of doing this is that you can capture and make sense of the team's current capabilities in a simple, visual form before you get into the details of working out who should be doing what to meet the organisation's goals.

If you want to get more scientific with it, you can go further by rating each member of the team on their level of expertise or development on key strengths. Below is a standard scale used in many situational leadership or competency models:

Strengths rating

1. Low level of expertise
2. Partially developed level of expertise
3. High/broad level of expertise
4. Fully developed expertise

The advantage of the rating scale is that it highlights the priority tasks where each member of the team can best contribute to the organisation. It also draws attention to the areas where there's excellent potential for additional training and development to build overall strength levels (e.g. to advance from a high level of competency (3) to a fully developed 'top performer' level of expertise (4)).

Once you've pooled all the data, take a moment to review what the matrix/grid/map says about the team:

- What are your initial thoughts and observations in describing this team?
- Which domain or category appears to be the team's most dominant? What does this tell you about what this team is really good at?
- What are the team's dominant strengths or talents? How might these contribute to the team's success?
- What are the weaknesses of the team? What frustrates you about this team?
- Do you see any potentially powerful partnerships on the team?

Ideally, you want this to be a transparent, collaborative process that allows all team members to get involved in chatting about their strengths and weaknesses openly and honestly. Relationships and interactions become stronger when everyone understands their teammates, talents and what makes each of them special, setting a positive stage for making team changes that will bring exceptional results.

STEP 2: WHO DOES WHAT?

Here comes the tricky part … working out who does what for a top-functioning team. *Belbin's Team Roles* is a tried-and-tested method to turn to for creating powerful, balanced teams and project groups, offering a way to align jobs and tasks according to people's strengths and preferred styles of working. If you're not already familiar with Belbin's model, there's lots of info out there on the internet, but I'll give you a bitesize run-through here. In short, Dr Meredith Belbin spent nine years researching what people do in successful teams, and he famously observed that individuals tend to assume *nine distinct team roles*. These are categorised into three groups – action-oriented, people-oriented and thought-oriented, like this:

Belbin's Team Roles

ACTION-ORIENTED	Shaper	Challenging and dynamic. Thrives on pressure. Has the drive to overcome obstacles.
	Implementer	Disciplined and reliable. Converts ideas into practical action.
	Completer-Finisher	Conscientious and accurate. Ensures timely completion of tasks. Polishes and perfects.
PEOPLE-ORIENTED	Coordinator	Mature and confident. Clarifies goals and acts as a chairperson. Delegates effectively.
	Team Worker	Perceptive and diplomatic. Encourages cooperation, builds morale and averts friction.
	Resource Investigator	Outgoing and communicative. Explores new opportunities and develops contacts.
THOUGHT-ORIENTED	Plant	Creative and free-thinking. Generates ideas and solves difficult problems.
	Monitor-Evaluator	Serious minded and strategic. Analyses the options and judges accurately.
	Specialist	Dedicated and self-starting. Provides in-depth knowledge and specialised skills.

Source: Belbin Team roles, www.belbin.com

This doesn't mean that all teams must have nine people. But it does mean that nine team roles generally have to be covered so that a team doesn't fall short of its full potential. Some people can comfortably try their hand at two or even three roles.

Belbin's Team Roles is a cool tool for figuring out what's missing from your team and for building on everyone's strengths as a whole, while also managing their 'permissible weaknesses'. Use it to work out what your team needs to give it the best chance of success and to check whether individuals are in the right jobs for their skills and abilities. For instance, if you're lacking a *Completer-Finisher* on the team, then it's likely that you'll have to constantly push and chase people to finish off tasks. No *Monitor-Evaluator* on board? Then far too many errors might be slipping through the cracks. If you're experiencing too much conflict between colleagues, then there would appear to be a strong call for a *Team Worker* and/or *Coordinator* to take the lead in pulling everyone together again. Is it just a case of your team needing an all-round step-up in performance? Then make sure you have a *Shaper*, *Implementer* and *Resource Investigator* on the scene. Different roles are also important for different circumstances, challenges or organisational priorities. For example:[4]

- New teams need a strong *Shaper* to get started.
- Competitive situations demand an *Innovator* with good ideas.
- High-risk areas are best assisted by a good *Monitor-Evaluator*.

Find more info at: www.belbin.com

Whether you opt to use the Belbin approach or simply work from your own 'homemade' strengths matrix, the aim is to allocate activities, objectives or responsibilities evenly amongst team members in ways that play to their individual strengths or the areas that they're looking to develop in, not just according to their role or position. This involves an element of *individualisation* in setting slightly different expectations for each person and tailoring your moves as leader to capitalise on their unique strengths. Few jobs allow people to spend 100 per cent of their time working in their strength zones, but you can intentionally increase the ratio to let people spend a greater proportion of their time on what they're best at.

---

[4] Department of Trade & Industry. 'People development & teamwork'. [Online] Available from: http://www.businessballs.com/dtiresources/TQM_development_people_teams.pdf

Max out team performance by letting your people 'own' the activities in which they're happily displaying their natural talents. For instance, if Sandra excels at helping customers solve problems, then look to put her in a client-facing position where she can thrive; or failing that, markedly increase the time she spends on customer support activities. Work out ways that people can automate, delegate or eliminate their weaker activities as much as possible, freeing them up to work on their respective strengths. For example, if Luke has a talent for strategic thinking, then allow him to invest more time in tasks where he can be free to generate visionary ideas, and strip back or reallocate his non-essential activities.

STEP 3: GETTING THE BALANCE RIGHT

Done well, a strengths-based approach can help you prioritise your efforts and focus your resources to grow your team at optimum efficiency, while also delivering superb results in the short term. Remember, a great team should always be a mix of styles that balance each other out. If all team members have similar styles of behaviour you end up with an inbred, unstable team that's bordering on defective. There's nothing to offset people's weaknesses so it's almost as if they're magnified, and people's strengths are echoed pointlessly.

An exaggerated example would be a team where everyone is an extrovert. Things could get pretty rowdy with people competing for the tasks that they want to work on, rather than cooperating to make sure everything's done. Throw a few introverts into the mix and the dynamic changes. A sales team full of amazing 'closers' wouldn't do half as well without strong 'openers' to kickstart conversations with complete strangers and whet their interest for the product or service. Pooled together, each person's strengths can overcome the weaknesses of the other. All you have to do is let them loose on the things they're great at.

That goes for you leaders too. Research by Tom Rath and Barry Conchie for Gallup found that the most effective leaders were not necessarily well-rounded, but they could create teams that 'made up' for the strengths they did not possess themselves.[5] The most cohesive and best-performing teams had

---

[5] Rath, Tom and Conchie, Barry (2008). *Strengths Based Leadership: Great Leaders, Teams and Why People Follow*. New York: Gallup Press.

strengths that spanned four distinct domains of leadership: *executing*, *influencing*, *relationship building* and *strategic thinking.*

- Executors know how to 'get things done'. They are best at implementing solutions and doing what it takes to turn a goal into reality.

- Influencers are great at selling ideas inside and outside the organisation and at helping their team reach a broader audience. These are the ones who'll speak up, make sure your group is heard and win you followers.

- Relationship builders are the essential glue that holds a team together. Through personal connection and care, they keep the team's collective energy high and create a stronger organisation by forming positive partnerships.

- Strategic thinkers are the ones that keep the team focused on the bigger picture. They are constantly absorbing and analysing information and helping the team navigate the best route for future opportunities.

Team tricks at Microsoft CEE

When I first inherited the Central and Eastern Europe (CEE) division at Microsoft, it was an average 'so-so' team in terms of its performance ratings. We overhauled our approach using a combination of strengths-based leadership and positive psychology, and within just a few years we became the best-performing region worldwide for four years running. No other regional team had ever achieved that level of success before, and no other team has managed it since. There was no mystery to how we did it. Based on StrengthsFinder and Myers-Briggs Type Indicator (MBTI) profiles, I reshaped and reorganised the team to match people's roles to their apparent strengths and proficiency level, and switched the focus to maximising their effectiveness rather than fixing their weak areas. It wasn't necessary to recruit lots of new people to build my power team; only 2 per cent of the original team was altered, but it was essential to make each person's talent count in a more profound and complementary way. Leadership is good, but *'Leadershift'* is even better if you can move people to be more of who they are.

As a positive leader, you set an example for your team. The example is not to be amazing at every job or every position, but to know your strengths and use them to your greatest advantage. At the end of the day, leadership is all about moving from the *I* to the *We*. The whole notion is that team members can 'take over' the areas where their teammates have lesser talents, with everyone doing what they do best to achieve success.

T-E-A-M

'TOGETHER EVERYONE ACHIEVES MORE'

Developing team strengths

As you've probably gathered by now, the strengths-based leadership approach we've been talking about in this book differs from 'conventional' leadership in quite a number of ways. A key one of these being that it urges leaders to change the way they view their team and to act as facilitators, coaches, motivators and guides rather than strict, hard-headed superiors. Positive leaders don't waste time micro-managing their team, dictating their every step and picking out their faults, but they do inspire and support people in developing their strengths so that they can do what they love and love what they do while upgrading their performance at the same time.

My best advice for introducing a strengths focus to your team's development is to start small. Pick two or three areas for each member of your team to work on through training or coaching. Or try it on a small project team as a pilot. This will give your team the chance to gain some quick wins and build the motivation to keep striving for positive growth. The *Strengths Action Plan* from the previous chapter will give you some action ideas to work with. If you're happy with the results from your test-run, you can then look at incorporating a strengths-based scheme into your formal processes, such as performance appraisal discussions.

Training is vital to liberate and capitalise on strengths. Finding our talents is like discovering diamonds in the rough, and training offers a way to hone and polish them until they sparkle. It's about adding the *knowledge and skills* to transform an innate *talent* into a powerful, knock-out strength. Refer to the following carefully defined terms:[6]

- Talents are your naturally occurring patterns of thought, feelings or behaviour. Your various themes of talent are what self-assessment tools like the StrengthsFinder 2.0 actually measure.
- Knowledge consists of the facts and lessons learned.
- Skills are the steps of an activity.

It's a sad truth that a lot of organisations don't see the value of ongoing skills training and development. They'll regularly spend 50–70 per cent of their budgets on people's salaries and yet invest less than 1 per cent on training them to sharpen their strengths.[7] One of the greatest services you can do as leader, however, is to offer your people targeted opportunities to exercise and grow their talents, and in turn boost the growth of the company as a whole. Training is an investment in potential, not a wasteful expense. When you invest in your people, you open up a new world of prospects not only for them but also for yourself. The stronger and more indispensable your team becomes, the more they are able to take care of business for you. So in the end, it's like taking a whole load off your shoulders. Here are some active steps you can take to open career growth opportunities for your team:

STEP 1: SET LEARNING AND TRAINING GOALS

People's existing strengths should drive their learning/training goals in the short term and their career development needs in the long term. Instead of waiting for your team members to come to you, approach them directly and help them set focused goals for training their strengths and re-aligning their career path. Let them know what qualities you see in them that could best help them meet the expectations of their role. But also make it clear that if they have a favourite strength they'd like to develop, you're willing to support them all the way. If they want to work on maximising their public speaking, IT knowledge, negotiation skills, their creativity or assertiveness, then be sure to give them your wholehearted encouragement. Their eagerness mingled with

[6] Buckingham, Marcus and Clifton, Donald O. (2001). *Now, Discover Your Strengths: How to Develop Your Talents and Those of the People You Manage*. London: Simon & Schuster.
[7] Sharma, Robin (2010). *Leadership Wisdom from the Monk Who Sold His Ferrari: The 8 Rituals of the Best Leaders*. London: Harper Element.

your backing will motivate and energise them to put in the effort that's needed to increase their ability to add value to the team.

STEP 2: ESTABLISH A DEVELOPMENT PLAN

In the context of the goals just agreed, figure out the most appropriate learning and development opportunities for your colleague. These can include any combination of formal, off-the-job training courses, events, e-learning programmes and seminars, or training through on-the-job activities such as shadowing, job rotation, mentoring, secondment, special projects, using workbooks/manuals, etc. Basically anything that will help your team member marshal and apply their targeted strengths.

To illustrate this process, let's say Jack on your team has an Input strength (based on his StrengthsFinder 2.0 assessment), and he loves amassing hordes of information and using it to make the right choices in his job. Working closely with Jack, think of learning tasks or special duties he can take on that would improve his resourcefulness and also help others in the organisation. Here are some ideas:

- Assign Jack a mini-project to devise a new system for easily storing and locating information. This could then be openly shared with everyone on the team to inform their decision making and research.
- To keep his Input strength primed, give Jack the freedom to schedule regular time in his workday to read books and articles that he finds stimulating.
- Identify Jack's specialist subjects and send him on a formal study course to help him become a qualified expert. This will position him as an authority in the team that others can turn to for information, support or answers to their questions.

Nowadays, we're spoilt for choice in terms of all the training and learning methods available to us. Take into account people's learning styles and preferences when picking out which learning tools to use. Some people learn best by hearing, others by seeing and a third group by doing. Distance learning and computer-based training courses are great for self-directed learners, but those needing practical challenge or management experience may benefit more from job rotation or delegation of extra responsibilities to increase their exposure to different tasks. Some of the bigger corporates, like GE and Unilever, actively move their younger talent around different locations and divisions worldwide, so that they can build the breadth of experience to become successful leaders of multi-functional teams across diverse cultures.

STEP 3: DON'T FORGET TO FOLLOW UP

Once your colleague has had the opportunity to learn and practise their new skills, they're going to need some feedback on how they're getting on. This doesn't have to come directly from you; it can be from a peer or through self-evaluation. What matters is that time is taken to review their progress in building their strengths and any relevant adjustments are made for future training or career opportunities. Make sure to celebrate great results as they happen to keep those motivation levels at a steady high.

Your leadership learning

It's not only your team that needs training, you do too! The qualities and strengths that make someone an authentic, powerful leader don't just develop out of thin air. Like a garden plant, they must be seeded and consistently nurtured to take root, sprout and ultimately flourish. Learning and improving as a leader is best achieved in the place where it all happens – on the job. That's not to imply that booking onto corporate training sessions, reading the latest management books or running along to seminars of the hottest speakers won't help. They can do a great job of getting you kitted up with skills and teaching you a bucket load of technical knowledge on business subjects like accounting, marketing, operations or finance. But leadership isn't about knowledge or technical acumen alone; it's about enabling and inspiring people to achieve great things – and experience and practice is a huge part of it.

PRACTICE MAKES PERFECT (ALMOST!)

Knowledge that stays unapplied is meaningless. All leaders should take a leaf out of their favourite sportsperson's book and practise, practise, practise! No matter how naturally gifted or knowledgeable they are about their sport, every successful athlete and sports star knows that practice is inevitably what makes their performance great. And it works just the same for CEOs, entrepreneurs, team supervisors and leaders of all kinds. Lasting success as a leader isn't based on what you know; it's based on *acting* on what you know (your 'know-how' not your 'know-what'). It's widely believed that 70 per cent of leadership development comes from experience, 20 per cent comes from coaching and just 10 per cent comes from classroom instruction.[8] For first-time leaders, applying their strengths and knowledge builds confidence because it provides assurance that they can do what needs to be done; and over time they get to know how to do it even better.

SELF-AWARE OBSERVATION

The best kind of practice happens when you take the time to reflect on what you're doing and why. This brings us right back to Chapter 1 and the need for *self-awareness*. As you move from one experience to another, you build up your own storehouse of triumphs, disasters and feedback. Like any other skill or ability, learning to be a leader is a process of objectively observing yourself in action, and adapting and improvising your approach based on your discoveries. Through self-assessment, you'll have a more direct route for achieving an even bigger impact with your strengths and you'll be greatly aware of what's going on, why it's happening and where you're headed.

You don't need to go overboard with self-reflection and put together some gigantic plan for your future development. Simply focus on writing yourself some leadership resolutions to use as cornerstones for your efforts to develop.[9] Ask yourself these questions:

- What are your resolutions for your own practice of leadership?
- In what directions do you want to develop and improve?
- What are the important challenges for you and how will you develop strategies to deal with them?

[8] Lombardo, Michael M. and Eichinger, Robert W. (2001). *The Leadership Machine: Architecture to Develop Leaders for Any Future*. Minneapolis, MN: Lominger.
[9] Pedler, Mike, Burgoyne, John and Boydell, Tim (2010). *A Manager's Guide to Leadership: An Action Learning Approach*. Second edition. Maidenhead: McGraw-Hill Professional.

LOOK TO YOUR ROLE MODELS

While my aim in this book is to show you how to be the very best, most authentic version of yourself, that doesn't mean you can't learn anything from other people. Everyone learns from role models, whether they're aware of it or not. It's natural to pick up habits, good and bad, from the people around you – your parents, your boss, your peers, teachers, coaches or celebrity figures in the press. This kind of learning is often unconscious. That's why it's important to actively seek the right role models who can teach you the right kinds of lessons. If you pick up lousy habits from the wrong model early in your career, they can become deeply entrenched and difficult to drop later on.

I'm not saying you should go cloning someone you admire by copying all their words and actions. But there's nothing wrong with tapping into different leadership examples and stealing little pieces of DNA from those you identify with and whose authenticity rings true to you. Draw up a list of three people that you admire or consider to be true leaders and think about the qualities that make them special (my main role models are Buddha and Bill Gates!). Consider the specific lessons or messages about leadership that you can learn from these leaders. Use your observations of these leaders to accelerate your learning.

Exercise 3.1: Top role models

1. My role model: _____

   Qualities: _____

   Lessons/message: _____

2. My role model: _____

   Qualities: _____

   Lessons/message: _____

3. My role model: _____

   Qualities: _____

   Lessons/message: _____

Note that you can learn just as much from negative examples as you can from positive ones. Always take heed when a fellow colleague or leader messes up or behaves without integrity, for instance, by belittling people in front of others or taking credit for someone else's achievements. Even the most positive, influential leaders can make innocent mistakes; they're only human after all. Leadership mishaps, errors or plain bad examples can all provide valuable, deeply impacting lessons about what not to do or how not to be. Take the lessons on board, but avoid repeating them like the plague!

Coaching: a strengths approach

Behind every great sports team is a great coach, and so it should be with any business team as well. These days, it's almost universally accepted that coaching is a mandatory part of any leader's role, along with leading, motivating and guiding teams and individuals. This is especially true for a strengths-based leader as their role is, in practice, not all that different from the job of a good coach.

Coaching is often confused or used interchangeably with mentoring, but the two are very distinct learning/management methodologies. My dear friend Anne Scoular, managing director of London-based coaching firm Meyler Campbell, makes the difference clear for us:[10]

> 'Traditional mentoring (or training or advising or consulting) _puts in_ advice, content, information. Coaching, by contrast, _pulls out_ the capacity people have within.'

From a strengths angle, coaching involves coaxing out people's strengths and aiming them towards success through a constant process of building trust, building skills and building independence. Good coaches hold back from 'telling' and micro-managing, and instead focus on 'asking' and empowering individuals to develop their own approach or solution to their particular challenge. There's an old proverb: 'Tell me, I'll forget. Show me, I'll remember. Involve me, I'll understand.' This light touch is what coaching brings to energise, liberate and unlock the potential of each person on the team to

---

[10] Scoular, Anne (2011). *The Financial Times Guide to Business Coaching*. Harlow: Pearson Education.

achieve first-class performance. Coaching should treat people like adults, not children who are incapable of independent thought. If done right, it facilitates individuals to become more analytical and self-aware, and to develop insight and critical thinking skills for themselves. The only way your people will grow and become self-sufficient is if they climb their own mountains. You can listen, advise, support and encourage them, but you can't climb the mountain for them!

As a regular check-in activity, coaching will inject a strengths culture and mindset into your team, encouraging it to go viral throughout the organisation. Though suffice to say, it can be a real challenge for leaders to maintain the continuous effort of coaching and supporting people in the 'live' work environment. When you're crazy busy, it's easy not to pay much attention to team members who are doing well and don't cause any problems. After all, they're not actively demanding or requiring your attention. But this means missing out on valuable opportunities to give one-to-one feedback, to communicate what's expected of them and to keep them driven and motivated to excel.[11] Whether they appear to or not, your people want your attention and interest, and they want guidance in growing their strengths to meet and exceed their expectations. Coaching is your chance to do all that and more.

THE UGROW MODEL

For coaching to work well, it's best treated as a routine process where you get together with each of your team members for frequent check-ins to share information about strengths development, celebrate success, discuss any additional help needed and tackle budding problems before they balloon into something bigger. The famous GROW model developed by performance coaching pioneer (and former racing driver) Sir John Whitmore provides a handy framework for carrying out balanced coaching sessions.[12] I like to use my own variation of the model called UGROW, where U stands for *Uniqueness* (as in your personal uniqueness/authenticity). This sets the stage

[11] Ashman, Joann Warcholic and Shelly, Susan (2011). *Play to Your Team's Strengths: The Manager's Guide to Boosting Innovation, Productivity and Profitability*. Avon, MA: F+W Media Business Now.
[12] Whitmore, Sir John (2002). *Coaching for Performance: Growing People, Performance and Purpose*. London: Nicholas Brealey Publishing.

for personalised, strengths-based coaching, which then follows the traditional GROW structure: *Goal, Reality (current), Options* and *What's Next?* (or *Will*):

1. Uniqueness: Who are you? (Working out what makes you unique and brings you meaning)

It's unfortunate that people try to plan aspects of their lives and solve problems without first taking time to identify what their personal uniqueness is. A person's uniqueness is authentic and is tied to what inspires them most. This first stage in the UGROW process is about guiding your team member to conduct an honest and genuine self-assessment of themselves and what their life purpose is. This can be daunting and scary. It's not easy for someone to reach inside and re-think why they decide one thing and not another, but it's the most valuable thing they can do to create more clarity for their lives. Believing in their uniqueness is the starting point to being able to fulfil their true potential and find a sense of meaning in what they do. Questions on personal uniqueness are powerful, but the answers must come from the heart. Here are some things you could ask to help the process:

- **Strengths:** What are your 'go-to' talents and skills (e.g. I'm good with people/ideas/computers/information/things/numbers/children)? What do people say you're good at (e.g. you're a natural sales person/leader/nurturer/relationship builder/creative)? How do you use your unique strengths for meeting challenges or overcoming problems? Which strengths do you most enjoy using? Which skills would you rather not use every day?

- **Values:** What do you hold most dear to you (e.g. honesty, teamwork, accomplishment, learning, optimism, stability, discipline, growth, generosity)? What do you tend to prioritise when making decisions? Are you aligned with your values in this particular situation? Are you living your values consistently?

- **Passions:** What excites and energises you? What are your favourite work activities and personal interests? What do they say about you? When does time seem to fly by?

- **Purpose/contribution:** What do your answers to the above questions reveal about you? Given your strengths, values and passions, how can you best contribute to others (in the team, organisation or society in general)? What difference can you make in this situation or as a whole?

2. Goal: What outcome are you aiming for? (Defining what you want to achieve)

With their personal uniqueness forming the basis of the conversation, the next stage is to figure out which direction the team member is heading. Your aim is to get them clear on what they want from this session and where it is they want to go. Structure any longed-for change as a specific, measurable goal to be achieved, and guide people in setting these goals based on their core competencies and strengths. Some relevant questions here could be:

- What will success look like in relation to this goal?
- How will you/we measure our success?
- What would be good about achieving this, for you and the team?
- What talents/strengths will you use?
- How enthusiastic do you feel about this goal? (Reflects their energy and motivation, usually linked to the presence of strengths and passion)
- How confident do you feel about achieving it? (Indicates whether they have the necessary level of skill)
- Is this goal aligned with what's most important to you? (Check that it takes into account their values)
- Does this goal fit with your overall career objectives? Does it fit with those of the team?

3. Reality: What progress have you made towards your goal? (Exploring the current situation, relevant history and future trends)

The next stage encourages your colleague to consider where they are now, i.e. their current reality in terms of behaviour, progress, etc. Spend time here so that they can get to the heart of things and lay out the key facts on the table to be looked at. Offer specific examples of feedback if you have them and consider whether there are any obstacles to moving ahead. Once the situation is clearly in view, it's surprising how easily ideas on how to make further headway can show up. Some reality questions to use here include:

- What progress have you already made in moving towards the goal?
- What specific actions did you take?

- What strengths have you made use of?
- What's been the impact on you or the team so far?
- If an ideal situation is 10 (i.e. achievement of the goal), what number are you at right now?
- What could help you get further with this?
- What are the major constraints/obstacles to moving forward?

4. Options: What are all the things you could do as a step forward? (Coming up with new ideas for reaching the goal)

Now that your colleague's got a good idea where they are and where they want to go, the next step is to brainstorm the options they have for getting there. Offer your own suggestions carefully, and help them define and refine choices by considering the upsides and downsides of each one. Use open questions like the ones below to branch out far and wide for possible options:

- What are the possibilities you see at this point?
- What else could you do? (Repeat this question to stimulate more ideas)
- What's worked in the past?
- What have you seen work in similar situations?
- What strengths or talents can you bring into play?
- If you had unlimited resources (budget, people, tools, etc.), what might you do?
- Who might be able to help?
- Would you like some further suggestions from me?

5. What's Next? What actions will you take? (Deciding on a concrete plan of action)

This final step is all about gaining commitment to action and creating a plan to leverage the option that's been selected. Remember that you want the person to 'own' their performance improvement and taking the time to plan out their next steps helps them do this and will boost their motivation too. Develop strategies for managing potential obstacles and agree any support that could be provided. Some questions you can ask include:

- Which of these options would you like to commit to?
- What will you do?
- What will be the first step?
- Will it meet your goal?
- Could you do more?
- When will you do that?
- How confident do you feel about doing that?
- How enthusiastic do you feel about doing that?
- How can you keep yourself motivated?
- Who will you talk to? Who else needs to know about your plans?
- What support do you need?
- When do you need to review progress? Daily, weekly, monthly?

The great thing about the UGROW model is that you can apply it to a whole range of situations, issues and problems – even ones the team member has been stuck in for a long time. In addition to encouraging people to reach greater heights, use it for course-correcting, to address skill-based deficits or to find ways to remove barriers to performance. *Feedback and coaching* should also be your first port of call to nip any unpleasant situations in the bud. When you're a leader, you have an obligation to ensure that everyone is doing their bit for the team and that any underperformance is dealt with swiftly. Carrying complacent, unwilling or problematic passengers can be crippling to morale in a team, and worse still, can build ill feeling over the long term. Poor performance is like a highly contagious disease. The longer it goes unchecked, the more everyone suffers.[13]

A BIG, BAD WEAKNESS

You'll often find that the reason behind most performance issues is that the person is working in an area of major *weakness* which slows them down, holds

---

[13] Clemmer, Jim (2003). *The Leader's Digest: Timeless Principles for Team and Organization Success.* Toronto: Clemmer Group.

them back and generally frustrates them. To be clear, a strengths-based approach does not completely ignore weaknesses. Weaknesses that don't bear any relevance to the job or performance are harmless; they are simply 'non-talents' and can, as a rule, be overlooked. But any weakness that's seriously impacting someone's ability to perform at their best presents a different matter altogether. Persistent problems would indicate there's definitely a need to manage this as a significant weakness. For instance, if your colleague is continuing to make far too many errors after repeated feedback, or they're developing an increasingly negative attitude towards you and others, then it's time for you to step in and troubleshoot. Negative outcomes to keep an eye out for include:[14]

- **Behaviour/actions:** decreased productivity; frequent mistakes; poor quality work; arriving late; disorganisation; absenteeism; inappropriate email or internet use; relying on others to do certain tasks; away from office/workspace for long periods of time; avoiding certain assignments; missed deadlines.

- **Attitudes:** negativity towards others; lacking in initiative; frequent complaining; blaming others; argumentative; disinterested in the job; no enthusiasm; not involved in the team; is 'cliquey' and excludes certain people; gossiping about others; being uncooperative; being overly withdrawn; resisting authority.

Use coaching to isolate the irksome weakness and openly discuss its impact. Chew over these questions:

- What is it about the weakness that makes it such a challenge for the team member?
- How is the person's performance being affected by this weakness?
- Is this weak task critical to their role and the organisation?
- Is the weakness a potential derailer?
- Does it stand out to others on the team and impact on their performance?
- Does it cost money because of waste or inefficiency?
- Does it create interpersonal friction?
- Are you losing customers or clients because of it?

---

[14] Holliday, Micki (2001). *Coaching, Mentoring and Managing: Breakthrough Strategies to Solve Performance Problems and Build Winning Teams.* Career Press.

If the weakness is found to be critical for performance (individual, team and organisational), it doesn't matter how awesome the person's strengths are, they will no doubt struggle to be fully effective if it's not brought to heel. For instance, a manager who is majorly lacking in empathy and never listens could seriously alienate her team. The fact that she's an ace organiser and master delegator will pale into insignificance beside her inability to form trusting, respectful relationships with her team members, who find her downright arrogant and cold. The long-term effects of a weakness such as this can be tragic.

OVERPLAYING STRENGTHS

Believe it or not, sometimes performance problems can result from strengths.

Your strengths can work against you if you overplay them. Any strength that's used too much or used in the wrong context can easily become a weakness. I must admit, for many years I had a tendency to 'overexpress' my natural leadership and Activator strengths. Not only did this lead to me coming across as too demanding, impatient and overly forceful with my team, but it was a huge source of burnout as I became a workaholic in my relentless pursuit to get things done. While it's tempting to double down on the core strengths that have made you successful in life, it's important to consider the limits of those strengths and the points at which they start to work against you. 'More' is not always the winning formula.

Strengths also become a problem when they're abused. Your strengths are the best indication for how *you* should do things, but other people also need to be allowed to use their strengths in the way that best suits them. If you embrace your strength as the only truth – 'This is the way I do things best, therefore we are all going to do it this way' – you ignore other, possibly better, alternatives and cause havoc with your relationships in the process. The result is limited vision and lopsided leadership: too much of one thing made worse by too little of its complement.[15] As executive coach Dr Joelle Jay puts it: 'Your strengths improve your impact. They are not the way the world should

[15] Kaplan, Robert E. and Kaiser, Robert B. (2013). *Fear Your Strengths: What You Are Best at Could Be Your Biggest Problem*. San Francisco: Berrett-Koehler Publishers.

work'.[16] If you suspect a member of your team is overdoing things or abusing their strengths, help them explore why it could be happening.

DAMAGE CONTROL STRATEGIES

So, what do you do when someone's struggling to get their head around a certain task/skill, their attitude is sub-par or things just aren't working out in general? You have three options, *Learn, Refocus* or *Exit*:

1. **Learn.** Sometimes poor work output arises due to lack of knowledge or skill, rather than talent. A team member who only has 25 per cent of the knowledge and skills required for the job won't be able to achieve optimal performance, no matter how fired up or motivated they are. The solution is simple; help them get the learning they need. This could involve gaining factual knowledge such as learning product features or protocols, or practising technical skills.

   If the problem *is* lack of talent and you're faced with a significant weakness, then it's a case of learning to perform the weakness to a reasonable level of competence. Some activities like listening and communication are practically baseline requirements for any role, especially leadership. They can't be escaped and not being able to do them can undermine a person's entire performance. Look at different training and development options to mitigate the weakness and help your teammate get a 'little better at it', e.g. formal courses or programmes, experiential learning or the support of a mentor. Don't go overboard and waste too much time, the aim is simply for them to become 'good enough' so that the weakness is minimised and doesn't exert such a negative impact on your teammate's performance.

   Learning is also a great strategy for regulating an overplayed strength. I used *coaching and mentoring* successfully to 'tone down' the excessive application of my leadership and Activator strengths to just the right amount for the situation at hand. You might want to look outside the organisation to find a coach or mentor who adopts a

---

[16] Jay, Joelle K. (2007). 'The best of you and the rest of you: Making the most of strengths-based leadership'. White paper. *Pillar Consulting*. [Online] Available from: http://joellekjay.com/documents/09090422-the-best-of-you-and-the-rest-of-you.pdf

strengths-focused approach, perhaps for a specified period of time (usually six months). Another option is to request a mentor from within the organisation to act as a role model and help the person explore different ideas for turning the weakness around. Good mentors will tend to take a coaching approach, supporting the team member in thinking for themselves and working to their own agenda, but they also bring the value of their personal wisdom and experience, which can be a great help.

2. **Refocus.** Learning not doing the trick? Then consider these tactics for diverting focus away from the weakness:

- **Stop doing it:** Can the team member just stop doing that particular task? If they can scrub it off their to-do list without any obvious ramifications, then it's problem solved! The added benefit is that they'll have more time to spend on their strengths.

- **Reshape the role:** Can you refocus and reorganise the person's work to reduce the extent to which they have to call on their weakness? Do this by making tweaks in their job description or by moving the task in question to the in-tray of another team member.

- **Design a support system:** Help your colleague find creative 'weakness workarounds' to help them get by. If they're disorganised, provide task management tools or resources (e.g. visual apps like DropTask) to keep them on track. Or allow flexible work arrangements if they have a short attention span, such as brief bursts of concentration interspersed with regular breaks.

- **Use strengths to compensate:** Encourage the team member to use one or more of their strengths to compensate for the weakness. Keep the emphasis on the outcome, not the process; and figure out which strengths will help to achieve it.

- **Find a complementary partner:** Find someone who will be energised by the task in question and enlist their help. For instance, a creative firebrand can work with someone that takes a logical and systematic approach to problems for more rounded decision making. Swap tasks around if necessary to compensate one of the latter member's weaknesses for one of former's strengths.

- **Call on the team:** By analysing people's relative strengths, you can reallocate the so-called 'weak task' to another team member who has the behaviour as a strength. The aim should always be to distribute and manage the team's workload in a way that maximises each person's opportunities to play to their strengths while minimising the need to play to their weaknesses.

- **Redeploy to another job:** Is your team member in the wrong job? Then redeploy them to a role more suited to their strengths/skills and which will be much better for them in the long term. Move them to another part of the organisation if necessary.

These strategies may not be perfect, but more often than not, you'll find they tend to work to everyone's benefit.

3. **Exit.** Unfortunately for us leaders, sometimes we have to make painful decisions and deal with their consequences. If your colleague doesn't improve after a number of trials with the above strategies (and only a small minority will not) then you need to acknowledge that you made a recruitment error and cut them loose. The evidence doesn't lie. Whatever you do, don't ignore the issue and persist with trying to develop them. This is usually a waste of time and badly demoralising for the team member involved. Don't engage in public hangings in an attempt to make an example of them either. Not only is this humiliating to the victim, it instils fear in the rest of the team that they might be 'next' to suffer. Sometimes a person is simply not suited to the work style of the organisation and they need to be set free to find a new situation in which to unleash their productivity. It's best not to beat about the bush – if you've decided you need to let someone go, do it quickly, but do it with honesty, not cruelty.

part two

**Personal mission and
ultimate vision – positive
purpose (the 'WHY')**

What is the 'WHY'? (working with your personal mission)

'The most beautiful fate, the most wonderful good fortune that can happen to any human being, is to be paid for doing that which he passionately loves to do.'
ABRAHAM MASLOW, AMERICAN PSYCHOLOGIST

It's time to bring out the powerhouse of leadership – the titanic, almighty, *Very Important Purpose* (VIP). Purpose lies at the crux of any successful venture, team, or indeed, person. True inspiration and happiness come when we start with the WHY and search for a higher meaning in the work we do and the value we bring to the world. Purpose defines *why* we're doing what it is that we do, faithfully reminding us what we are about and what we really want. It's the biggest energiser in the world – our reason for being and doing. Children are always asking 'why?' . . . and it's not just to deliberately annoy us grown-ups!

No doubt you've come across this old saying: 'Find a job you love and you'll never work a day in your life.' As a leader, you have an immense responsibility to yourself, and that's to find a job, a business, an industry, a profession, a team, an environment, a partnership, a lifestyle – anything – that you love. The truth is, we all need our own *personal mission* – the enjoyable quest that gives us our get-up-and-go and fills our life with moments of 'flow', where time flies and we find that we're inevitably doing our best, most satisfying work. In pursuing a mission that we love, we can be confident that we're doing what really matters to drive positive change and spark firecracker results, and we can eliminate those pesky distractions that get in the way of our ideal path.

Leading your own life

Successful businesses have been creating mission statements for years to define their core strengths and values, to provide thrust and direction to their daily work, and to affirm *why* they do what they do. A personal mission is much the same – but it's a declaration of who *you* are, what *you* stand for and what *you* want to put out into the world.[1] That's right – it's personal! I'm not exaggerating when I say that finding your personal mission can truly be the most significant activity you do to lead a first-rate version of your own life.

YOUR REASON FOR BEING

Your mission is the cornerstone for your whole existence – the promise to yourself, your work, your family, your industry, to society and the world. It's an articulation of what you're all about, including how you make decisions and how you create boundaries. And it's a powerful instrument for any high achiever because it provides a win–win path for both success AND happiness.

[1] Steinbrecher, Susan (2014). 'Why you need to create a personal mission statement'. *The Huffington Post*, 1 October. [Online] Available from: http://www.huffingtonpost.com/susan-steinbrecher/why-you-need-to-create-a-_b_5642112.html

YOUR REASON FOR DOING

Your mission is the most direct route to making your highest dreams (or visions) a reality, acting as your conscious 'call to action'. It brings a laser-like focus, commitment and intention to what you do on a daily basis and determines the valuable difference you can make in your life. As you'll see in the next chapter, having a vision – an ultimate end result – is crucial for inspiring yourself and others to reach for bigger, grander things . . . but it's through your mission that you actually make it all happen. So why not make the journey to get there an enjoyable one?

Everyone has a purpose, a mission in life, but masses of us don't even realise it. You might feel like you don't have one right now . . . but of course you do. The thing is, nobody else can tell you what it is; you need to work it out for yourself. After all, only you know in your heart what's most important to you. You can't simply hope that the right job, the right employer, the right lifestyle or relationships will be handed to you on a plate. In the Western world, we're faced with a mind-boggling number of choices in how we live our lives. Until you narrow down your mission in a meaningful way, you'll be like a modern-day nomad wandering about hoping to 'discover your true self' and start building your life, but without any sort of map or blueprint to construct it from. Chances are you'll end up in the wrong district, disappointed and dissatisfied, and way out of sight of your reason for existence.

Once you decide which choices are most likely to bring you happiness, everything – achievement, gratification – becomes easier. Your mission gives you the solid framework you need for all your decisions and actions, both the day-to-day ones and the metamorphic, life-changing ones. You're clear on why you exist and what you need to do. Gone is the frustration and self-doubt and you begin to feel (perhaps for the first time) that you're fully in charge of your life.

Benefits of having a mission

Crafting a mission based on good, healthy principles brings scores of benefits in that it:

- refocuses your energy on personal priorities and passions
- provides a basis for making major, life-directing decisions

- allows you to develop the strengths and personal qualities that will unlock your full potential
- identifies the obstacles that are blocking you from achieving your goals
- acts as an invisible hand to guide you
- keeps you working in line with your core values and beliefs
- offers a compass for smaller daily decisions in the midst of fluctuating circumstances, stressful conditions and high emotions
- makes it easier to flow with changes
- gives you permission to say no to distractions
- rids you of the need to have everything figured out and categorised. You don't need prejudgements, prejudices or assumptions to accommodate reality when you're living by your mission.[2]

For your mission to be wholly engaging and energising it must be what *you* want. This may seem 'duh' obvious, but far too many people fall into the trap of doing what's expected of them or what they think they should do to match other people's achievements. Rachel might train to be a doctor to follow in her father's footsteps, or Philippe might start his own business in the hope of keeping up with his entrepreneurial peers. Focus on what's right for you, not for anyone else. If you allow someone else to set your mission or base it on superficial reasons (like money, ego, power or fame), the intrinsic drive just isn't there. You're letting your goals come from the outside, rather than from within, so any motivation and satisfaction you feel will be short-lived. Choose your mission for yourself and you'll be all the more ready to go out and get it, and more importantly, commit to it.

Job vs career vs calling

When it comes to creating a happy and purposeful life, how we perceive the work we do can actually matter more than the work itself. Research on workers

[2] The Community. 'Business mission statements'. *Stephen R. Covey* [Online] Available from: https://www.stephencovey.com/mission-statements.php

in every conceivable occupation by Yale psychologist Dr Amy Wrzesniewski and her colleagues reveals that we tend to have one of three 'work orientations' (or mindsets) about our work.[3] We either experience it as a job, a career or as a calling:

- **Job:** People with a 'job' see work as a chore, a means to an end, with the focus being on getting paid at the end of the week or month to support their lifestyle outside of work. They work because they have to rather than for personal fulfilment or the betterment of the company/society, and their work is kept strictly separate from their personal lives. These individuals 'do the job' but perceive little meaning in the daily drudgery and can't wait to clock off for the weekend or holidays.

- **Career:** People who are on a career path are driven by the need to advance and succeed. These people are happiest when they're 'winning' and look forward to the next jump in the hierarchy, raise or any other opportunity to step up their power or prestige. Careers with a clear 'upward ladder' are appealing to those with this orientation, and they tend to rate themselves by what rung they're on in relation to their colleagues and peers. They'll willingly make sacrifices for the company if it means they get that office on the top floor! Though engaged, they can quickly become dissatisfied if they're not forging ahead at the pace they want.

- **Calling:** People with a calling view work as a positive end in itself; they love what they do and their eyes light up when they talk about it. The external rewards (money and advancement) are still important, but they're mainly motivated by intrinsic reasons. Their work is a form of self-expression and personal gratification, and it's viewed as a privilege rather than a chore. People with this orientation are more likely to feel that their work draws on their personal strengths, is connected to their personal values and contributes in some small way to the greater good – like the janitor who sees his role as making the workplace/hospital/school a cleaner, healthier space for others. Or the worker on the assembly line who imagines people enjoying the products she is making. Folk with a calling will go to the 'next level' to adapt their duties and develop relationships to make their work even more meaningful and satisfying.

[3] Wrzesniewski, A., McCauley, C. R., Rozin, P. and Schwartz, B. (1997) 'Jobs, careers, and callings: People's relations to their work'. *Journal of Research in Personality*, *31*, pp. 21–33.

Fascinatingly, these orientations play out in all manner of professions, from hospital cleaners, hairdressers and clerks to engineers, CEOs, doctors and salespeople. Most are fairly evenly divided – with about a third of workers falling into each category.

Wrzesniewski's research found that those with a calling orientation report higher satisfaction with their lives and work, and are more likely to 'craft' their jobs to fit their strengths and interests. A *positive mindset* is key. People with a calling feel good about what they're doing, no matter what it is. This is fortunate as it's not always easy to discover what sort of work can yield greater satisfaction and wellbeing. But we're all able to *choose* how we view our employment and cultivate greater feelings of engagement in what we do. People who focus on the negatives of their work – the deadlines, the pressure, the slog – miss out on the positive opportunities right in front of them. A calling orientation represents a 'portable benefit' for those with a positive outlook in that they can bring meaning and pleasure to a variety of work experiences.[4] They can find delight even in the most ordinary and unglamorous daily tasks, like mopping the floor or making cups of tea.

And here's something even better about people with callings – not only are they happy and fulfilled, they're often super-successful too. By giving more to their work in terms of passion and ability, they get more back from it, including financial rewards. At this point of the book, it's no secret that we often perform best at the things we find most engaging. In pursuing work that gives us meaning and pleasure, not only does our motivation increase, so do our strengths and skills – and with that our success.

Recognising your own orientation towards your work is the start to defining what you need and want in your professional life. For one, it can help you find ways to motivate yourself and craft a better work mission without having to change jobs. You don't have to blow up everything that already exists to live a better life, tempting though it may be when you're under constant stress and strain! Sometimes it's just a case of making a few small changes, such as getting involved in more teamwork, re-adjusting your working hours or

---

[4] Brooks, Katharine (2012). 'Job, career, calling: Key to happiness and meaning at work?' *Psychology Today*, 29 June. [Online] Available from: https://www.psychologytoday.com/blog/career-transitions/201206/job-career-calling-key-happiness-and-meaning-work

moving desks. At other times, a radical career change or fresh start is absolutely the right thing. You might have been climbing so fast up the professional ladder only to come to the realisation that it's leaning against the wrong wall. What then? A bit of self-reflection can help you make the switch to a new career or field that could well prove more satisfying. I found my calling as an authentic leader, strategist, coach and mentor when I began homing in on what I could do to inspire others to better their lives and the world around them, rather than losing myself in the never-ending scramble to hit the next performance target.

Exercise 4.1: Do you have a job, career or calling?

Do you see your current work as a job, a career or a calling?

Write a description of your typical workday and evaluate your activities according to how pleasurable, invigorating and meaningful they are. By zooming in on day-to-day tasks like this, you can identify important patterns in how you perceive your work. On the whole, are you looking at it through a lens of positivity or necessity? You can even ask the same question of work you've done in the past.

Take a moment to think about how your current work orientation affects your motivation and your overall career/life satisfaction. Does it impact on your desire to continue with your career or to find a new one?

If you need a bit of help determining your work preference, you can take the free 'Work–Life Questionnaire' developed by The University of Pennsylvania. Go to the Authentic Happiness site and select the quiz from the 'Questionnaires' drop-down list. It should only take a few minutes. (Note: you will be asked to register. Just create a username and password.)

Here's the link: https://www.authentichappiness.sas.upenn.edu/

How did you get on? Congratulations if you made it into the calling category. It means you've already found a strong sense of purpose and job satisfaction in what you're doing. If you see your work as merely a job or career and are mentally stuck on the grind not the gain, consider whether you need to change your outlook or priorities. Big improvements can be made by training yourself to obtain more feel-good 'flow'.

GETTING INTO THE 'FLOW'

A question for you:

Is there anything you do regularly that makes you lose track of time?

We all know what it feels like to be so utterly absorbed in doing something – completing a crossword puzzle, playing a sport, making music, writing a report, cooking a meal, gardening, closing a business deal, executing a project, painting a 'masterpiece' – that our sense of time disappears and we discover hours have flown by when it seemed like just minutes had passed. Our attention is focused entirely on what we're doing to the point that everything around us fades away, and we fail to hear the phone ringing or our name being called. Shockingly, we might even miss lunch! These energising, often joyful, experiences are what the brilliant psychologist with the difficult-to-pronounce name, Mihaly Csikzentmihalyi, termed *flow*.[5]

According to Csikzentmihalyi, people are happiest when they're in this state of flow, which he describes as 'being completely involved in an activity for its own sake. The ego falls away. Time flies. Every action, movement and thought follows inevitably from the previous one, like playing jazz. Your whole being is involved, and you're using your skills to the utmost'.[6] Athletes call it 'being in the zone' while artists label it 'aesthetic rapture'. The more you are in the flow or 'the zone', the more you are at your best – it's an optimal experience where you have:

1. **Complete involvement in what you're doing:** You have intense focus and sharp concentration, and aren't interrupted by unruly, wayward thoughts.

2. **Great inner clarity:** A translucent understanding of what you want to achieve and how well you're getting on.

3. **Active control over the situation and what you're doing:** You just seem to 'know' how to respond to whatever happens next and what the outcome will be.

[5] Csikzentmihalyi, Mihalyi (1990). *Flow: The Psychology of Optimal Experience*. New York: Harper and Row.
[6] Geirland, John (1996). 'Go with the flow'. *Wired*. September, Issue 4. [Online] Available from: http://archive.wired.com/wired/archive/4.09/czik_pr.html

4. **The knowledge that the activity is doable:** You have the necessary skills to complete it successfully.

5. **A merging of action and awareness:** A sense of harmony and ecstasy in the moment where everything is 'clicking' and it feels almost effortless. The frustrations of everyday life are removed and there's a feeling of being outside everyday reality.

6. **No ego:** There's a loss of self-consciousness in favour of the task at hand, and you aren't preoccupied with worries about yourself. You enjoy a sense of serenity and transcending beyond the boundaries of the self.

7. **No awareness of time:** 'Where did those last few hours go?' You aren't watching the clock and are fully absorbed in the present moment. Hours pass in what seem like minutes.

8. **Intrinsic motivation:** A feeling that the activity is intrinsically rewarding in and of itself. The end goal is often just an excuse for the process.

Tellingly, there's a paradox that comes with this notion of flow. While it's no bombshell conclusion that most people prefer leisure to work, research by Mihaly Csikszentmihalyi and Judith LeFevre found that people actually have more flow experiences at *work* than they do at home.[7] As a matter of fact, they occur three times more often for people at work. This contradicts the commonly held view that happiness is about leisure and relaxation, while work is about hard effort and struggle, or even punishment. Our best, most productive moments usually occur when our body or mind is stretched to its limits in a voluntary effort to accomplish something challenging or worthwhile. People rarely experience flow when they're in a passive state of rest and relaxation, such as when they're chilling on vacation or watching TV. The happiness that comes with flow is of our own making, and we emerge from the experience even more complex, self-confident and capable – now that's not something we can often claim after a lazy night binge-watching serials on Netflix.

---

[7] Csikszentmihalyi, M. and Lefevre, J. (1989). 'Optimal experience in work and leisure'. *Journal of Personality and Social Psychology*, *56*, pp. 815–822.

The flow model

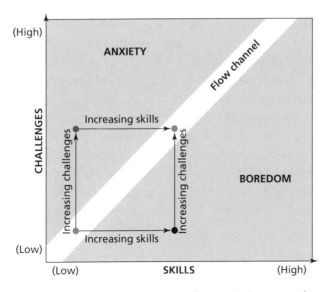

Source: Adapted from van Gorp, T. and Adams, E., *Design for Emotion* (Morgan Kaufman, 2012).

- **High challenge/low skill:** If the challenge/difficulty of a task is high and our skill level is low, then we experience frustration and anxiety. The task is over-challenging for us = BURNOUT.
- **Low challenge/high skill:** If the challenge/difficulty of the task is low and our skill level is high, then we experience boredom. The task is under-challenging for us = BOREOUT.

When we're pushed too hard to complete a task, beyond our stretch zone, we start to associate our work with pain, worry, frustration, disappointment and unhappiness. Our focus is on getting it out of the way rather than enjoying the process; and flow is clearly absent as we sit in the 'anxiety' quarter of the graph above. On the other hand, if the task is too easy for us and there's no struggle at all, we get bored and lose out on the satisfaction of overcoming a worthy challenge. Again, there's no flow as we float around in the 'boredom' zone of the graph, lost in tedium and easily distracted. What we need is that sweet spot that's not too hard and not too easy, but *just right*. The task must test us, but not torture us. As indicated by the flow channel on the graph, we experience flow when we strike a balance between the difficulty of the task and our skill at performing it.

High Challenge + High Skill = Flow

So, the secret to happiness in the workplace doesn't exclude the possibility of hard work and exertion. We need to be active and continually challenge our skills to create conditions that foster flow. A tennis player will play a better, more enjoyable game if she competes against an opponent who is slightly more skilful than she is. A pianist will benefit by practising a piece of music that's a touch harder than the one he locked down yesterday. But thankfully, there's no need to go overboard. We don't have to work totally flat out and overexert ourselves to get our best performance; that will just lead to burnout. Knowing this, we can better recognise and realise opportunities for working on tasks that present us with the right level of challenge, where we not only perform our best but also enjoy what we're doing. The result = peak experience (*happiness*) and peak performance (*success*). We can't force it, but we can invite flow to occur more often by setting up the right conditions.

TRIGGER FLOW IN THE WORKPLACE

For each of us, there are hundreds of opportunities to expand ourselves and create these flashes of intense living and productivity. A positive leader who is mindful of the need to spark higher levels of engagement and happiness in their team will want to grab hold of some of these ideas. Companies like Microsoft, Ericsson, Patagonia and Toyota are taking advantage of Csikszentmihalyi's wisdom to assign work that challenges people to the right degree and consequently get the best out of their teams.[8] There are certain things you can do to fan the flames of flow, both personally and business-wide.

1. **Tackle tricky tasks:** But not too much! Choose activities that will stretch your skills and provide you with new feelings, experiences and insights, without being overwhelming. To encourage flow, a task has to be stimulating, one that you love doing and can actually complete, otherwise flow won't occur and you'll be tempted to jack it in. If it's too boring and tedious, you won't enjoy it or grow from it, and you'll be prone to wilful thoughts and distractions. On a personal level, a flow task can be anything you want that challenges you to learn or upgrade your strengths – working on your novel, cooking dinner for eight people, learning how to ski, inventing a new app, and so on. On the career front,

[8] Marsh, Ann (2005). 'The art of work'. *Fast Company*, 1 August. [Online] Available from: http://www. fastcompany.com/53713/art-work

defining your *personal mission* will help you shape your job or work tasks to fit you and your strengths like a glove (see next section). The way you practise your strengths will look very different to the way I practise mine, and that's how it should be if we're all to play to our uniqueness.

2. **Set micro milestones:** Ones that can be reasonably achieved. Small, clear and concrete goals add motivation, focus and structure to what you're doing. Pick one thing every week to intentionally focus on getting better at with regard to your key strengths. Working steadily towards an ideal picture of success helps you stay the course and nudges you into that enraptured feeling of flow.

3. **Follow up with feedback:** As you progress towards your goals, you must have clear, timely feedback along the way. This can be feedback from other people, or from your own self-awareness/observations that you're making progress with the task. Through balanced feedback, you can adjust your efforts in a way that helps you stay in the flow and maintain high productivity levels. Learn how to give and receive feedback and make sure open feedback mechanisms are in place within your team or organisation. I like to voluntarily ask for feedback from people I work with to make sure my message is clear whenever I publish an article or blog post online (it helps me keep my Communication strengths honed).

4. **Sharpen your focus:** All sorts of things can take your attention away from the task at hand. If your focus is constantly being interrupted, you're not going to be able to get into or remain in an engaging state of flow. Endless multitasking is the enemy of flow. You need to concentrate fully on what you're doing and give it everything you've got. Log out of Twitter, turn off your phone and eliminate all other distractions. Learn to use strategies to improve your concentration so you're more effective during the day (e.g. prioritise using task management tools, schedule blocks of time for dealing with emails, reorganise your workspace, listen to music or 'white noise' apps, set a timer on your flow activity).

5. **Elevate your energy levels and emotional state:** Pay attention to your bodily sensations and how you're feeling. Physical symptoms of nervousness are normal and will naturally ease off once you get going. If your energy levels are low and you're feeling sluggish, then do something to pick yourself up. Eat a healthy snack, read something motivational or go for an energising walk. Keep tabs on your emotional wellbeing too. If you're in an aroused, angry, anxious or worried state, do something to cool you down, like meditation or

talking to a friend, or maybe hire a coach to help you experience mindfulness and greater happiness at work. You really need to be calm and collected to build up the right momentum for flow.

Exercise 4.2: Measure your flow

ACTIVITY 1: PAST FLOW

1. Identify a specific time or activity when you experienced a sense of flow.
   - When did it occur?
   - What were you doing?
   - Where were you? (work, home, etc.)
   - What factors helped you experience flow in that moment? (e.g. your skill/ability versus the level of challenge)
2. Describe the specific things you did or principles you followed to enjoy a sense of flow.

ACTIVITY 2: FUTURE FLOW

1. Pick a task during which you'd like to feel more engaged.
2. Are you currently in the Burnout (over-challenged) or Boreout (under-challenged) zone?
3. Determine how you can raise your skills or increase/decrease the challenge level to improve the possibility of flow.
   - To raise skill, consider what personal strengths, knowledge, resources and professional relationships you could call on or build upon to help you accomplish the task effectively (e.g. get more training or new equipment to help you with a particular talent).
   - To raise challenge, look for creative ways to learn and grow more from the same activity (e.g. contribute more in group discussions; play against a slightly stronger opponent, etc.).
   - To decrease challenge (and consequently your stress levels!), explore opportunities for delegating, prioritising or asking for help.
4. Are there any other actions or principles you can follow to encourage flow?

Download a template for this exercise at http://positiveleaderbook.com/measureyourflow

Crafting your personal mission

As a leader, you have to wear multiple hats in your life. Your personal mission can unite all the roles you play into one all-encompassing purpose and help you craft your current work so that you're not just 'doing a job', but experiencing a calling. It's not often that a job will come tailor-made for you; you have to manoeuvre it that way deliberately. Once you know who you are and what you stand for, you can start deliberately finessing your job so it's filled with greater meaning and balance. To do that, you must first look inside yourself to figure out *what makes you great, what your values are and what you're passionate about.* This information isn't always immediately obvious. It involves quite a bit of self-reflection as you have to dig deeply into your most basic beliefs, values and motivations, and try to recall the full range of experiences you've found uplifting and worthwhile. However, this process is necessary to fully connect with the 'Why' behind your life and become master of your own destiny. I have a fool proof system for creating your own personal mission that never fails to bring more success and happiness into the lives of people that I coach. It involves examining three core aspects of yourself, as shown in the curvilicious diagram below:

Personal mission

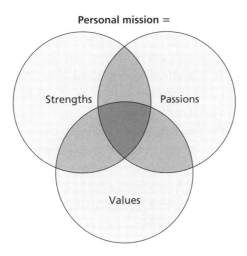

Personal mission =

Strengths

Passions

Values

Looking at where the circles overlap can help determine what kind of work would make you happiest, that is, work that corresponds to your strengths, values and passions. We can begin the process of finding the right mission by asking these three crucial questions:

- What are my *strengths*? (i.e. What am I good at?)
- What are my *values*? (i.e. What gives me meaning and provides me with a sense of purpose?)
- What are my *passions*? (i.e. What gives me pleasure? What do I enjoy doing?)

Let's work through them one by one.

1. WHAT ARE MY STRENGTHS?

If there's anything Part 1 of this book taught us, it's that we all have super powers – things we do extremely well. These strengths often feel very natural to us, an intrinsic part of who we are, and so we often take them for granted. But it's important to see them as a measure of what makes us special. Our strengths are a key means to performing our best and, as such, they're a necessary aspect of our personal mission. When we really play to our strengths, we feel motivated and energised; we have more 'flow' experiences and can build a more rewarding life. If you haven't already worked out what your strengths are in Chapter 2, you can take a quick inventory of your strengths using this fuss-free approach:

- **Past successes:** Identify past successes and figure out what strengths were commonly played out during those times. These successes could be at work, in your community, at home or even from your childhood. Write them down. For instance:
  - developed a new, successful marketing angle for an established product that had seen a recent drop in sales
  - helped organise a fundraising event at my child's school that raised a record sum for charity
  - devised a personal study system that enabled me to achieve a top grade in my exam for my latest professional qualification.

  There are some common themes here. All successes relate to organisation and creative problem solving – signature strengths that you can choose to bring into play more intentionally as part of your personal mission.

- **Current strengths:** Write down all your strengths and the roles you play in life right now. How have you seen them at work in the past few weeks? Are you satisfied with how you're currently using your strengths? Your work should draw out a variety of your natural talents and skills to bring more 'life' and energy to what you do on a daily basis.

- **Future contributions:** Make a list of the ways you could use your strengths to make a difference. If you could be a 'world authority' in one thing, what would it be? In an ideal situation, how could you contribute best to: your family; your employer or future employer; your friends; your community; the world in general?

Not only does having an acute awareness of your strengths give you greater value and power (bonus points for your leadership career), it can also lead to passion (bonus points for your happiness). After all, work is most fun when you're actually good at it. By following a path that uses your strengths, you'll very likely start falling in love with what you do.

2. WHAT ARE MY VALUES?

A big clue to what you really really *really* want is hidden away in your core values. Your deepest values define what matters most to you and are the guiding rules and moral codes you live your life by. They represent your priorities and determine how you measure your success at work, at home and in your community. By knowing your values, you can wisely make decisions and plans that honour them, and you can de-clutter your life to focus on what's really important.

Crucially, you can use your values to assess whether a career or job will actually feel good to you in the long run. If you continually have to do things or follow directions that run against your personal values, it'll be hard to muster up any enthusiasm for the job, and this can translate into more serious problems over a longer period. For example, if one of your core values is 'family' and you have to work 60+ hours a week or go on regular trips away from home, it's likely that you'll experience a lot of internal conflict and anxiety because you won't be able to spend much time with your family. Similarly, if you value 'honesty' but you're often asked to carry out tasks that require you to bend the truth (either in what you say or do), then your job will be a constant source of stress to you. Things just won't feel right because you'll be out of touch with your values. You need your values to be authentic in order to feel comfortable in your own skin.

Develop a list of what you think your values are. Use the following questions to help you:

- What is important in your work?
- What would you contribute money to or volunteer for?
- What things do you like to read about, watch on TV or surround yourself with?
- Who do you admire? These could be people that you know personally or who 'wow' you from afar. Are there people in your life who impress or even intimidate you? (Often your personal values are elements that you admire in others)
- What topics or causes would you speak up or fight for? (What values does your stance represent?)
- What or who do you care about deeply (e.g. industry sector, purpose or people)?
- What principles or personal qualities do you want to demonstrate more of?

Answer these questions quickly without thinking too much. When you've finished, look at the values you listed and see if you can choose the three to five that you consider most important of all. These are the ones that you would like to be in a position to express every single day. If you're stuck, scan through the *checklist of values* below. Are there any that jump out or call to you? Feel free to add in others if your priorities aren't listed here:

Accomplishment	Discipline	Friendships
Adventure	Diversity	Fun
Authenticity	Efficiency	Giving/generosity
Balance	Enthusiasm	Growth
Bravery	Excellence	Harmony
Commitment	Fairness	Health
Compassion	Faith	Helping others/society
Creativity	Fame	Honesty
Dependability	Family	Humour
Determination	Freedom	Inspiration

Integrity	Peace	Serenity
Justice	Perseverance	Service to others
Kindness	Power	Spirituality
Knowledge	Prosperity	Success
Learning	Recognition	Teamwork
Love	Relationships	Tradition
Loyalty	Respect for others	Trust
Nurturing	Responsibility	Variety
Openness	Risk-taking	Wellbeing
Passion	Security	Wisdom

If you're going to be happy at work, you should never compromise on your core values. Often what we think matters most in our jobs and lives, such as achieving material success and outstanding profits, doesn't match up with what really gives us meaning. Sooner or later, something has to give and before we know it, we completely burn out, crack up or fall into an unhealthy, depressive state. This is exactly what happened to me and I'll share my experience with you in Chapter 7. To help you avoid that mistake and lead a good example for your team, don't stifle your values, use them as an internal GPS to keep you on track with your purpose and get you through any discouraging circumstances. Refer to them in both times of happiness and hardship.

3. WHAT ARE MY PASSIONS?

Notice how the most brilliant leaders have real passion for what they do. Leaders in business or in any other field can't expect to get others buzzed up about their work unless and until they are buzzed up about it themselves. Passion is a powerful precondition for über-successful leadership, firing up our self-starter energy and setting us in motion towards our goals. It's this lust and zeal that fuels us on to achieve remarkable results, and by creating teams that are just as positive and passionate, we can become unstoppable.

Leaders who love what they do work harder and put in the hours, but the key difference is . . . they don't see it as work. They'll happily get out of bed to do what needs to be done, and they'll do it with spirit and energy. Why else would Warren Buffett and Bill Gates still choose to work? It's not like they're strapped for cash and desperately needing to put clothes on the kids' backs and food on the table – they do it for the *love*. Leaders who love what they do demonstrate passion by:[9]

[9] Boyer, Lyn. *7 Secrets of Sensational Leaders*. Sarasota: Leadership Options.

- their willingness to take risks to fulfil their mission
- remaining committed in spite of hardship or misfortune
- continually learning and searching for better ways to reach their goals
- seeking out others who will join them in their quest.

Let's be realistic though. Even if we generally love what we do, it's likely our job will still involve some menial or unpleasant aspects. We can't just turn our backs on them because they don't send us into spasms of ecstasy or fill us with gladness. You might not enjoy scrutinising complex balance sheets or sacking people (I definitely don't!), but as a leader that's still part of your job. All of us are bound to have 'shitty days at the office'. The key is not to turn your nose up at the bad stuff, but to make sure the vast majority of your time is spent on the things you really enjoy. It's the balance that counts. If you don't enjoy your line of work and you're not prepared to do something about it (even small changes in the right direction can make a world of difference), then you may as well give up, go home and get clear about what you *do* like. I would give the same advice to anyone on your team too. You're either passionately in the game for excellence or you aren't really a player.

Business authors Robert Kriegel and Louis Patler cite a study of 1500 people over 20 years that proves the value of finding and focusing on your passions within your career.[10] At the outset of the study, the participants were divided into three groups. Group A (83 per cent of the sample) were embarking on a career chosen for the prospect of making money now in order to do what they want later. Group B (the other 17 per cent of the sample) had chosen their career path for the reverse reason – to pursue their passions. They would do what they wanted to do now and worry about money later. The results of the study were astounding:

- At the end of the 20 years, 101 of the 1500 sample had become millionaires.
- Of all the millionaires, all but one (100 out of the 101) were from Group B, the group that had chosen to pursue what they loved.

It seems the myth might just be true – if you find your bliss (and work hard at it), world-changing success will 'magically' come.

So how do you work out what your passions are in the first place?

---

[10] Kriegel, Robert J. and Patler, Louis (1991). *If It Ain't Broke. . . . Break It!* New York: Warner Books.

Step 1: Do a self-audit of what you like and love

To start with, do a self-audit of the tasks and responsibilities you enjoy or love to do. Make a list of them. Don't let your inner critic edit your thoughts; the whole idea is to find out what your true desires are, not shred them to pieces. Here are some questions you can ponder on to find passionate possibilities for your mission:

- Out of all your current work tasks, what would you gladly do for free?

- When was the last time you were in a state of flow and totally lost track of time? What were you doing?

- If you had a free hour to surf the internet, what would you explore?

- What environment do you love being in? (e.g. do you love working on your own or in a team? Do you like being outdoors or indoors? Do you love travel or hate it?)

- Imagine you won 150 million pounds, euros, dollars (or any other currency) in the lottery but you still had to do some form of work. What would you spend your days doing?

- What careers do you find yourself dreaming of? What jobs do others have that you wish you could do? The sky's the limit.

- What three to five companies would you love to work for?

- What do you love helping people with? How do you most commonly help others?

- What would you do if you knew you could not fail? (If you had a magic potion that gave you immunity to failure, what would you be driven to do?)

- At the end of your life, what would you love to be remembered for?

- What do you find yourself doing anyway? What are your areas of interest?

- How do you spend your free time? What do you look forward to doing after you're done with everything that's required of you?

- What sparks your creativity? (In sport, business, at home or anywhere.)

- What do you like to talk about? (Your favourite topics of conversation are major indicators of what you're really interested in. Ask your friends what gets you animated and makes your eyes brighten up.)

- What gives you energy? (Spend a few days mapping your energy and engagement levels at work, and notice what makes you peak.)

Here are some examples of general passions to get you thinking:

Acting, writing, sailing, teaching, travelling, designing, cooking, exploring, making/playing music, talking, technology, singing, making a difference, politics, inspiring, building using your hands, arts and crafts, healing, dancing, reading, exercising, being around kids, interviewing, planning, inventing things, performing, meditating, family relationships, sports, gymnastics, nature, tasting, fishing, campaigning, debating, researching, networking, making people laugh, learning, de-cluttering, entertaining, photography, mentoring, organising, skydiving . . .

Step 2: Try new things

Another way to figure out what your passions are is to get into the habit of trying new things. Life often pushes us into certain directions and we get lodged into a rut, never thinking (or always fearing) to do anything different. Waiting for your 'one true passion' to throw itself at your feet before you feel confident enough to strike out in a new direction is counter-productive. You may as well resign yourself to being stuck in the mud forever.

We learn who we are in life by getting out there and testing reality, not by sitting on the sidelines. We live in a fast, frenzied, global world and I highly recommend to people that they move around a bit and experiment with new things. Look for temporary assignments, evening classes, sabbaticals, outside contracts, advisory work, executive programmes or even moonlighting opportunities to help you test the water and get experience in new departments or industries. Speak to knowledgeable people, do your research, give it time and keep looking until you stumble onto something you really love. Trial and error is the name of the game. In some ways passion is becoming a luxury because people are realising that they have to take some risks if they're to re-launch themselves and live a more avid life. But these risks aren't wasted. The skills and experience you gather through experimentation will mean all the more career capital for you in the long run. So just do something, anything, to gain some momentum. You might be amazed at what you discover about yourself. Wouldn't it be great if we could all adopt retail magnate Harry Gordon Selfridge's motto? – 'There's no fun like work.'

Strengths + Values + Passions

Once you've explored the three areas – strengths, values and passions – put them together to find patterns or themes that overlap. Each piece alone is valid, but you need to have all three elements in play together to complete the puzzle. Going back to our triple-circle diagram, where the circles intersect is where you unlock your full potential and achieve three-way wins in your life. Ideally, you need to focus your personal and career goals on the activities and interests that fall here. Here's my personal example to show you what it looks like.

Jan's personal mission

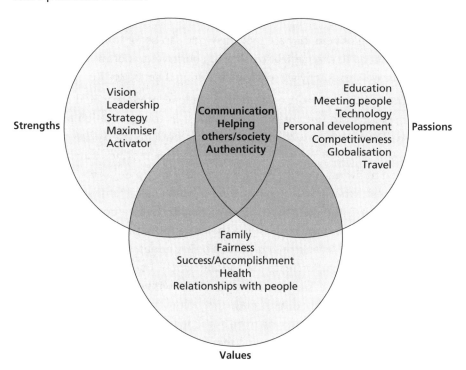

STEP 1: REVEAL YOUR MISSION

Taking the activities in which your circles overlap, combine them into one powerfully charged and purposeful mission – one that defines and captures the essence of who you are. The commonalities might not be obvious at first. Our purpose doesn't necessarily come pre-packaged so give yourself time to learn what makes you tick. This is a process after all.

Finding my personal mission

After having a go at the triple-circle diagram, I realised that I was spending far too much time on business/performance priorities and neglecting my own values with regard to my family, authenticity and personal wellbeing. In my mind, it was crunch time all the time at work, so it's no wonder I eventually collapsed under the pressure of trying to stay on peak form. I felt disconnected and out of touch with my genuine self because I wasn't acting according to my deepest values and passions. However, the circles revealed to me that I could craft a personal mission that would take into account more aspects of my personality and give me permission to bring forth my authentic self by being real, open, transparent and honest. At the same, I realised I could use my self-learning, insights and experiences to teach others how to become more of who they are too. The world can be far too 'samey', and I think we need to change that by allowing ourselves to portray our distinctive personalities as they are, without 'watering them down' for business.

Looking at where my circles overlap, what kind of work would provide an opportunity to use my skills and interest in communication to build stronger connections with others and give back to the wider society, while still allowing me to be me? Coaching, mentoring, training and speaking at events are all activities that allow me to engage with what I'm good at, what gives me pleasure and what's consistent with my values. Today, I find it tremendously rewarding to be in a position to help people understand themselves and their strengths, practise greater optimism and follow their calling. And as a side bonus, I get to talk about the 'big' topics that fascinate me and the actions I believe can make the world a better place, such as balancing wealth with purpose, intelligence with emotions, learning with play, technology with human potential, and so on. Coaching allows me to be authentic while I'm cheering people on towards their goals or bringing them back to line when they wander off course. What's more, I can pull into operation my talents for communication and being able to bond quickly with others for a special, meaningful purpose each time. So, in a nutshell, my mission or 'why' is: *to unlock human potential around the world*. And there's nothing else I would rather be doing. I wake up every morning thinking how lucky I am to be able to feel happiness and passion doing what I do. I want you to be able to experience that feeling too. The teachings in this book are part of how I manifest this mission, so I hope they prove useful to you.

What's your mission? Does it involve working with children; conserving the environment; running your own business; entertaining people; fighting discrimination; designing beautiful clothing; helping the sick and infirm; creating clever campaigns – what? You might even have the same mission as me, but perhaps you need to pursue it in a different way, through politics, education or teaching? Once you've identified the mission that would be most significant and enjoyable to you, and that calls on your strengths, make sure you write it down (in the form of a positive statement) or draw a picture, diagram or chart to represent it. Make it jazzy. You should feel direction, inspiration and motivation whenever you look at it. Carry it with you, post copies in visible places at home and work. Surround yourself with your mission so it feels real.

STEP 2: MAP IT OUT

Next, determine what you can do on a micro and macro level to start working your mission:

Micro mission

Don't assume that you have to leave your job or your organisation in order to create more gratifying work. Highly ambitious changes sometimes fail because they're too much to handle all in one go. Often it's best to go for some small wins first. Think about how you can redesign your role or make changes around the edges of your job to bring it more in line with your mission. What adjustments can you make to improve your day-do-day activities and match them to your strengths, values and passions? For instance:

- **Take on more:** Ask if you can participate in different meetings or a different department; offer your services for certain projects; train newcomers; take ownership of extra tasks or client relationships; volunteer to organise an event in your area of interest. Try to start doing the job you want or seek higher levels of involvement, even if it's only in a minor way at first.

- **Tell your boss:** Make it known to your boss that you want more challenges to fit your talents, values and personal career goals, and that you hope to reduce the amount of work you find uninspiring. They could have their own ideas or opportunities that might not have crossed your mind.

- **Experiment:** Craft your own little experiments by doing something new for a short period to see how it feels. For instance, try tweaking things about in your work environment, or test out a new coaching style with members of your team. Set clear goals to challenge yourself in the areas you want to develop, even when your job doesn't require it.

- **Improve your connections:** Change the quality and/or amount of interactions with others you encounter in your job. Want more teamwork? Think about ways to get involved in activities that span different departments or which encompass group goals. Or join a book club or health club with your co-workers. Want to work alone more? Look into opportunities to work from home or on solo projects.

- **Check your outlook:** If you can't introduce any actual changes, ask yourself what potential meaning, pleasure and growth already exists in what you do, like the janitor who sees the potential inherent in his role to improve everyone's health, environment and wellbeing. Can you inject some happiness boosters throughout the week – brief activities to rejuvenate you and bring more enjoyment to your work?[11] Like scheduling time to read interesting articles into your planner perhaps. Remember, the mental construction of our daily activities defines our reality more than the specific activities themselves.

- **Take your mission home:** What other outlets do you have for your strengths, values and passions outside of work? Maybe you could try putting aside two hours a week to practise a hobby that excites you, be it sports or music or whatever. Or do something fun and challenging to raise funds for a local charity, like running a half-marathon with your kids. Perhaps you could devote one day a month to community service. Alternatively, you could put more energy into your relationships with friends and family to improve your overall happiness and life satisfaction.

Macro mission

If you've tried aligning your responsibilities with your mission but your job still feels more chore-some than cheerful, it may be time to take more drastic action. What large-scale changes can you make to experience your work as a 'calling'? Are there alternative sources of income that offer a better set-up for you? Is there a different role in the business that will allow you to bring in your specific strengths, values and passions to achieve success? Or is it smarter to

[11] Ben-Shahar, Tal (2007). *Happier: Learn the Secrets to Daily Joy and Lasting Fulfillment.* New York: McGraw-Hill.

jump ship to a more progressive or suitably matched employer? Knowing your mission allows you to connect with companies that have similar values and beliefs, and helps you better weigh up the pros and cons of any new career opportunity. You could even strike out on your own and make your 'be my own boss' dream a reality. The decision's all yours.

STEP 3: LIVE YOUR MISSION

The final step is to go ahead and live your mission. Set positive goals for the short and long term based on your micro and macro actions. These should help you focus on success (what you want to achieve) rather than failure (what you want to avoid) and point your career in the direction you want it to go. Then, in the iconic words of big sports brand Nike – *just do it*.

Your purpose can change as you go through different life stages, so it may be worth revisiting the triple-circle exercise every now and then to keep your mission tip top fresh. It's also a good idea to keep a record of activities, thoughts and feelings to assess your progress on personal and professional goals. If anything, this is essential for your self-awareness and to keep a check on your biggest priorities. A little nudging, correction and fine-tuning might be needed to guarantee those three-way wins.

A mission for everyone!

A positive, go-ahead leader can use the same triple-circle approach for the benefit of his team, division or entire organisation. Everyone is inspired (and de-spired) by a different and diverse set of personal factors; by that I mean strengths, values and passions of course. What works for one member of your team in stoking their fire won't necessarily work for another, and therefore a one-size-fits-all approach isn't going to do much good. No one wants to be 'just another number' or 'one of the crowd', so you have to be able to connect with people as human beings. A leader who shows great awareness and sensitivity to people's wellbeing and personal uniqueness can play a massive role in influencing drive, nurturing talent and making normal life more rewarding for their team.

In my view, the best way to show your support and use your leadership to serve others is *by helping people find their mission*. This is no easy task, even if you're already chummy with your team members. Trying to understand the individual and what makes them feel valuable is difficult enough; but it becomes even harder when crossed over with the demands made by each job and the organisation itself. Small business owners and entrepreneurs are usually ahead of the game here, as in many ways they're accustomed to this form of personal leadership. It will take a bit of time to get everyone working in accordance with their strengths, values and passions, and there's bound to be some relationship building, dialogue and job tailoring/crafting experimentation involved. This can be frustrating in today's never-stand-still world where everyone expects things to happen in a moment's notice. Like I said earlier, it's a process, but an important one. When your people can perform activities that they enjoy, find meaningful and are good at, they'll put in double – no, more like triple – the commitment and performance effort towards the success of the organisation.

Being visionary (inspiring the dream and making it happen)

'*The empires of the future are empires of the mind.*'
WINSTON CHURCHILL, ENGLISH STATESMAN, WARTIME UK PRIME MINISTER

Do you have a vision of how you want your life or business to be? Is it clear? Does it feel real? Does it make you squirm with excitement? Purposeful leaders are forward looking. They create an inspiring and compelling picture of the future in their imagination, one that others can also see, feel, understand and completely grab onto. American civil rights activist Dr Martin Luther King knew all about the *power of vision* when he delivered his famous 'I have a dream' speech. The 'hot' vision or dream is what fires our imagination and keeps us looking ahead towards a beautiful horizon. It's what makes the risks of leadership and moving out of our comfort zone not only possible, but worthwhile.

To be visionary as a leader, you have to be able to inspire and be inspired. Renowned self-development speaker and author Dr Wayne Dyer talks of *inspiration* as 'being in-Spirit'.[1] When we're in-Spirit, a vision or idea takes hold of us and we feel connected to our source of power and totally on purpose. This inspiration comes through having a meaningful *mission*, one which activates our unique strengths, values and passions. Leaders who are inspired by their 'why' are able to envision a glittering future in which they add something special to the world as a result of doing what they are here to do. What's more, they can also get everyone around them feeling and doing things 'on purpose' in order to achieve the dream and make it a reality.

Higher inspiration

There's an interesting old fable that illustrates the different ways we can interpret our goals in life:

Building a vision

A traveller arrived in a small town and stumbled upon a construction site where a group of bricklayers were working. He asked each worker what he was doing:

'I'm laying bricks,' grumbled the first, who looked fed up.

The second, who was working more energetically, briefly stopped to respond: 'I'm building a wall.'

Approaching the third worker, who was humming a tune as he worked, he received the happy response, 'I'm building a cathedral.'

The fourth, working a little way off, put down his tools, looked up at the sky and responded with a warm smile, 'I'm serving God.'

The four bricklayers were all doing the same job. However, each had a different vision of its purpose and, in turn, experienced a different level of passion and commitment in doing the work. If you were asked to pick which bricklayer

---

[1] Dyer, Dr Wayne W. (2010). *Inspiration: Your Ultimate Calling*. London: Hay House.

would make the better leader, it's pretty obvious who would be the most capable of inspiring you to reach for bigger and better things! The fourth bricklayer was performing the same task as the others, but he was awake and aware of what it meant on a more magnificent scale.

Leadership involves choices and commitments. As with the bricklayers, we can choose which kind of purpose we follow – a higher visionary goal or a lower 'just-get-through-the-day-and-go-home' one. The story reminds us that there is great value in cranking up your perspective to find the grander, more upscale meaning in the work you're doing. If you love what you do and believe it to be worthwhile, then you'll have the passion to fuel you on your journey and to carry others along with you on a wave of inspiration. Let's face it – nobody's going to want to follow you to the Land of Apathy.

TO INSPIRE AND BE INSPIRED

Outstanding leaders understand the purpose of their work. They see the 'why' behind it and have a profound belief that it connects with something greater than themselves. Such leaders are inspired by what they're doing and where they're going. To use an old moth-eaten cliché, they can zoom out to see the 'bigger picture'. And not only that, they ensure others can see the picture in wide frame too by building a shared vision that appeals to their audience's hearts as well as their minds. Throughout history, all the most exalted leaders have done this in some shape or form. It's often argued that before the Second World War, Winston Churchill had been a middle-of-the-road political leader; there was nothing particularly special about him. It wasn't until he found his honourable purpose to 'defend Britain and win the war' that he became the great heroic leader we still harp on about today.[2] The war triggered his 'why' and whipped up the latent strengths, values and passions buried within him.

Providing inspiration as a leader is not an optional extra or 'add-on' to the job, it's your topmost priority. Extensive research carried out by leadership consultants John Zenger, Joseph Folkman and Scott Edinger over a four-year

[2] Gell, Anthony (2014). *The Book of Leadership: How to Get Yourself, Your Team and Your Organisation Further Than You Ever Thought Possible*. London: Piatkus.

period to determine what makes a top leader showed that the ability to 'inspire and motivate high performance' was the single most powerful predictor of being perceived as an extraordinary leader.[3] There aren't all that many natural visionary leaders in the corporate world. Most CEOs, entrepreneurs and executives have to learn and earn their way to becoming inspirational through what they say and how they act.

Technological visionaries

In IT, there have been a great many innovators but only two true visionary leaders who changed the world – Bill Gates of Microsoft and Steve Jobs of Apple. Perhaps I'm biased, but I always look to Bill as an inspirational example. When he first came out with Microsoft's bold vision of 'a computer on every desk and in every home' in 1977, the technology to achieve it wasn't even in place and people saw little need for computers in their everyday life. But Bill's vision painted a fascinating mental image of the future that mobilised people into action and transformed the way we all live, work and communicate. He turned what was once a passionate hobby into one of the most successful businesses of all time . . . and he made technology cool. I believe that because he was so blisteringly obsessed and committed to his mission, he was able to create a special emotional connection with employees and customers alike. Despite his quiet demeanour, he really is quite extraordinary in his unshakeable conviction and ability to glimpse the opportunities the future holds.

Going from one technological genius to another – Steve Jobs' extraordinary vision, fanaticism for design excellence and power of conviction completely reset the whole IT industry. While Bill was all about the productivity gains that could be offered to customers, Steve demanded and accepted nothing short of perfection in function, detail and design. It was well known that he pushed his team to the utmost limits, both technically and emotionally, to achieve the spectacular standards he envisaged. And gosh did they deliver!

---

[3] Zenger, John H., Folkman, Joseph R. and Edinger, Scott K. (2009). *The Inspiring Leader: Unlocking the Secrets of How Extraordinary Leaders Motivate*. New York: McGraw-Hill.

Visionary leadership

Do you have a vision that you passionately care about? Maybe you want to:

- make something happen
- change the way things are
- create something no one else has ever created before.

Can you breathe life into this vision and get others hoping and dreaming of it too?

Without a noble purpose or vision to guide us, our actions can often become reactive or arbitrary, driven by the latest events or even by random, fluke influences. Good planning can help to a point, but won't necessarily take us all the way. Planning is short term while inspiration is in it for the long haul. Leadership is about going somewhere, a journey towards a bright future. It's the vision rather than the plan that tells you where you're going and what success can and should look like. Hence why Dr Martin Luther King had a dream, not a plan! In his 'I have a dream' speech, King described his vision of a world where people live together in mutual respect, and where his children 'will not be judged by the colour of their skin but by the content of their character'. His vision forced a moral awakening on equality and civil rights across America and changed the course of history forever.

If you don't have a vision – an ideal and unique image of what you, your team or the organisation can become – then where exactly are you leading your people?

Being inspirational is linked to the concept of *transformational leadership*, first introduced by leadership expert James MacGregor Burns in 1978[4] and further extended by Bernard M. Bass in 1985.[5] A transformational leader takes people from point A (good or bad) to point B (good or better). You, the leader, are the vehicle for this journey and your fuel is *inspiration*. Without you,

---

[4] Burns, James MacGregor (1978). *Leadership*. New York: Harper & Row..
[5] Bass, Bernard, M. (1985). *Leadership and Performance Beyond Expectation*. New York: Free Press.

nothing happens. So you have a special responsibility to engage your integrity and power to:

- articulate a clear, exciting vision that others can buy into
- provide meaning and challenge to people's work by activating their higher-order needs
- arouse positive emotions in your followers
- lead by example by being authentic and playing to your unique strengths, values and passions
- help your team find their 'why' and align their own strengths, values and passions to activities they find enjoyable and rewarding
- manage your energy well to stay 'Zen' in the heat of battle.

A transformational leader stirs up people's emotions and garners trust and respect from their followers. They *inspire*. A manager, on the other hand, looks after the day-to-day nuts and bolts involved in delivering the organisation's strategy. They *plan*. Inspiring is spiritual (in-Spirit) and emotional, more than practical. Planning (the 'what' and 'how'), though useful, simply doesn't generate the same raw passion, devotion or momentum as inspiration (the 'why'). Looking back at my overall career, I believe I behaved like a manager 60 per cent of the time and a leader 40 per cent of the time. It took me a while to get to grips with it. Managers can motivate people to carry through ideas and 'do the work', but only leaders can bring together great teams and create an emotional connection and shared purpose to lead them somewhere worth going.

All that being said, the 'what' and 'how' still have their place in the big scheme of things. Planning and purpose are both necessary. You may have heard the maxim that goes, 'Not all dreamers are achievers, but all achievers are dreamers.' We need to dream, but we need to act at the same time. Leadership isn't something that we can just leave to chance. As unglamorous as it sounds, we all have to do our homework and look as far down the pipeline as we can. Without exercising a strategy and taking persistent steps forward, dreams will remain dreams and never come true.

Achieving the impossible

Your vision won't just happen in one giant leap; it will take a series of baby steps to get there. The journey calls for much *faith, conviction and a positive mindset* to keep folk aiming high and striving for success. This is no picnic. Travelling from point A (where you are now) to point B (your vision) might involve going over some bumpy, uneven ground, and there could be several tough obstacles along the way. No matter how well your journey starts off, threats or challenges can emerge that you haven't anticipated, throwing you into a crisis. Even the best-laid plans don't always work out as intended. It's at these times that positivity can prove elusive. Being in a position of authority, it's up to you to help your people be tenacious and stay fired up when work gets toilsome and all they want to do is give up and dive under the duvet.

The faith to climb mountains

One way to really make your dreams happen is to use the power of belief and a positive mindset. Let me share an example of how I unlocked my team's potential to achieve what they thought would be impossible. I used . . . a story. That's it. However, it wasn't my story that made the difference to my team's performance. It was someone else's. After two years of running the Central and Eastern Europe (CEE) division at Microsoft, things were progressing reasonably well. We were all working at full tilt and making use of our strengths – results were showing and we were growing. But I knew at a gut level that we hadn't delivered our full potential. We needed to make a bigger impact, but it felt like what we were trying to do in the marketplace was impossible. My team hit back saying 'enough is enough' and complained that they were being driven too hard. They were drained and didn't believe they could achieve much more. I needed someone who had accomplished something really crazy and outrageous to show them that our goals were within reach. That's when I pulled in mountaineering legend and explorer Reinhold Messner to speak to my management group. He was the first man to climb to the top of Mount Everest without supplemental oxygen when nobody believed it could be done, and I wanted him to show my team that achieving the impossible *was* possible!

When he and fellow adventurer Peter Hebeler first announced that they would be attempting the climb without oxygen apparatus, everyone thought it was futile. They were labelled 'lunatics' by members of the climbing and medical communities and were told by nine out of ten experts that it wasn't feasible. The physiological demands for climbing

▶

Everest were known to be tortuous and they were putting themselves at risk of severe brain damage. Quick, accurate decision making would be needed to cope with the weather extremes, steep icy slopes and biting cold. And without enough oxygen during the ascent, it would be difficult to think clearly. The oxygen levels at the summit of Everest were only considered enough to support the body at rest, not in motion. Though it took almost everything out of the two climbers, they concluded the feat on 8 May 1978. Two years later Reinhold did it again, completely solo this time. He reached his career peak in 1986 when he became the first man to climb all 14 mountains across the globe standing above 8000 metres.

Reinhold Messner's story totally changed the mindset of my team. He is clear proof that you can be an inspirational leader whatever your field. We were all blown away by the discipline and faith he had demonstrated on his climbing quests. It's fair to say that, after his speech, our motivation went through the roof, as did our renewed commitment to achieving our goals. Even the sceptics in the team experienced a shift in their perspective. Doing our best wasn't enough anymore; we were ready to do 'whatever it takes'. We even adopted a new motto: 'what the human brain can imagine, it can achieve', which we repeated over and over like a mantra until it penetrated into everyone's subconscious and became embedded in the team culture. Four years later we were Microsoft's best performing region worldwide. Reinhold's exceptional leadership qualities showed us we could get there. His inspiring speech cost just €4000, but our Finance specialists estimated that because of it we generated an additional $1.2 billion in revenue for Microsoft.

> 'If you find your path and take it, you will have strength and direction and a goal and nothing and no one will be able to stop you.'
>
> Reinhold Messner, record-breaking mountaineer and adventurer

YOUR SUBCONSCIOUS SAT NAV

Every great feat that has ever been accomplished or invention that has ever been created began as a picture in someone's imagination – a vision. Your vision is a mental image of the world which does not yet exist. Time spent imagining it is never wasted as it keeps your mind firmly focused on what you want. This is hugely important because your *mind* is your greatest asset . . . or it can be your worst enemy. Your subconscious mind houses a sophisticated guidance system, like a sat nav. Its job is to act on or seek out whatever you consistently focus your attention upon (hopefully, the vision of your ideal future). Intriguingly, your subconscious doesn't know the difference between what's real and what's fake. The electrical signals are all the same. When your subconscious mind receives information from the conscious mind, it accepts it as the whole and entire truth, no matter if it's positive or negative. Once you 'programme' your subconscious sat nav with a target location (idea, suggestion or image), the subconscious proceeds to navigate towards it. It does this by, for example, alerting you to opportunities, drawing you to the right people and providing the impulse to take action.

Your subconscious doesn't think for itself or question things, it simply does as it's told. That's why it's hugely important that you deliberately only feed it positive images. Your mind will direct you towards them like a magnetic force. So, if you imagine that you can be successful in what you're trying to do, then you *will* be successful. But you have to have faith that it's possible. As leading motivational speaker and author Brian Tracy points out, 'All great men and women have been people of faith . . . They have had an attitude of calmness and confidence and a belief that there was a power greater than themselves that was helping them.'[6] It's really important that you *believe* you can do it and not let destructive, negative emotions interfere with the calm, positive attitude your subconscious needs for ideal functioning. Even when they're not actively doing anything, successful people are thinking about their vision, visualising it, imagining it and feeling it already accomplished. Ultimately, you have to be a CMO – a *Chief Mind Officer* – as all great performance is fuelled by what happens in the mind.

BELIEVE IN YOUR TEAM

Don't be afraid to expect the most from your people and push them out of their comfort zones. Your belief in the unique strengths and skills of your team can be very powerful. It reflects your confidence and trust in them, which is a galvanising factor in producing world-class achievements. This is known as the

---

[6] Tracy, Brian (1995). *Maximum Achievement: Strategies and Skills that Will Unlock Your Hidden Powers to Succeed*. New York: Simon & Schuster.

Pygmalion effect – when your belief and confidence in another person's potential brings it to life. Pygmalion was an ancient Greek sculptor who fell in love with an ivory statue he had carved of his ideal woman, named Galatea. She embodied his every hope, dream and possibility, and he prayed to the gods to make her a reality. They granted Pygmalion his desire and she became the woman he already believed she was. The takeaway for you here is: believe in your team and they will reward you for it with loyalty, commitment, results and more.

Bear in mind that you also have to be just as committed yourself, more so in fact. All exceptional leaders 'show up' and never get bored of the story they're helping to create. You need to lead the way for your team and show them (through what you say and do) that you will fight to the end to achieve your goals. If you're not all that fussed about the vision, your team will quickly pick up on your lack of faith and disinterest, and they won't be bothered either. Show that you're fully committed and willing to do what it takes – stretch yourself, step out of your comfort zone, make sacrifices where necessary, be creative, take strategic risks and have self-discipline. Your presence and dedication will inspire others to stay the course. Never give up on being the best leader you can be – 'keep on keepin' on' and your team will follow your inspirational lead.

TAKE A POSITIVE CUE FROM SPORTS

In many ways, sports psychology is far more advanced than business psychology when it comes to encouraging people to reach for the stars and unleash their full potential. Czech ice hockey coach Marian Jelinek highlights that there are two inspirational drivers that talented sportspeople tap into to gain a competitive edge:

1. **Play for enjoyment:** Athletes follow their 'calling'. They engage passionately with a meaningful purpose or activity which allows them to use their strengths in ways that they enjoy.

2. **Need to win:** Athletes have a crystal-clear vision and a desire to be 'the best'. They visualise what success looks like and use practice and persistence to get there, while also managing their energy effectively.

For all of us, both of these aspects need to be brought together in equal measure if we're to be successful and happy in the work we do. If you only go after victory, you'll be successful (perhaps even a champion in your field), but you'll burn out before long if you're not having fun. Likewise if you only play for enjoyment, you may gain satisfaction from using your skills but you'll never challenge yourself enough to become more than a run-of-the-mill player as you'll be lacking that competitive desire to win.

For athletes in peak physical condition, success is less about technical skill and more about what happens in the mind, and the most accomplished athletes always look through the lens of positivity in order to arrive at the top of their game. A core habit of any major sports personality is his or her ability to 'think like a winner'; what I call *Premier League thinking*. An optimistic and ambitious outlook can be fundamental in elevating and amplifying performance, and more hopeful athletes often rack up greater achievements. If you don't play the 'mental game' well and are beset by self-doubt, fear and anxiety, then you have no chance out there on the real-life playing field. This same principle applies just as much in the business arena as it does in sport. Whether you're a manager, doctor or artist, you can become a Premier League player by using positive self-chat, habits and imagery to build up the mental determination to win.

Empirical studies have found a positive relationship between the 'need for achievement' and business success.[7] Individuals with a strong achievement orientation tend to:

- set high standards for themselves and those around them
- constantly look for better ways to accomplish a task
- anticipate problems
- take risks to achieve their goals
- accept responsibility for performance results.

These talents trigger behaviours that ultimately lead to successful economic outcomes and business performance. If, like the best athletes, leaders learn to practise positivity and their 'sport' gives them pleasure, they can truly become winners and achieve extraordinary things in their own lives and for their organisations.

---

[7] Bharadwaj Badal, Sangeeta (2015). 'The psychology of entrepreneurs drives business outcomes'. *Gallup*, 1 September. [Online] Available from: http://www.gallup.com/businessjournal/185156/ psychology-entrepreneurs-drives-business-outcomes.aspx?utm_source=giessen&utm_ medium=search&utm_campaign=tiles

LESSONS IN REACH AND RESILIENCE

Beliefs are self-fulfilling prophecies, so while you need to set super-high expectations for yourself and your team, you also need to have the confidence that you can rise to meet them. When you commit to achieving something, you demonstrate faith in your ability to see it through, to bringing about your envisioned future. You create your reality rather than reacting to it. If you encounter a problem, look for the opportunity it brings; if things go haywire or you fall behind, keep pointing and looking ahead towards your brighter future (the vision). Given my love of sports, it may not surprise you that the life lessons that have been most valuable in guiding much of my decision making and behaviour in business were picked up through my experiences playing tennis as a youth:

Lessons from tennis

1. **You are alone in the court as much as you are in your life.** No one but you is in control of how you act and react in relation to the events and happenings in your life. Your attitude is all up to you. No matter how much you're struggling, you can choose where to put your focus – on the pain of today or the glory yet to come. Use whatever mental magic you like to condition and retrain your mind. Try positive self-talk, visualisation, reframing your thoughts, relaxation exercises or taking time off from bad news.

2. **You play to the last ball.** Never give up on your vision. Reinforce it with every interaction, in both word and deed. Your potential is not fixed by your previous achievements or where you've come from, but rather by what you believe. *The map is not the territory* – it's only your filter of it. You can create a new map that more accurately reflects your new reality; a blueprint that your mind can use to create your life the way you want it. The more you move your mindset, the more power and momentum you generate towards your vision.

When I was laughed at and taunted for wanting to play pro tennis as a chubby child, I was left with a choice. I could run home crying to my parents and give up my dreams and ambitions there and then. Or I could suck it up and do what needed to be done to get fighting fit and get my game on. The ball was in my court, literally, and I decided to go for it. I trained hard every day in any space I could find – the utility room in the winter, the hall at 4am – anywhere. It was my lesson in resilience. At the same time I envisioned myself being successful; I really pictured it in full colour. One year later, I beat the reigning champion and became number one at the tennis club – no more fat guy!

What does the future look like?

We've been talking about having a dream or vision throughout the whole of this chapter, but what exactly does that mean and how do you go about creating one? A vision is a realistic, convincing and attractive depiction of where you want to be in the future.[8] Your vision is your 'Mount Everest', the majestic mountain you just *have* to climb – the epic end result that challenges you to move out of your comfort zone to achieve something special or go somewhere better than you are right now.

A concrete and compelling vision does a lot of things. It:

- paints a seductive picture of the future (usually five to ten years from now)
- creates clarity for setting new goals
- illuminates the direction people must head in
- enables strong workforce buy-in
- energises and empowers people in focusing their efforts
- inspires and moves people emotionally to connect with a worthy purpose
- helps to shape the organisation's long-term strategies
- embodies the organisation's culture and values
- sets the scope of priorities and guides planning
- helps people at all levels to make decisions
- provides a marker to measure achievement
- attracts/engages and retains talent
- aligns people and activities across the organisation
- helps manage change and bring hope for the future
- reflects what's unique about you or your organisation.

A vision can be simple or complex; it can be as vague as a dream or as pinpoint precise as a SMART goal – but it must never ever be dull. A vision absolutely *must*

[8] Manktelow, James. 'What is leadership?' *Mind Tools*. [Online] Available from: https://www.mindtools.com/pages/article/newLDR_41.htm

create tremendous energy. If it doesn't give you or others a buzz, then it's not fit for the job. For Facebook founder Mark Zuckerberg, making the world a better place through social sharing is the ultimate dream. What lights him up and keeps him going through the tough times is the guiding ideology that if people have access to more information and are more connected, they'll have greater understanding and empathy – and it follows that we'll all live in a better world.

All visionary leaders are a bit crazy. They have dreams bigger than the times they live in. My advice is don't be scared to aim for the outrageous or to think the impossible. It's usually the crazy people that change the world. They disrupt the status quo and shake things up. Doing things differently is the only way to achieve evolutionary results and make positive change. Some visionary leaders, like Sir Richard Branson, get a thrill out of setting themselves huge, apparently unachievable challenges and trying to rise above them. Others, like Sir Stelios Haji-Ioannou, the founder of easyJet, make it their business to overtake complacent giants and pull the rug from under 'the way things are': 'Taking on the big boys is what I do for a living, and I keep doing it industry after industry – and it has never failed me.'[9]

THE VALUE OF VISION

Strategy and actions follow directly from the vision. Without a focused and defined picture of where things are headed, you're susceptible to being pulled away from your real, authentic self, and worse, you risk losing the respect and loyalty of your team – with disastrous consequences. A leader is defined by their followers. Without any followers that believe in you and your vision, are you really leading? Failure to provide a captivating vision or guiding 'North Star' can leave people feeling adrift and wandering off in all sorts of directions – HR is going one way, finance, production and sales are all going another way. The result is that some departments end up taking a wrong turn or going nowhere at all! When we don't put the time and effort into thinking about where the business is going, we can fall into the habit of chasing short-term goals, wasting resources on ineffective strategies, or shamefully, making repeated mistakes.[10] But when we consider our future in a hopeful way, we're

[9] Gell, Anthony (2014). *The Book of Leadership: How to Get Yourself, Your Team and Your Organisation Further Than You Ever Thought Possible*. London: Piatkus.
[10] Lopez, Anthony (2010). *The Legacy Leader*. Mustang, OK: Tate Publishing.

more likely to make full use of our strengths, manage our energy better and say no to obligations that aren't aligned with our interests.

People move towards the pictures they see in their minds, and so you need to be able to produce a rich results-oriented image of what success looks like and how things will be when the vision becomes a reality. An inspirational vision is more than just any old goal; it's your big 'win'. It translates dry objectives into something more tangible and attainable – something people can not only see, but that they can feel themselves being a part of; something that they are moved to pursue. The strongest leaders know how to work their own strengths and those of the organisation, and as a result, they operate superbly in their comfort zone. But being comfortable is not where the big wins are. Creating an innovative, 'pie-in-the-sky' vision that leverages those strengths can shape the whole business in the best way possible to succeed in the future. Being a visionary leader doesn't mean ignoring the trends in your industry; of course you must take into account how the market is likely to evolve and how your competitors are likely to behave. If anything, the best visions are those that tap into some real analysis of opportunity and potential innovation to create a more vivid and meaningful picture to everyone being led.

The difficult task is in 'selling' the vision, communicating it with clarity and passion in order to propel people to do what needs doing to get there. Not all leaders can be great speakers, but you can enhance your visionary communication skills by discovering, visualising and practising your own authentic message. Tell the story of your vision and use metaphors to bring it to life. Your goal is to inspire and motivate, not dictate. Don't try to map out the entire journey for people or compile endless lists of marching orders. A vision is a 'dream with direction', not a dream with full GPS navigation, so keep it simple:

- Here's where we are going.
- Here's why we need to go there.
- Here's your important role in helping us get there.

The process for getting there will become clearer as you all proceed and will evolve through your mission and strategy. When people share a common vision, there is huge momentum for success. Make it an adventure and let people use their own ingenuity to conceive what needs to be done. Set them free to experiment and take calculated risks. Talented people want to be part of something bigger than themselves. They want to feel that their ideas, endeavours and exertions have helped produce something momentous: 'How cool. I helped to create that.' This is how you get the kind of passion, purpose and positivity which aligns psychological wellbeing with high performance and encourages people to go the extra mile for the organisation.

Go on, dream a little

- Frame your vision as the best-case scenario, one that can create win–win benefits for everyone involved. What will it look like for each of your primary stakeholders? What key outcomes will evidence your success?

- Imagine that you or your company will be appearing in a publication in five to ten years' time. What will have been your biggest accomplishment? How would you like to appear to the outside world?

- Focus on the end result, not the process for getting there. Picture the incredible success you can realise from going in this direction. Put lots of graphic detail into the image to make it vivid, and see it actually happening.

- As well as seeing your vision in your mind's eye, imagine the *excitement, satisfaction and thrill* you'll experience when you get there. Feel as if you've already succeeded.

This visualisation technique can take some getting used to, especially if you're not comfortable with creating vivid images in your mind. Practising at night before you go to sleep is a great way to feel your vision within reach and inflame a positive outlook.

STEP 2: I – INSPIRE

The next step is to figure out how you can *communicate* your vision clearly and passionately. This is especially important if you're a leader in business as the vision isn't just about you. You have to consider others and how to rally their engagement and partnership, so that in the end all parties are motivated to do a bang-up job. Use the following guidelines:

- Begin by structuring your team around your vision based on their *strengths*. This is a powerful way to win people over as they can be authentic and do what they enjoy while working collectively to build the vision.

- Help others understand your *true intentions*. Be strong, straight and sincere in communicating your vision. You've got a series of arguments and facts that have convinced you that this is the right course – so use them on your team. Don't leave people guessing what you really stand for, otherwise they'll never fully engage with you or your dream.

- Focus on a short list of *key benefits and outcomes* that taps into the desires of others and provides a detailed picture of where you intend to be, who you want to be and what you can confidently achieve. What words and phrases will you use to communicate these outcomes/benefits to others?

- *Make it sexy and simple.* Your goal is to tell the story in a way that excites people and enlists their support for the common cause, and to infuse them with the belief that getting there *is* possible. Try not to make a huge rah-rah speech that goes on forever but says very little – give people a simple tune to whistle. Save the 'boring stuff' like deadlines and budgets for another time. Leadership professor and author John Kotter suggests a useful rule of thumb: 'Whenever you cannot describe the vision driving a change initiative in five minutes or less and get a reaction that signifies both understanding and interest, you are in for trouble.'[11]

- Think about the kind of *environment* in which you're going to unveil your vision and how broadly you'll disseminate it, e.g. in team meetings, one-on-one, through managers and supervisors, during speeches, via written newsletters. Create a plan for getting feedback and involving others in shaping the vision.

Write down your ideas and practise communicating your vision. Make sure you express it in a way that sounds authentic and encourages hope and aspiration. Practise out loud frequently to yourself and others until it feels natural. If you don't believe it, no one else will believe it either.

STEP 3: N – NAVIGATE

The vision is the bedrock of your success, but it doesn't guarantee you'll be victorious. Your vision can only become a reality if you take action and put in the hard work and diligent effort needed. How will you *live* the vision and make it happen? Here are some suggestions to point you in the right direction.

- Develop a plan for ongoing communications about the vision to keep it at the forefront of everyone's mind. Display it prominently in different formats and places that people can easily see. Use posters and flyers in your facilities, at company events, workshops and update meetings.

[11] Kotter, John P. (1996). *Leading Change*. Boston: Harvard Business School Press.

Talk regularly about how your actions, campaigns and products back up the vision. Repetition is essential. Constantly sell the vision. Keep it alive!

- Identify any roadblocks that need to be removed in order to move forward. Obstacles that can hold back the new vision include things like inertia in people, negative beliefs or entrenched systems. You have to be ready to dislodge these before they discourage others in your team and cause the momentum of your vision to come to a standstill.

- Be open to changing the vision in response to feedback. Encourage your team to make reasonable concerns known. If there are requests for major adjustments from several quarters, it's possible you may have missed a vital ingredient in cooking up the vision, and something needs to be amended or added to improve its flavour.

- While looking ahead to envision your future path, it's also important to *stay in the present*. That means inspiring a shared dream but also bringing relentless positivity and progress to your team on a day-to-day basis. Remind people that they're not laying bricks; they're paying homage to a higher power by building a cathedral. Your vision liberates you, so you can enjoy the here and now while you're in the middle of pursuing it.

MAKE A VISION STATEMENT

Some leaders find it helps to establish a *vision statement* or even a visual representation to describe their ultimate desired end-state. The best vision statements for organisations are short, snappy and 'Twitter friendly' – they condense a lot of information into an inspiring, memorable and clear declaration that can be quickly understood by most people.

Vision statement examples

A just world without poverty. Oxfam

To be Earth's most customer centric company; to build a place where people can come to find and discover anything they might want to buy online. Amazon

▶

> To be the company that best understands and satisfies the product, service and self-fulfillment needs of women – globally. Avon
>
> To enrich and delight the world through foods and brands that matter. Kellogg Company
>
> At IKEA our vision is to create a better everyday life for the many people. IKEA

What's the difference between a vision statement and a mission statement?

A mission statement answers questions like:[12]

- Why does my/our business exist?
- What is my/our work?

While a vision statement answers the questions:

- Where do I see my business going?'
- What do I/we intend to do?'

The mission statement describes the present state and purpose of the company – the overarching strategy for accomplishing the vision, i.e. what the company does, who it does it for and how it does it. It's narrower, more specific. The vision statement has a broader reach, defining the optimal state (mental picture) the company wants to achieve at some point in the future.

Motivation: the 'motive' to act

While feeling inspired is crucial for taking action towards your BIG vision and fulfilling your utmost potential, the reality is that we all sometimes need a kick in the butt to get started or keep going on the day-to-day stuff. *Inspiration* and *motivation* are not one and the same. Your inspiration is the internal *pull* that keeps you in line with the future you want, while motivation is the everyday *push* to psych yourself up and do what's needed to be done to make the tantalising dream happen. If you're a football player, you might dream of your team becoming number 1 in the Premier League (inspiration), but you still need to be pumped up to play your best in every match (motivation).

---

[12] Arline, Katherine (2014). 'What is a vision statement?' *Business News Daily*, 11 December. [Online] Available from: http://www.businessnewsdaily.com/3882-vision-statement.html

Motivation is what will get you out of bed in the morning to get stuff done. It will prod you to take control of the individual actions, steps and feelings necessary to get where you want to be – to finish the proposal, chase the next sale or make it to that conference.

Though positive psychology has been having a real 'moment' in the world of academia for its revolutionary potential in motivating people, a hefty portion of Fortune 500 companies are still using incentive theories and programmes that were proven ineffective decades ago. These outdated approaches to motivation are based on the idea that people work in accordance with how they're paid. The expectation is that people will work hard to get great results when there's an attractive reward or bonus in store for them. In other words, it's all about the money! A lot of businesses are big on this because it's easy, it's measurable and it can be formularised. And to a certain extent, it works. You can pay people to do what you want, when you want . . . over and over again. Money *is* a motivator, but it's not the ideal way to influence people in the long run (your budget couldn't handle it for one). There are a horde of other factors you can take into consideration if you want people to feel happy about going to work. On the whole, it's much better to *inspire* people so that they do something because they want to do it. As a performance driver, inspiration is more enduring than extrinsic motivation – people will give their all whether you dangle more money in front of them or not, during good times and bad. When motivation is tied to the inspiration of 'why' you are doing what you are doing, you can provide an environment that will justify your team choosing to invest their most precious resources – namely, their strengths, their energy and their emotional commitment – into their work.

So how do you go about doing that then?

The first clue is in Maslow's much talked about 'hierarchy of needs' model.

Climbing up Maslow's pyramid

Leaders can get a tonne of insight into what drives their own motivation and that of others from the well-known work of US psychologist Abraham Maslow, published in 1943.[13] Far from being 'old hat', his theory is still just as valid today as it was back then, and leaders would do well to recap its intuitive

[13] Maslow, Abraham, H. (1943). 'A theory of human motivation'. *Psychological Review*, *50*(4), pp. 370–396.

wisdom on how to build sustainable motivation. It's based on the premise that whatever we do as humans, we do it to satisfy our needs. In other words, we are all 'needs junkies', driven by our cravings. Maslow's model divides our needs into five categories, which come in a set pecking order. As one desire is satisfied, another pops up to take its place:

- **Physiological:** what we need to stay alive, e.g. food, water, air, sleep, shelter, warmth.
- **Safety:** what we need to be free from harm, e.g. steady employment, a safe place to live, health, law, protection from danger, financial security.
- **Social:** the need to belong and for love, affection and intimacy. Relationships, e.g. friends, partner, family. Involvement in social community and work groups.
- **Esteem:** the need for things that foster self-worth, confidence, social recognition and accomplishment, e.g. status, power, cars and, of course, good old money! Respect for others and respect by others.
- **Self-actualisation:** the 'holy grail' of happiness. This highest level is focused on self-awareness and personal growth, e.g. individuality, creativity, spontaneity, fulfilling personal potential, lack of prejudice, faith and transcendence.

Maslow's hierarchy of needs

The way I like to look at it is that the first two lower levels are *motivational needs*. Without a steady job, decent work conditions or enough money to cover our necessities, we're going to be unhappy. That's pretty obvious. So we're highly motivated to satisfy these needs to avoid nasty, unpleasant feelings or consequences. Once they're satisfied, however, we no longer think about them – they become the norm. The three higher levels of the pyramid are concerned with our relationship bonds, aspirations or personal development goals. These are what I call *inspirational needs*; they don't stem from a lack of something, but rather from a desire to grow and evolve as a person. We have to feel inspired *internally* to find meaning, build engagement and become self-actualised, rather than motivated *externally*.

In China, India and other fast-evolving economies in the East, there's a much stronger appetite to learn and compete (in both individuals and organisations) because people have a bigger purpose to satisfy their lower needs. The first two Maslow needs are huge motivators when they're unmet. People will readily knuckle down for fair pay, reasonable conditions and civilised treatment. While over in the West, it's a peculiar case of 'we have enough to live but nothing to live for'. We've mastered the majority of the Maslow levels with the exception of *self-actualisation* – that sublime penthouse at the topmost tip of the pyramid. Self-actualisation is the quest to become self-aware and reach your full potential as a person, to find and express your 'calling' in life. Unlike the lower level needs, this need is never fully satisfied. As you evolve psychologically, there are always more and more opportunities to continue to grow. If these desires aren't met, people can get restless and frustrated, even if they are technically 'successful' in all other respects – say, with an amazing career, adorable kids and all the comforts civilisation has to offer.

Big companies have no issues satisfying the foundational elements of the Maslow pyramid. They're increasing salaries and annual leave, improving working conditions and providing security through contracts of employment, pensions and medical insurance. Many are going further to encourage social connections and a sense of belonging through teamwork and social activities. But they're still not taking proper care of the peak of the pyramid. Results from employee satisfaction surveys across the board show that people are generally happy with how employers are meeting their material and security needs. However, they're not getting enough feedback and recognition from their managers. Without praise or feedback, it's difficult for people to grow and become self-actualised, or to feel a vital part of the business. It gives the impression that leadership isn't paying attention to what they do and that their contribution isn't important. This ignorance and lack of interest is essentially fuelling an *engagement crisis* across all industry sectors. To their credit, however, there are the odd few companies that seem to have got the hang of it. The Virgin Group is an excellent example of a business with a healthy, people-first culture that encourages individuals to spend time working on things they enjoy and find meaningful, and where people are recognised for great effort via feedback, work variety and autonomy.

New research by consulting firm Bain & Company and the Economist Intelligence Unit on over 300 executives points to the productive power of an inspired and engaged workforce, rather than a simply satisfied one.[14] Results showed that satisfied employees were productive at an index level of 100 while engaged employees produced at 144, nearly half as much again. Meanwhile, inspired employees scored a monumental 225 on the same scale, leagues ahead of the others! These figures prove that mastering the art of inspirational leadership is what truly counts in building an impressive organisation. But you can't inspire employees to their full potential until you first satisfy and then engage your team, progressing up the *pyramid of employee needs* shown below. It's the Maslow order of things in corporate style:

The pyramid of employee needs

INSPIRED EMPLOYEES...

Get meaning and inspiration from their company's mission	Are inspired by the leaders in their company

ENGAGED EMPLOYEES...

Are part of an extraordinary team	Have autonomy to do their jobs	Learn and grow every day	Make a difference and have an impact

SATISFIED EMPLOYEES...

Have a safe work environment	Have the tools, training, and resources to do their jobs well	Can get their jobs done efficiently, without excess bureaucracy	Are valued and rewarded fairly

Source: Used with permission from Bain & Company (www.bain.com).

[14] Garton, Eric and Mankins, Michael C. (2015). 'Engaging your employees is good, but don't stop there'. *Harvard Business Review*, 9 December. [Online] Available from: https://hbr.org/2015/12/engaging-your-employees-is-good-but-dont-stop-there

Meaning is the new money

One thing evident from the Maslow model is that *money* is not the premier motivator in our lives. Obviously, if we don't have any, then we become dissatisfied and will work full steam ahead to get it. Most of us need a certain amount of cash to buy life's essentials and support our lifestyle; and some of us like toys or travel more than others! We hanker after money for security (housing, food, saving for a rainy day) and status (to brag that we're somebody). Some of us want to be dirty-rotten-filthy-stinking-rich, while some of us simply aim to be 'well off'. There's nothing wrong with that – the mindset of wanting money is essential to success and can contribute to our enjoyment of life, for instance, by liberating us from certain chores or work we don't find meaningful. Beyond a certain point, however, it doesn't make any difference to our motivation or happiness.

Money is only a means to an end . . . it's not THE end. Cash, status and other tangible trappings that show we've 'made it' professionally only lead to a temporary spike in our wellbeing, so they don't keep us motivated for any sustainable length of time. Sometimes they even cause us a great deal of misery. A lot of powerful, high-income jobs often come with increased stress and time pressures, making us tense and reducing our capacity to savour life's small pleasures. In a 2005 study of 792 financially affluent adults by PNC Advisors, more than half reported that wealth didn't bring them more happiness, and almost one-third of those with assets greater than $10 million said that money actually brought more problems than it solved.[15] I believe it was the famous American architect Frank Lloyd Wright who observed that 'many wealthy people are little more than the janitors of their possessions'. This implies that well-off, materially minded people are trapped in their lifestyle and aren't making the most of themselves – and research backs this up. In their paper titled 'The Dark Side of the American Dream', psychology professors Tim Kasser and Richard Ryan demonstrate that people for whom 'making money' is a primary objective are less likely to actualise themselves and reach their full potential.[16]

---

[15] Kristof, Kathy, M. (2005). 'Money can't buy happiness, security either'. *Los Angeles Times*, 14 January.

[16] Kasser, Tim and Ryan, Richard M. (1993). 'The dark side of the American dream: Correlates of financial success as a central life aspiration'. *Journal of Personality and Social Psychology*, **65**(2), pp. 410–422.

The best leaders (the most happy and successful ones) are motivated far more by doing something worthwhile than by quick, easy money or the latest gadgetry. Equally they know that long-lasting success is built on helping people identify, pursue and achieve self-actualisation. When people grow as people, they automatically ripen into valuable, effective team members. I'm always saying that you can buy the use of people's hands or brains for money, but you can never buy their heart. A leader who doesn't understand this simple fact may try to solve people problems and dissatisfactions in their team by raising pay. But all that does is supply more of a response to a low-level need than is necessary, and overlooks the higher levels altogether. Nobody's going to say no to the extra cash (now that would be stupid!), but their frustrations will still be there. Getting a pay rise won't necessarily do anything to make someone love their job. It will just stop them from hating it.

In his enlightening book *How Will You Measure Your Life?*, Harvard Business School professor Clayton Christensen suggests that instead of chasing more money or a more prestigious ego-boosting title to make you happy and satisfied, you need to be asking yourself a different set of questions:[17]

- Is this work meaningful to me?
- Is this job going to give me a chance to develop?
- Am I going to learn new things?
- Will I have an opportunity for recognition and achievement?
- Am I going to be given responsibility?

It used to be the case ten years ago that, during interviews, I would talk to a potential job candidate about the conditions and security we could offer them at Microsoft – money, stock options, and so on. But in recent years, it started to become more of a balanced discussion and I often got asked the question: 'If I join you, will I be able to change the world for the better?' It's also my experience in working with young people through youth organisations such as Junior Achievement (which teaches entrepreneurship and work readiness) and AIESEC (international student exchange) that they are much less materialistic than the baby boomers and Generation Xers. The millennials (those born in

[17] Christensen, Clayton M., Allworth, James and Dillon, Karen (2012). *How Will You Measure Your Life?* New York: HarperCollins.

the 1980s and 1990s) want to work for organisations that are committed to social values and responsibility, and they aspire to make a difference to others. According to 2014 research by professional services firm Deloitte:[18]

- More than 70 per cent of millennials expect their employers to focus on societal and mission-driven problems.
- 70 per cent want to be creative at work.
- More than two-thirds believe it's the management's job to provide them with accelerated development opportunities in order for them to stay.

Evidently, *purpose* is a much bigger draw than *profit* these days, as is the need to socially interact, enjoy flexible work arrangements and learn new skills. For leaders, this means learning how to engage the young generation as sensitive, creative and passionate contributors in the workplace, including providing them with a remixed set of rewards. Convergence of the generations is also paramount, so millennials, baby boomers and Gen Xers can all work comfortably side by side, each bringing their unique strengths and experiences to the fold.

---

[18] Bersin, Josh (2015). 'Becoming irresistible: A new model for employee engagement'. *Deloitte University Press*, 26 January. [Online] Available from: http://dupress.com/articles/employee-engagement-strategies/

The big picture (building a winning culture)

'Culture eats strategy for breakfast.'

PETER DRUCKER, BUSINESSMAN AND 'FATHER OF MODERN MANAGEMENT'

A positive leadership approach is based on the notion that you can achieve wealth in success and happiness, not just on a personal level, but on an organisational one too. Every organisation needs to look at ways of enriching or upgrading who and what they are. Positive leaders set an agenda for excellence with a big vision that brings people together, but they don't stop there. They work hard to build a fun, friendly workplace culture where people are energised to perform to the best of their ability. These leaders spread a mood of optimism and openness so that everyone can find satisfaction in their work, while at the same time making sure the goals of the organisation are met.

A positive culture

The culture of an enterprise or team isn't an easy thing to pin down. Perhaps the simplest way to put it is that it represents 'the way we do things around here'. This 'way' is shaped by a huge range of influences, including the type of industry the company operates in, the products/services it offers, what its priorities are and the tasks it needs to carry out. But most of all, culture is fashioned by the *people* of an organisation – their work habits and norms, how they get on together and how they are treated. In this sense, it can be positive or negative. It either facilitates and supports organisational success or undermines and inhibits it.

A healthy, vibrant organisational culture with lots of 'people equity' boils down to great leadership of course. Go behind the scenes in any organisation or team with a stand-out culture and 99 per cent of the time you'll find a leader that develops and enables people rather than coercing and enforcing them; a leader that can break down boundaries and bind people together with a winning drive. David Hanna, a principal with consulting and development firm RBL Group, once wrote, 'All organizations are perfectly designed to get the results that they get'[1] – whether good or bad, better or worse. You can't avoid having a company culture, it will happen either way, whether you like it or not. But you can determine what kind of 'vibe' it will have by where you put your focus and the messages you send. As a leader of your own team, division or organisation, you play a massive part in defining and communicating the culture – but you aren't necessarily part of the culture yourself. The best leaders operate via their own personal set of values and rules, and they don't hang about in any organisation if it means that they're constantly required to break them. I believe this personal level of influence is often underestimated, but that it can have a huge impact in engaging people with the organisational identity. People need authentic leaders to look up to and align with, and are turned off by those who simply spout the standard company speak.

CHANGE THAT STICKS

The task of fostering a thriving culture doesn't happen at 'internet speed', it takes time and perpetual work to take hold in an organisation. It can be even

---

[1] Hanna, David, P. (1988). *Designing Organisations for High Performance*. New York: Addison-Wesley.

more challenging if you've been appointed to reform a toxic culture marred by conflict and obstruction. Leaders who are new to an organisation are often eager to shake things up and make their mark, so they run in with all guns blazing, aiming for fast, short-term results. I'll admit, I've gone down this route with almost every new team I've inherited, but it's not a tactic I would endorse if you've got a really sick culture and downtrodden, cynical bunch on your hands. Positive leadership isn't about making aesthetic changes to stamp down on problems and get quick outcomes, or about holding people to unachievable standards, it's about creating a great place to work. When you're new to an enterprise, it helps to give yourself a grace period at the beginning to work out the 'lay of the land' and get your bearings so you know what you're dealing with. Use your eyes, ears and instincts to figure things out from the first principles instead of making assumptions. Examine people's feelings about working there, appraise their habits and behaviours, and above all, check their energy levels.

Sometimes establishing a positive workplace culture can happen relatively quickly. Leaders that instil trust and confidence in their team can bring about fast changes with effective initiatives, such as letting people make decisions, investing in their growth, sharing information and data, trusting them to do the right thing, giving them opportunities to collaborate and be socially active, and allowing them to take risks without fearing a backlash if they make a mistake. But, if you want to build a winning culture that lasts, you have to be prepared to carry on building every day and reinforce it with every step. You can create conditions that are conducive to top flight performance and happiness by *empowering employees* – giving them the freedom, control and independence to succeed. *Dr GRAC* is a method recommended by personal development mastermind Stephen Covey to make your discussions explicit and give clear guidance to your team. The acronym describes five elements that will help you cover all bases when working out how to best give others responsibility – DR (Desired Results), G (Guidelines), R (Resources), A (Accountability) and C (Consequences). Visit http://positiveleaderbook.com/measureyourflow for guidance on how to empower employees effectively using the Dr GRAC method.

Set a mission for your team

Your culture is part of why you exist as a team and how you succeed. On that account, a crucial ingredient in developing a positive, strengths-based culture is being careful about how you define success. Despite being a bit of a mathematical whizz myself, I always encourage leaders to put *purpose* before numbers when determining their team's long-term strategies and outcomes. We live in an age where strict target setting is the mandate in driving achievement, and this can make it tricky for people to keep in touch with a deeper sense of purpose. When the work environment is overrun with complexity or ambiguity, imposing tight, specific goals can heap a mound of extra pressure on your team without any real motivational or inspirational benefit. They might know 'what' the target is, but do they know the 'why' behind it? I find that it's much better to create a *mission* that conveys the spirit of the organisation and sets a blueprint for excellence, rather than enforcing lots of demanding financial goals. If well thought out, the mission provides a collective definition of your existence as a team, giving you clarity and alignment around your joint 'why'. It acts as an anchor for your strategy, helping it evolve much more easily. Concentrating energy on your mission means you don't have to constantly be thinking, 'what's next?'

Your team mission shows your commitment to defining and living a positive, happy culture. So, whatever it is, make sure it's an inspiring one based on the tangible meaning and significance you bring to your customers and the wider world. This will make your team feel good about the work they do, even during those times when they might be stressed or overworked. Ask: How are you making life better for people?

Microsoft on a mission

Microsoft's latest mission is a lot more thoughtful than it used to be, focusing less on technology and more on how it handles its relationships with others: 'To empower every person and every organization on the planet to achieve more'. It might sound idealistic and ambitious – impossible even – but it echoes a powerful growth ethos where individual and organisational potential is cultivated. It also reflects the evolution of Microsoft's culture to become more responsive in how it deals with its customers and partners. In an email to his employees, CEO Satya Nadella wrote, 'We fundamentally believe that we need a culture founded in a growth mindset. It starts with a belief that everyone can grow and develop; that potential is nurtured, not predetermined; and that anyone can change their mindset. Leadership is about bringing out the best

▶

in people, where everyone is bringing their A game and finding deep meaning in their work.'[2] A company's mission affects people's feelings about working there and the way they go about things, feeding into and reinforcing the culture day by day. It has to resonate with people at a deep level if it's going to animate, galvanise and energise them, reminding them 'why' they are part of the company in the first place. Indeed, the really great thing about Microsoft's new mission is that it takes things 'back to basics', mirroring the same excitement that Bill Gates produced when he first envisioned a PC on every desk and in every home.

Real-world mission statement examples

To refresh the world. To inspire moments of optimism and happiness. To create value and make a difference. Coca-Cola

To invent the next industrial era, to build, move, power and cure the world. General Electric

The Adidas Group strives to be the global leader in the sporting goods industry with brands built on a passion for sports and a sporting lifestyle. Adidas

To give people the power to share and make the world more open and connected. Facebook

To establish Starbucks as the premier purveyor of the finest coffee in the world while maintaining our uncompromising principles while we grow. Starbucks

To embrace the human spirit and let it fly. Virgin

To be our customers' favorite place and way to eat and drink. McDonald's

Spread ideas. TED

[2] Bishop, Todd (2015). 'Exclusive: Satya Nadella reveals Microsoft's new mission statement, sees "tough choices" ahead'. *GeekWire*, 25 June. [Online] Available from: http://www.geekwire.com/2015/exclusive-satya-nadella-reveals-microsofts-new-mission-statement-sees-more-tough-choices-ahead/

How do you work out your own team, department or company mission?

In exactly the same way as you figured out your personal one (see Chapter 4). Examining your collective *strengths, values and passions* will help you identify the true 'pulse' behind the whole enterprise. This may take some thinking about and plenty of discussion with key stakeholders (customers, employees, shareholders, etc.). Where your strengths, values and passions intersect will reveal your reason for being in business. Use your findings to define a mission that symbolises to the world who you are as a team and why you do what you do.

STEP 1: WHAT ARE YOUR TEAM/COMPANY STRENGTHS?

What can you be best at or get great results in? It's crucial to start with strengths and use your uniqueness if you want to win in your field.

- Think of your strengths in business, starting with the nature of your *product offerings*. What do you sell? What determines the level of quality? For instance, is one of your core strengths that you offer low prices and great value, or can you boast lots of cool, flashy product features?

- Next look at the level of *service* you provide. Consider things like installation, sales, shipping, customer service, assembly, consulting, technical support and money-back guarantee. Try and nail down what you're really good at.

- What strengths do your *people* have? Look at the roles played by you and each of your colleagues, your work norms and mindset. How do they contribute to the overall culture of the enterprise?

- What *resources* (capital, technology, equipment) do you have at your disposal to help you perform and achieve your goals?

STEP 2: WHAT ARE YOUR TEAM/COMPANY VALUES?

Values are positive intentions that speak to the heart of people and allow you to define how your organisation is different in meaningful ways. They represent what you stand for as a team and help your people feel proud of what they do. In practical terms, your values are 'rules of success' that give you a clear benchmark from which to build the positive habits and policies that underpin the culture of your organisation – in fact, they probably do this better than any hard-line measures you could put together. What are the most important values or principles that drive you to deliver your purpose and vision? To get a sense of your real values, speak to people at different levels in your organisation to glean their input. It's as simple as asking, 'What's important to us?' Pay attention to the language they use. Try and sum up the underlying philosophies that guide the way you work using simple speech rather than techno waffle or MBA lingo. Adopt straightforward, concise terms like 'teamwork and collaboration', 'acting responsibly' 'speed and agility', 'demonstrating fairness', 'curiosity and learning', 'fun and craziness', 'open communication', 'trust and respect' or 'customer service'. Remember, your values have to be understood on the ground floor and on the front line, not just in the boardroom. If your values don't mean anything to anyone, you'll never get them to translate into tangible results. The objective is to find those that actually contribute to defining your culture and what's different about your behaviour, not to drum up a list of generic platitudes.

Nailing down your values also requires you to consider your customers as well as your colleagues. What can you offer your customers? How do you make their lives easier, better or more successful? What do they really need from you? Your answers to these questions should help you determine which shared values, attitudes and practices would be most beneficial for you to emulate. Yet another thing to contemplate is public perception. Think about the image you want to create in the minds of your customers, partners, suppliers and the world at large. When people look at your company or team, what would you like them to see?

STEP 3: WHAT ARE YOU PASSIONATE ABOUT AS A TEAM/COMPANY?

Passion is significant to your destiny as an organisation. It's the spark that ignites and energises you as a team to achieve something special and reach your true potential. Help people discover and align their passions with the overriding passions of the organisation and you can rest assured you'll be knocking on success's door. When leaders and teams share a core passion, enthusiasm spreads like wildfire at every level of the organisation, and the energy can be felt almost as soon as you walk in the building. You don't even need to agree on the details, the passion you share will unite you on common ground and represent the standard by which all decisions are made. It's often the secret ingredient needed to overcome seemingly insurmountable obstacles and conflicts too. A passionate purpose impacts on your image with customers as well as employees. As bestselling author of *Start With Why*, Simon Sinek, puts it, 'People don't buy what you do; they buy why you do it.'[3] Your passion tells people why they should do business with you. They can see it and feel it all around you, and it rubs off on them.

Richard Y. Chang, author of *The Passion Plan at Work*, suggests that you look to many sources inside and outside the organisation for clues of your passion.[4] Explore your individual passions as a leader and what you share as a group. Many organisations are founded on passion – entrepreneurs often start their own companies as an extension of what makes them come alive. Outside the organisation, what passionate advantage do you have with your customers and partners? As well as your present passions, evaluate your organisation's history to identify passions that might have fizzled out or been neglected. Can they be successfully revived? Look towards potentialities in the future too. Your passion often defines the direction you take as a business, linking to a vision or end result that makes you tingle with excitement and engages you as a team. The result of this 'passion review' process is a window into the heart of the organisation. Are you passionate about people, entertainment or power? Engineering excellence or entrepreneurship? Find out what drives your organisation and embrace it.

STEP 4: LIVE THE MISSION

Now for the fun part. Take your strengths, values and passions and put them together to find your mission. What opportunities are you passionate about that will allow you to build your strengths while expressing your core values?

AEISEC: 'What starts here changes the world'

I've been a member of the supervisory board for AIESEC (the world's largest international student exchange organisation and platform for

▶

---

[3] Sinek, Simon (2011). *Start With Why: How Great Leaders Inspire Everyone to Take Action*. London: Penguin Books.
[4] Chang, Richard Y. (2001). *The Passion Plan at Work: Building a Passion-Driven Organization*. San Francisco: Jossey-Bass.

facilitating leadership potential) for eight years. When I first started working with them, their mission was, truth be told, a bit vague and flat. It fell far short in impressing, inspiring and inflaming people's passions as it merely stated what they did and what they were (i.e. a global, non-political, independent, not-for-profit organisation run by students). As such, it didn't embody a clear 'cause' that pulled people together. For me, it was plain to see that their mission was strikingly at odds with their exhilarating energy and spirit, and it failed to reflect the positive change they were striving for in developing the business leaders of the future. The issue behind this was that AIESEC's leadership team changed every year and it was tasked with managing a huge global network. The dynamic nature of how AIESEC was run meant that their commercial focus was very practical and motivational, and this was mirrored in the mission. A motivational mission can work well in the short term, energising people for up to a year or so, but an *inspirational* mission captures the heart and enables an organisation to survive year after year. It has much more 'added value'.

When you listen to AIESEC's young leaders describing their ideas for activating responsible, integrity-based leadership, embracing diversity, conquering the digital divide and promoting a golden, sustainable economy, it's obvious that the business of the future will be very different. According to the organisation, doing good and doing well will no longer be mutually exclusive possibilities as they go all out for 'peace and the fulfilment of humankind's potential'. Through coaching, I helped the student leaders view their purpose through a big-picture lens with the intention of creating a more compelling, overarching mission that would encapsulate everything their organisation stood for. Being a bright bunch, they quickly came to realise that their essence was the ability to change the world for the better. Now AIESEC's rallying cry is: 'What starts here changes the world'. It's positive, it's purposeful, and it unifies everyone to the cause. This upgraded mission (which has lasted for approximately six years so far) expresses AIESEC's strengths by way of global and business reach, the team's passion for pushing frontiers and its core values in diversity, excellence, leadership, integrity, participation and sustainability. As it proudly announces on its website, AIESEC is without doubt 'a youth organisation on a mission'.

Once you've got your own noble mission all figured out, document it. Post it in a prominent place. Circulate it around. Make it as visible as possible so that your people can live and breathe your mission day in and day out. Keep it short and simple, so that it goes viral and people can remember it easily. Think of the KISS principle – 'Keep it Simple, Stupid'. You want your mission to be fairly specific so that it will prompt goal setting and tracking, but you also want it to be general enough so that it won't date. Work out transparent ways of measuring how well you're doing in meeting or not meeting your mission, and celebrate any progress publicly.

Celebrate success

Downplay internal competition and reward collective wins so everyone feels part of the big successes. Taking a moment to celebrate milestone achievements can be great for team building and helps workers feel appreciated for their contributions to the company, not like meaningless cogs. It lets the team know how important they *all* are and gives them a chance to bond and reminisce about shared projects or activities they've played a part in. Celebrating doesn't just mean gathering people together for 15 minutes to pop the champagne and toast your triumphs; you can find other unique ways to reward and praise your team that will make work more fun and enjoyable. And they don't have to break the bank. Simple things like themed dress-up days, family-friendly picnics or surprise pizza parties can all do the job in celebrating a win and saying thank you for a job well done. Whatever you do, don't just send an email out to everyone when something good happens saying 'let's celebrate'. That's a poor cop-out by anyone's standards and will only leave people feeling deflated. Celebrate for real. Do something!

When rewarding first-class individual achievements, get the whole team involved. And avoid making profit the only king. Remember, people want to work for a meaningful cause, so don't just reward revenue goals but include other key performance indicators such as outstanding customer service, innovative employee suggestions, excellent health and safety or even exemplary attendance records. This sends a clear message about the things that are important to you as a company. In his idea-packed book, *Performance Breakthrough*, business coach Mike Goldman recommends an

'Above and Beyond the Call of Duty' (ABCD) award.[5] This is a reward for people who've done something outside the scope of the job in order to help a client, co-worker or supplier. Nominations can be made by anyone in the organisation and an 'all hands' meeting is held each month where the stories behind each of the nominations are told. This is much more powerful for encouraging positive behaviour and team morale than your typical top-down employee of the month award, which often induces rivalry and 'dog-eat-dog' competition.

HAVE FUN TOGETHER

If you really want to establish a positive environment that breeds happiness and high performance at work, then you need to get serious. Serious about having more fun that is! There's a general attitude amongst hard-nosed leaders that any form of play shouldn't be allowed in the workplace; that it's time-wasting and frivolous, and takes people away from the real business of work. They couldn't be more wrong. Businesses that make a point of encouraging fun and play are, by and large, the ones that get the best work out of people. A serious atmosphere without any reprieve for employees sucks the enjoyment out of work, turning it into an endless chore of deadlines, meetings and emails. When leaders inject fun, social gatherings and celebrations into the workplace, they create a family-like atmosphere that helps people derive more meaning from their jobs and ensures continuity, excellence and loyalty for the business.

Encourage social gatherings where people can get to know each other beyond the work they do and feel part of a community. Casual social activities are ideal for mingling with your team and make it easy for people to break down barriers and form personal connections while having fun. They also help teams work together better on future projects and initiatives, and boost wellbeing as a whole. A 2013 study at the London School of Economics found that 'talking, chatting, socialising' with colleagues is the only activity that results in happiness levels that are similar to those experienced when not working.[6] When I was running the CEE team at Microsoft, we would organise a pizza lunch every

[5] Goldman, Mike (2015). *Performance Breakthrough: The Four Secrets of Passionate Organizations.* Second edition. New York: Highpoint Executive Publishing.
[6] Bryson, Alex and MacKerron, George (2015). 'Are you happy while you work?' CEP Discussion Paper No. 1187, *Centre for Economic Performance*, February. [Online] Available from: http://cep.lse.ac.uk/pubs/download/dp1187.pdf

month. At the time, there were 25 nationalities represented on the team and, each month, people would take it in turns to talk about their respective country. This was fantastic because everyone got to learn about each other and the diverse cultures that made up the team. When you're part of a multinational organisation, being culturally aware pays huge dividends in creating greater collaboration and bringing about a sense of kinship.

For some organisations, the crazier the gathering, the better. Quirky team traditions and silly theme days all reflect a positive, fun workplace. Google, the paragon of positive culture, uses fun office challenges to motivate its employees – ever seen the movie *The Internship*? This is something that companies of any size can easily imitate and gives the team something to look forward to. For instance, you can organise 'decorate your area' competitions, cook-offs, karaoke contests, spoof video filming challenges, spelling bees, bingo games, ping pong matches, video game wars, bin basketball – you get the idea. There's no limit to the ways in which you can infuse fun into the workplace. And you can offer small rewards for the winners, such as a gift card to a local restaurant. Fitness and wellness activities are also gaining popularity as fun ways to break up the day and get employees moving. Set up a trampoline or mini golf course in the office, organise a sports day, install a Nintendo Wii or introduce on-site yoga classes to relieve stress. You could even stipulate 'walking meetings' where people can be both productive and active at the same time.[7]

---

[7] Housh, Will (2015). '5 inexpensive ways to create a company culture like Google's'. *Entrepreneur*, 22 January. [Online] Available from: http://www.entrepreneur.com/article/240172

part three

Energy management –
positive process (the
'HOW')

Slave to success (burnout and stress)

'Performance is actually improved when our lives include time for renewal, wisdom, wonder and giving. That would have saved me a lot of unnecessary stress, burnout and exhaustion.'
ARIANNA HUFFINGTON, CO-FOUNDER OF *THE HUFFINGTON POST*

Ever find yourself completely worn out by the time Friday evening comes around? Whether in business, family life or in our social circles, we're all run ragged trying to cram as much as we possibly can into each and every day. This accelerating sense of urgency can be attributed to the amazing (but stress-carrying!) developments of our digital age. We have data all around us on a non-stop, 24/7, all-you-can-eat basis, and the immediacy of communication (from smartphones to Skype to Twitter to Bluetooth) is having a drastic effect on how we manage our time. Top that off with a chaotic and constantly-changing work environment and it's no wonder we feel the need to run our lives at breakneck speed and be on full-time 'inbox monitor' duty.

For business leaders, this frantic lifestyle can carry a truckload of advantages. There are abundant opportunities for creative decision making and innovation, as endless information offers a huge wellspring of inspiration for fresh ideas. And capitalising on the hustle and bustle of change with flexible commercial approaches can in turn lead to incredible growth in the marketplace. But there's obviously a flipside to this manic climate. The hasty search for immediate gains and the need to keep on top of things can just as swiftly deplete your energy. The result? You may soon find yourself in danger of 'burning out'.

Energy shutdown

Being busy-busy is such a feature of modern life that no business leader can say that they aren't feeling the strain. It's clear that, in today's 'perform or perish' economy, CEOs and other executives are expected to do more than ever before, and with less time to do it in. There are project deadlines to meet and speeches to make, and everyone expects you to have the answers to all their questions, foolish or otherwise. The sheer number of different tasks you have on the go at any moment can leave you feeling spread out wafer thin. Then there are the knock-backs and roadblocks that every time-starved, out-of-balance boss has to deal with along the way. Indeed, being a leader is a great way to discover the legitimacy of Murphy's law: 'If anything can go wrong, it will.' Entrepreneurs often get it worse as people expect the founder of an organisation to somehow be superhuman. It comes as no surprise then that, according to a study by the Harvard Medical School faculty, 96 per cent of senior leaders have reported feeling burnt out to some degree, with one-third describing their burnout as extreme.[1] *Burnout* is defined by the Merriam-Webster dictionary as 'exhaustion of physical or emotional strength or motivation usually as a result of prolonged stress or frustration'.[2] Take a look at some of the common symptoms:

- constant tiredness – low physical and emotional energy
- anxiety – feeling overwhelmed and out of control
- increased frustration with the job and with colleagues

---

[1] Kwoh, Leslie (2013). 'When the CEO burns out'. *The Wall Street Journal*, 7 May. [Online] Available from: http://www.wsj.com/articles/SB10001424127887323687604578469124008524696
[2] Definition of 'Burnout', http://www.merriam-webster.com/dictionary/burnout

- poor sleep patterns
- physical ailments – headaches, gastrointestinal problems, skin conditions, etc.
- difficulty in concentrating
- increased irritability
- loss of pleasure (in work, but also generally in life)
- a pessimistic outlook and negative attitude
- decrease in productivity and performance
- increased use of alcohol, tobacco, caffeine and drugs
- loss/increase in appetite

For high-level leaders, it's not just the 'pace' of life that's a problem but the 'weight' of it. The demands of the position can end up pushing you well beyond your capabilities, leaving you – at the least – feeling tired and low on energy throughout the day, or as the stress mounts over time, completely dreading getting out of bed each morning. Overworked and overburdened to the point of exhaustion, you feel helpless, resentful, trapped and downright frazzled – like you're at the edge of a 100-foot drop and about to be pushed right over it.

BURNOUT ACROSS THE BOARD

Cases of extreme exhaustion and burnout have been on the increase in the last two decades, and it's not just those in leadership roles who are feeling the effects – it's fast becoming an epidemic in every tier of the modern workplace. In April 2015, the results of a survey conducted by research firm YouGov – and commissioned by Virgin – were released. The purpose of the study was to explore the extent to which stress, anxiety and burnout impacted on UK employees:

YouGov survey findings: How stressed are UK employees?[3]

Over half (51 per cent) of full-time UK employees said they have experienced 'burnout' or anxiety in their current job.

---

[3] Preston, Jack (2015). 'Infographic: How stressed are UK employees?' *Virgin,* April. [Online] Available from: https://www.virgin.com/disruptors/infographic-how-stressed-are-uk-employees

> This figure was consistent amongst men and women and for employees in most age groups, except for those over 55, where only a third said they had experienced it in their position.
>
> Less than a third (32 per cent) of those working part-time said they had experienced these conditions (lending credence to the argument for flexible working and better work–life balance).

In response to bosses, demands for more, the phenomenon of 'presenteeism' sees people working longer and harder to prove they're 'up to the job', sacrificing their own physical and mental health in the process. At a time when employee engagement and wellbeing has become something of a Holy Grail for companies, this is really bad news. Employee burnout is toxic for individuals and toxic for organisations, as people who run on empty for excessive periods of time suffer a downturn in productivity, get sick easily and are more likely to make mistakes. Those employees with any sense will soon defect to a healthier job environment.

TIME IS NOT RENEWABLE, BUT ENERGY IS

When asked about the main factors behind their burnout, the majority of victims will point out the demands on their *time* as being the primary culprit. There's no denying that working longer hours to combat an overflowing in-tray hikes up the chances of physical and emotional exhaustion. We try to take control of these burdens through typical 'time management' methods – by organising our day meticulously, using day planners and to-do lists, setting up reminders on our smartphones – driven by the idea that the more we can squeeze into our day, the more productive (and hopefully the less stressed!) we will be. However, this is overlooking a vital point that every individual can benefit from. The key to avoiding burnout is not how we manage time; it's how we *manage energy*. After all, how effective and happy can we be when we're cramming numerous tasks into a single day, often on autopilot? Or when we're increasing the length of the working day in order to eke out the last bit of energy we have before we drop? Consider the following scenarios:

- You have a crucial deadline you need to meet, but throughout the day you find yourself distracted by a pile of other bitty tasks that command your attention (responding to emails, filling in paperwork, etc.) As the day wears on, you feel squeezed and under pressure – your deadline is looming and you've made nowhere near as much progress as you should have. Mad panic! You frantically rush to get it done before the cut-off.

- You've made dinner plans for the evening with your spouse/family and are eagerly looking forward to spending some warm and fuzzy 'quality time' with them. Your working day is chock-a-block as you try to fit in as much as you can, so that when the evening arrives you won't have to be plagued by thoughts of unfinished work lying on your desk, and can just relax. But, sitting down for your meal you find yourself too sapped out to actually enjoy the occasion, no matter how much you wish you could.

- You set aside an entire day to work on a project, devoting 10 or 12 hours to it in order to be as productive as possible. Things start well, but as the day progresses you begin to feel tired and agitated, unable to give the project the level of concentration it deserves. The quality of your work takes a nosedive and you go home feeling not only drained and irritable, but disappointed that you hadn't met your expectations. What a bummer.

You're probably thinking, 'So what? That's just a normal workday to me.' The 24/7 work-to-the-bone culture dominates the whole business climate and these kinds of stressful experiences are part and parcel of our working lives. Be honest, you probably take pride in how many hours of overtime you can fit into your schedule, or on how quickly you can race through your daily tasks without any rest stops. The core problem with this line of thinking is that *time* is a finite resource, but we're trying to manage it by placing infinite demands on ourselves. Trying to fill our days to the brim implies that the workday never ends, and there's no time available for recovery or a personal life. It's easy to get pulled into a relentless stream of stressful activities to the point that we get used to the assault and fail to realise how damaging it can be to our wellbeing and the quality of our output. We don't see these work demands in the same way as the 'big stressors' in life like illness, moving house, a new job, a promotion, redundancy, divorce or a new baby. Yet all the research shows that it's the minor stressors on an everyday basis that will 'break the camel's back.'[4] Before we know it, the constant deadlines and cycle of *go, go, go* have burnt us right out. The 'I can handle it' attitude only pushes us off the rails even faster.

[4] Borg, James (2010). *Mind power: Change Your Thinking, Change Your Life.* Harlow: Pearson.

Squeezing more hours out of the day by skimping on sleep or neglecting our family is clearly not the answer, and we should be focusing on managing our energy instead. Unlike time, which is strictly limited to 24 hours per day for everyone, personal energy is renewable. You can't control the amount of time at your disposal, but you do have power over your energy. This is where the idea of *energy management* (as opposed to time management) can be utilised to transform not just your working habits, but the overall quality of your life.

> *'Performance, health and happiness are grounded in the skilful management of energy.'* Jim Loehr and Tony Schwartz, performance psychologists

In their hugely successful and influential book, *The Power of Full Engagement*, Tim Loehr and Tony Schwartz suggest that people often fail to see the significance of energy in both their professional and personal lives.[5] Drawing on their experience of working with world-class athletes, they explore the ways in which we can learn to control our energy, which comes from four main sources: *physical, mental, emotional and spiritual*. By careful management of the quantity and quality of energy we use each day, we can revitalise ourselves and refuel our energy 'tank' so as not to run out of steam.

That Loehr and Schwartz chose to turn their focus on business leaders is no coincidence. Most leaders live at such a furious pace that they lose sight of what's important – both in work and in their personal lives. They're operating in crisis mode, fuelled by adrenalin, with the minimum amount of time given to recovery and recuperation. This is surviving, not thriving. The paradox here is that exceptional leaders generate even more work for themselves, either through their own initiative or because others recognise their value. Successful people (entrepreneurs especially) are vulnerable to what's termed 'opportunity madness' – a condition in which they constantly create or get involved in alluring new projects that require even more time when they're already overstretched.[6] When leaders feel burnt out it undermines their energy, passion and imagination, and it spreads like a virus through the workplace, posing a significant hazard. Conversely, energetic and positive leaders inspire greater contributions from those around them.

---

[5] Loehr, Jim and Schwartz, Tony (2003). *The Power of Full Engagement: Managing Energy, Not Time, Is the Key to High Performance and Personal Renewal*. New York: Simon & Schuster.
[6] Patterson, Jerry, L. and Kelleher, Paul (2005). *Resilient School Leaders: Strategies for Turning Adversity into Achievement*. Association for Supervision & Curriculum Development.

Stress: how much is too much?

Stress is everywhere. Even when we're not stressed ourselves, we hear about it from others – co-workers, friends and spouses – 'Work is so stressful at the moment because of this office move', or 'I've got exams coming up, I feel so stressed'. The concept of stress itself is so familiar that we think nothing of it when it pops up in newspaper and magazine articles, or on the TV and radio. Stress goes hand in hand with the modern world, where the demands of time, technology and the economy on human beings are greater than ever before. But how much do we really know about stress?

Well, what you might not know is that a fair dose of stress here and there is actually good for you. Short-term stress is a sign that you're pushing yourself to the limits of your mental capabilities, and brings an adrenaline boost which can strengthen your performance and heighten your memory capacity. The pressure keeps you motivated towards your goals and increases your sense of challenge and fulfilment. Let's compare the mental with the physical to get a better understanding of this. When you're working out in the gym, for instance, the aim is to push your body beyond its comfort zone, taking it to the limit of what it can safely achieve (before it wipes out!). Consequently – after a sufficient period of rest and recuperation – your body will become stronger, fitter and healthier than it was before. The same principle applies to the mind: by exercising it to a level outside your comfort zone – *stressing* it, so to speak – then you can improve its capacity, assuming you also give it a decent amount of resting time.[7] This is what I like to call *positive stress*, and it's not the stress to worry about (if you'll excuse the pun). Exposure to this kind of stress can be great for keeping you focused when making important speeches and spurring you into action when urgent tasks call for it, so it's handy for tackling all the things that are ever-present on a leader's to-do list.

Negative stress, on the other hand, is when you strain yourself beyond what's considered healthy – the scenarios we looked at earlier being good examples of this. The feeling that you're losing control or are unable to cope with a situation turns it from a positive pursuit into a negative experience, sending your levels of the stress hormone cortisol soaring. We can live comfortably with the odd, infrequent bout of this, but when it becomes the norm in our lives,

[7] Mind Gym (2005). *The Mind Gym: Wake Your Mind Up*. London: Time Warner.

that's when we know we have a problem. None of us were designed to be permanently on high alert. Long periods of excessive pressure and feeling overwhelmed push us right to the end of the stress 'spectrum', to what's known as *chronic stress* – a tell-tale sign that you're on the slippery slope to burnout. Research abounds to show how this kind of toxic stress remains rife in the workplace. One recent example is a 2015 study of 600 UK employees by performance psychology firm Star Consultancy:[8]

Stress in the workplace: a few stats

The average staff member felt 'stressed, anxious and worried' on 84 days out of the average 240 in a working year.	28% said that they felt 'stressed, anxious and worried' at work twice a week.	62% cited stress as the main reason they don't always perform at their best.

The majority of workers pointed to increased workloads and deadlines as the cause of their stress.	Only 6% said that they had told their managers about their stress and anxiety issues.

If the average employee has these sorts of experiences, you can imagine how much worse it might be for business leaders. Indeed, 88 per cent of leaders report that work is a primary source of stress in their lives and that having a leadership role increases the level of stress.[9] Slashed budgets, layoffs, unrelenting competition and fear of what's around the corner are having a brutal impact on executives. Being in charge of others who are also stressed only exacerbates the problem. It can be tempting to see working beyond your means as a sign of success. Your sleep deprivation and caffeine addiction are worn like a corporate badge of honour – a symbol of your 'heroic' work devotion. But no matter how many gallons of coffee you drink a day or few hours' sleep you get, your performance won't be any better for it. As a matter of fact, it will be far worse. Research has found that a week of sleeping only four or five hours a night impairs your cognitive abilities to an equivalent

---

[8] PM Editorial (2015). 'Chronic stress dominates a third of UK working life, says research'. *CIPD*, 8 January. [Online] Available from: http://www.cipd.co.uk/pm/peoplemanagement/b/weblog/archive/2015/01/08/chronic-stress-dominates-a-third-of-uk-working-life-says-research.aspx

[9] Campbell, Michael, Baltes, Jessica I., Martin, André and Meddings, Kylie (2007). 'The stress of leadership'. *Center for Creative Leadership (CCL)*, White Paper. [Online] Available from: http://insights.ccl.org/wp-content/uploads/2015/04/StressofLeadership.pdf

blood alcohol of 0.1 per cent. That's to say, your quality of thinking is as bad as it would be if you were drunk! On the whole, high levels of stress in the workplace lead to:[10]

- poor decision making
- reduced performance and productivity
- an increase in mistakes which may in turn lead to more customer complaints
- increased sickness and absence
- poor commitment to work
- high employee turnover
- poor employee/workplace relations.

With such serious consequences, it really pays to keep an eye on your stress levels and those of the people you lead.

WHAT'S YOUR IDEA OF STRESS?

Stress can be a personal thing. What's regarded as stressful varies from individual to individual. Some people, by their nature, are more prone to stress, and even find everyday situations stressful. Others have a much higher threshold and may take what's typically considered to be a state of emergency in their stride. What one person would see as positive motivational pressure, another may find completely overwhelming. Sometimes this is down to whether they feel they have the strengths/skills to meet a particular demand. For instance, asking your colleague to prepare a business statistics spreadsheet for the senior management team when they don't know how to use Excel can bring on a panic attack: 'I'll never handle this.' But for someone who loves fiddling with formulas, it can be an exciting challenge. Likewise, if you have a fear of public speaking, being selected to give a talk at the regional directors meeting might cause you to come out in a cold sweat, especially if you've got enough on your plate already. But if you enjoy giving presentations and communication is one of your strengths, then you'll feel proud to be chosen. Your interpretation of the event will be a lot more positive. Most jobs today

---

[10] The University of Edinburgh (2012). 'Work related stress – Information for managers/supervisors'. Health & Safety Department, 29 February.

are deadline driven, so someone with a lack of organisational ability or poor time management will likely experience a general level of stress.[11] It's possible that the major factor that determines your stress levels is not what's going on 'out there' (in the environment), but what's happening 'in here' (in your thinking). The pressure of the task itself might not be the problem, but rather your perception of it. It's what you do with the pressure in your mind that turns it into stress.

Very rarely is stress caused by one single 'stressor'. It snowballs up to a point where your mind and body are unable to keep up with the onslaught. The anxiety alarm goes on and you never manage to switch it off. Sometimes, it's a minor, trivial event – landing on top of all the other things you've been dealing with – that topples you over into that stressful state.[12] The stress spiral means that little obstacles in the workplace and at home become magnified – molehills become mountains and small quarrels become full-on feuds. In every circumstance, stress is made worse when people feel they have little support or hardly any control over their work. Understanding what triggers stress is essential if you're to nip it in the bud as early as possible.

Common stress triggers at work[13]

1. **Demands:** work overload or work underload; high expectations; disruptive shifts and work rotas; poor work environment/conditions (facilities, hazards, buildings); lack of time; lack of knowledge or skills to do the job.

2. **Control:** lack of input and autonomy/decision making in work; authoritarian, 'command-and-control' management style; inadequate systems of communication; little influence over performance targets.

3. **Relationships:** poor work relationships; conflict with colleagues and bosses; discriminatory relationships and practices; harassment and bullying; lack of leadership; isolation at work.

4. **Change:** ineffective management and communication of change; job insecurity; future job change.

▶

---

[11] Rowan, Sophie (2008). *Happy at Work: Ten Steps to Ultimate Job Satisfaction*. Harlow: Pearson.
[12] Borg, James (2010). *Mind Power: Change Your Thinking, Change Your Life*. Harlow: Pearson.
[13] Adapted from: 'Causes of stress'. *Health & Safety Executive*. [Online] Available from: http://www.hse.gov.uk/stress/furtheradvice/causesofstress.htm

5. **Role:** job design/career mismatch; unclear purpose; boring/repetitive work; unclear responsibilities; role conflict.

6. **Support:** lack of support from colleagues; inadequate training or resources; lack of tolerance of mistakes; lack of recognition or feedback; work–life balance.

TAKE THE STRESS TEST

So how do we know when we're experiencing an excess of negative stress? The best method is through self-reflection. Look at yourself objectively and make an honest assessment, as you would with a loved one you suspect may be on the brink of burnout. It may help to ask someone you trust to give their opinion about your stress levels. If you're still unsure, take the stress test below to get some sort of guideline.[14]

Exercise 7.1: Stress Test

(Circle the number according to how each statement is relevant to your lifestyle.)

STRESS TEST	ALMOST ALWAYS	OFTEN	SOMETIMES	ALMOST NEVER
1. I feel disorganised and unprepared for the day	4	3	2	1
2. I find myself racing to get things done	4	3	2	1
3. I struggle to make time for enjoyable activities	4	3	2	1
4. I get frustrated or anxious when late for a meeting	4	3	2	1
5. I get slightly panicky when nearing a deadline	4	3	2	1
6. I have difficulty getting a good night's sleep (e.g. fitful sleep or not enough)	4	3	2	1

[14] Adapted from: Stress Management Society. 'How vulnerable are you to stress?' [Online] Available from: http://www.stress.org.uk/stresstest.aspx

STRESS TEST	ALMOST ALWAYS	OFTEN	SOMETIMES	ALMOST NEVER
7. I feel like I'm taking on more than I can handle	4	3	2	1
8. I feel like I don't have control over how my day develops	4	3	2	1
9. I delay my lunch breaks or omit them altogether	4	3	2	1
10. I feel exhausted once the working day is over	4	3	2	1
11. When I'm not coping well, I keep it to myself	4	3	2	1
12. I suffer from headaches or tiredness for a good portion of the day	4	3	2	1

When you feel like you've answered each question honestly and accurately, add up your score and see where you position in the guidelines below.

12–24:	25–35:	36–48:
Congratulations, you're currently in the safety zone! Although it's likely you still experience moments of negative stress, they've not become routine in your life and are unlikely to have consequences on your health and general wellbeing. There's always room for improvement, however, so keep reading PART 3 for tips on how to manage your energy to achieve maximum health and productivity.	Although alarm bells shouldn't be ringing just yet, this result suggests you may be experiencing symptoms of negative stress on a regular basis. The constant strain and your vulnerability to stress can become more aggressive and frequent if steps aren't taken to tackle it. Adopting an energy management plan pre-emptively will not only help prevent this, but will move you into the healthy – and happier – safe zone.	The warning signs are flashing! This result indicates that you're in the danger zone and that negative stress is a routine part of your life, perhaps affecting you daily. There's a high risk that you could end up burning out if an emergency plan isn't put into action. It's essential that you learn to manage your energy effectively and shake up your lifestyle drastically, so that you can regain control of your life.

The difference between happy, successful leaders and those who aren't isn't whether or not they suffer from stress, but how they deal with it when they do. Instead of drowning your stresses in booze or relying on caffeine to keep you going, turn to *energy management* to regain control over the pressures in your life and learn useful coping mechanisms. See Chapters 8 and 9 for productive energy-based strategies that can act as an antidote to stress.

Surviving burnout

It's both worrying and sad that being stressed, burnt out or depressed is often seen as a weakness in our society. Some bosses feel that by admitting to any form of tiredness or overload, they may as well declare that they're unfit to hold such a crucial, pressure-packed role. It's seen as out of character and un-leader-like to confess to being on anything but top form. Far from being a weakness, however, it takes a lot of strength to acknowledge that you're suffering and need help. If you had a business-related problem, would you simply ignore it and hope it went away? No – you would look at it to define exactly what the problem is and what's causing it. Then you'd consider potential solutions for tackling it before committing yourself wholeheartedly to a course of action. So why should it be any different when confronting personal issues? As for the stigma attached to mental illnesses, it's worth noting that some of the world's greatest thinkers and leaders have hit hard times, before overcoming them and going on to achieve wild success.

From Harvard to the mental hospital and back

In 2011, I had the beginnings of what you might call a 'breakdown', though I didn't realise what it was at first. It started a week after I'd returned to Europe from Harvard University in the States, where I'd been working with professors on the implementation of IT in areas such as health care, defence and security. My first symptom, rather surprisingly, was severe stomach pain, which got so bad that I was hospitalised in late October that year. The doctors performed all kinds of tests, but couldn't find anything wrong with me – physically I was fit, though I wasn't particularly healthy. But over the next two months, my health deteriorated rapidly in every way. I lost 20 kilos in weight and all my motivation and self-confidence went with it. I couldn't talk or write to anyone – I became disconnected from the world. I found myself lying in bed listless, lacking the energy to get up to do anything. I almost couldn't walk, that's how weak I was. By the end of December, things had gotten so bad that my wife was encouraging me to check into a mental hospital. Seeing no other hope, I eventually took her advice. My daughter Christyna was only 15 at the time.

A friend of mine, a well-known psychiatrist, came to visit me at the hospital and diagnosed me with clinical depression. At the time, it felt like it was happening out of the blue, but I realised afterwards that the year-on-year build-up of pressures at work and its conflicts with my family life had finally taken their toll. I was forced to take a good long hard look at my way of life. Like a lot of leaders, I had been burning the candle at both ends to get the job done, no matter what. The constant need to prove myself combined with all the travel and not taking time out for rest and renewal took everything out of me. It left me numb, and I lost passion and energy for all the things I used to love. For instance, I used to enjoy being around people, communicating and collaborating, but after getting depressed, I found even responding to simple emails draining. Sleep and staying in bed all day did nothing to refuel or energise me. Not only was it a deeply unpleasant experience to go through myself, but it was shocking and distressful for my family, friends and colleagues to witness. I was trapped by my own success and didn't see any real point in my life.

The doctors at the hospital were wonderful and did all they could to help. For my initial treatment, they gave me antidepressants but unfortunately they didn't work for me. They changed the type of antidepressant, but my condition still didn't improve. At this point, I started to entertain thoughts about dying. The idea of death felt almost comforting, promising an end to the bleakness. My entire perspective had turned black: I could only see black cats and black cars everywhere. I would get up in the morning and the day would get worse and worse as it went on. The only thing that kept me going was the temporary escape I would have when I went to sleep. As my despair worsened, it got to the stage that the psychiatrists at the hospital were considering the idea of giving me electric shock treatment, but I declined. Even though I felt like I'd hit rock-bottom, I couldn't bring myself to go down that route.

▶

Thankfully, with the third antidepressant I started to get a little better and eventually life brightened up again – as you might have guessed by my living to tell the tale. I'm very grateful for the doctors and other staff at the mental hospital for taking such good care of me during the darkest period of my life.

By the end of March 2012, several months after my admission into the mental hospital, my depression had lifted slightly and I felt ready (if not enthusiastic) to go back to work. The hospital released me and, step by step, I started to do a little bit of paperwork and watch some TV now and then. When I booted up my PC for the first time in six months, I was greeted by more than 7000 emails! That's when it hit me and I thought: 'Wow, I have to do something about this'. It was like rebooting Windows from a human perspective. I started responding to the emails as much as I could, and within two weeks I was feeling even better. I eventually resumed my work at Microsoft, but it never really felt like things were back to 'normal'. I started questioning why this illness had happened. Then my friend put me in touch with a doctor who practised holistic medicine. He asked unusual questions about my life that you don't normally get asked by a doctor, like whether I measured my time when running. He even asked: 'Was your mother a teacher, by the way?' She was! It was from her that I had adopted the idea of point scoring and grading to measure my achievements throughout my whole life. The doctor concluded: 'Since you were four years old, the only thing that has mattered in your life is performance,' At that point a light bulb lit up in my head. My whole world had revolved around material success, but there is obviously so much more to life than that. It was clear I had to change things; otherwise I was at risk of the depression being a recurring condition rather than a one-off. Success is like a drug. It's OK to have more provided it's a side-effect of your happiness. But virtues become vices when practised to excess – and success, like any drug, can ruin your life if you let it control you.

Following these revelations, I was referred to a special coach who helped me transform every aspect of my life, even down to my diet and exercise routine. I started eating more vegetables and fish, and less sugar, which I'd been consuming in excess for far too long. I had always exercised, but now I switched to more calming methods like tai chi.

It seemed strange that I was changing my diet and exercise methods to help my mental recovery, but that's just it. Restoring your wellbeing requires taking care of multiple streams of energy – your physical, mental, emotional and spiritual sources – not just the odd one or two of them. Good health is essentially a state when all aspects of your being are in robust harmony.

THE ROAD TO RECOVERY

Although the best way to combat burnout, stress and depression is preemptively with a positive outlook and good energy management, what happens when it's too late and you've already hit rock-bottom? The automatic reaction is to give in to despair, which is completely natural under the circumstances. However, the power to change your life still lies in your own hands: you just need to know how to use it. While I'd achieved some unbelievable and unimagined successes in my life before stumbling into depression, I was always thinking that I would be happy at some point in the future. It was never really there in the 'now'. The real big learning I got from my illness is that happiness is not one point. It's not one specific mood or moment in time that you can easily pin down. That's why waiting and hoping for happiness to arrive won't work – it will constantly evade you and remain lurking somewhere in the future. The best we can do is put in place the components to attract more joy, meaning and satisfaction in our lives, and to take good care of ourselves at all times, not just when something goes wrong.

This is a message that has never been more relevant than it is today, especially in the fast-paced, mile-a-minute business world. The long-hours lifestyle has become the 'new reality' and one we feel we need to adopt if we're going to be successful. But it's making us sick. A lot of professionals are running the rat race, trudging non-stop towards success, and this goes against the natural way of things. When we were cavemen, we would hunt intensively and then rest, hunt and then rest again, repeating this cycle to keep ourselves going. Today we are hunting, hunting, hunting for results around-the-clock, and then we wonder why we burn out, get depressed or have a heart attack! All professional athletes follow the caveman approach in their respective sports. How they regain energy is of paramount importance. Professional tennis players, for instance, are only playing in matches 20 per cent of the time, when they're expected to push themselves to the limit. The other 80 per cent of the time they are training to help improve their reactions, and getting plenty of rest and eating nutritiously to conserve energy for their next competition. Compare that to the 'corporate athlete' who is in the midst of stressful situations for 50+ hours per week, having to make decisions and take actions that carry substantial weight in an organisation's growth without regular periods of rest and recovery. And unlike athletes who have coaches, physiotherapists and fitness programmes to help them perform, CEOs or top-level leaders might only have a PA to manage their diary. They don't have regimes in place to help them get in tip-top physical and cognitive order, reminding them to eat right, take breaks and learn new things so that they can be at the peak of their game. But if a leader wants to perform like a top sportsperson, then they need to behave like one too. Leaders need to prioritise taking better care of themselves and should aim to find a lifestyle balance that will yield dividends when it's time to perform.

STRATEGIES FOR COPING

No one can look after your recovery better than you, and there are all sorts of ways you can conquer your mental and emotional setbacks to live a happy, balanced life. Happiness might seem like a million miles away right now, but it's a lot closer than you think. At the very least you can loosen the grip of negativity and anxiety over you. I'd like to mention a few things that helped me overcome my depression and made me stronger as a person. Hopefully, the following coping and prevention techniques will be as beneficial to you as they were to me:

1. Control your thinking

We perceive reality in a very narrow way. Psychology professor Tim Wilson estimates that the unconscious brain takes in 11 million bits per second of information, but the conscious mind is only able to process 40 bits per second.[15] This means that what we consciously think about is being drastically filtered. If you're always focusing on the negative aspects of situations, yourself, other

---

[15] Wilson, Timothy D. (2002). *Strangers to Ourselves: Discovering the Adaptive Unconscious*. Boston: Harvard University Press.

people and the future, negativity will continuously filter through to your state of mind, keeping you in a depressive or anxious state. Thinking saddening thoughts makes you feel sad. Thinking angry thoughts makes you feel angry. So, obviously the quickest way to change how you feel is to change how you think.

Make an active choice to challenge your negative thinking and turn things around with positive thoughts. For instance, keep a *negative thought diary* to track how many self-defeating and unhelpful thoughts you're actually having and what triggered them. Then go over each thought and ask yourself whether it's truly justified. Challenge yourself to write down something more realistic, helpful and positive to replace it. If you're thinking something like:

- 'I didn't win that crucial account, I'm a total failure. I can kiss goodbye to the sales manager promotion.'

Convert it to. . .

- 'I'm disappointed I didn't get the account. It doesn't mean I'm not good at my job; I've had some great successes. There are plenty of other opportunities to prove my suitability for the promotion.'

If it helps, think about what you would say to someone else in the same situation. Turning your thoughts around like this will cause your moods to follow suit, helping to remove obstacles to your happiness. Think of it like flipping a switch to go from darkness to light.

2. Ready yourself for change

The only constant in life is change. If you can't absorb change, it's hard to survive. Sometimes our lives can be engulfed by sudden and dramatic shifts, leaving us feeling completely overwhelmed and unsettled. Even small unexpected moves can catch us by surprise. Learning how to accept change, or even better, embrace it, can pay great dividends for your inner peace and personal growth. Here are a few tips:

- **Keep calm and carry on.** Although there might be intense change going on in one aspect of your life, it's important that you don't let it invade everything else. If you like to go on that Sunday jog in the park or have a meal out with the family every Friday, don't let the fact that you're moving to a new city or taking on a new role in your company stop you from doing it. The more you stick to your usual routine and carry on as normal, the less distressing the change will be.

- **Acknowledge your thoughts and feelings.** Allow change to unfold without fighting it and use mindfulness techniques to absorb the experience. By becoming aware of what you're thinking and feeling, you can achieve a state of calm amidst all the stress. It could also be helpful to talk to other people about it: maybe even those who're going through the change with you, such as work colleagues or family members. Try not to isolate yourself in a place of denial and resistance.

- **Look at the positives.** A change in circumstances doesn't necessarily have to be seen as something you 'just have to deal with'. By focusing on the positive side of change, you can use it as an opportunity for inner growth and self-development. Embrace the wisdom change brings while keeping an eye on your bigger purpose. An unexpected move can set you on a path to exciting new prospects that you might otherwise never have considered, making you all the better for experiencing it.

- **Give yourself time.** Change is something that takes time to get comfortable with. You might be feeling rattled or nervy right now, but don't let it bring you down – this is usually a temporary phase and you'll soon adjust to your new scenario. It might help during this 'settling in' period to treat yourself to a short break or a fun activity that you don't often get around to doing. Reward yourself for coping so well.

3. The art of detachment

A lot of people fall into the trap of becoming too attached to things like money, property, titles, or what's in their garage. It's almost like they're human *doings* or *havings* rather than human *beings*. Of course, there's nothing wrong with enjoying the nice things in our lives, especially when we've worked so hard to get them, but it's dangerous to get so attached that we identify ourselves with them. This puts our happiness at major risk should we ever happen to lose one of our precious possessions. By learning to control our thinking, living in the 'now' and being open to change, we can rise above the pull of worldly attachments and instead get a heightened perspective of life – one that allows us to enjoy the essence of just *being*.

4. Laughter is the best medicine

This is a simple observation, but it's so obvious that it fails to be obvious anymore. People, especially big bosses under pressure, rarely make time for fun and laughter in their hectic lives. And yet a sense of humour is one of the best resources you can call on for relieving stress and lightening your mood during a dark time. Aside from the health benefits of laughter (which are numerous), having a sense of humour about life's difficulties can normalise your experience and help you keep things in perspective, and it provides a great way to bond with others. Not everything needs to be taken seriously all the time, so don't be afraid to laugh at yourself once in a while. You could even attend a laughter school or introduce laughter training to your organisation to help bring back the joie de vivre. Great leaders see the funny side of even the most serious issues. Think of US President Barack Obama in some of his most powerful speeches. Until recently, there was even an engineer at Google with the title of 'Jolly Good Fellow (which nobody can deny)', whose aim was to solve unhappiness.[16] How funny is that?

[16] Bort, Julie (2015). 'This Google engineer's title is 'Jolly Good Fellow' and he's solving unhappiness and war'. *Tech Insider*, 18 September. [Online] Available from: http://www.techinsider.io/google-jolly-good-fellow-chade-meng-tan-2015-9

How to become a Chief Energy Officer (CEO)

'Everything is energy and that's all there is to it ... It can be no other way. This is not philosophy. This is physics.'
ALBERT EINSTEIN, NOBEL PRIZE-WINNING PHYSICIST

'Life is a marathon, not a sprint.' How many times have you heard this expression? Perhaps so many that you'd be happy never to hear it again! But while the message of pacing ourselves rather than constantly speeding through life is valid, it's not the whole of the story. Life (and leadership for that matter) *is* a marathon, but it's a marathon run in a *series of sprints*. Rather than keeping your pace steady to maintain stamina for the long run ahead, you're better off breaking down your big activities and 'giving your all' as you sprint towards each of them. At the end of each sprint you rest and recharge your energy, and then you sprint again, all the while keeping the finish line in mind. That's how you get to unleash your full potential and consistently hit the high standards you set for yourself and your team.

In this chapter, we'll look at how to turn you into a CEO. No, not the type you're familiar with, but another kind of CEO – a *Chief Energy Officer*. This will mean learning to manage both your own energy and the energy of your team to be maximally effective in the workplace. Through good *energy management*, you can optimise your peak energy times by taking strategic breaks, being proactive (not reactive) and minimising digital distractions. And you can build greater enthusiasm into your team by creating a work environment where everyone is encouraged to maintain their reserves of energy – physically, mentally, emotionally, and even spiritually.

The science of energy management

If Albert Einstein himself implies that there's a science behind energy, then it's difficult to argue otherwise. Hardly any of us really know how our energy works, however; probably because we don't consider it worth thinking about. Instead, we automatically believe that the best way to be productive is to max our output as much as possible by cranking out more hours at our desks and juggling lots of things at the same time. According to 2015 Eurostat figures, the UK has the fifth longest working hours in Europe – longer than France (13th place) and Germany (25th place). But market research firm YouGov reports that its output per hour is actually far less than the output of those countries.[1] Being 'busy' does *not* necessarily equate to being productive. More often than not, we're just spreading ourselves thin and letting our batteries go flat. A better understanding of energy would show that 'running the marathon in a series of sprints' is the optimal approach to managing our energy, and brings with it a whole host of benefits:

- lower susceptibility to negative stress, fatigue, burnout and depression
- more time for planning, preparation and reflection
- an increase in enthusiasm and engagement
- a higher standard of productivity.

[1] Dahlgreen, Will (2015). 'A seven hour working day is "most productive"'. *YouGov*, 14 October. [Online] Available from: https://yougov.co.uk/news/2015/10/14/british-people-say-7-hour-work-day-most-productive/

We all know that quality leisure and relaxation time *after* work helps us perform better the next day, but what about the suggestion that we take time throughout the day – even during working hours – for recovery? This might seem like an unrealistic and unmanageable task to the average leader out there, but not according to performance psychologist Tony Schwartz. He suggests that without mulitple breaks at work, people will conserve their energy to try and make it to the end of their shift without wearing themselves out, as they would while running a marathon. This, he argues, means that they're only reaching 25 per cent of their potential output across the workday; whereas what they could be doing is taking advantage of the moments when their body's natural alertness is at its highest, so they can reap a colossal 90 per cent output instead. Holding ourselves back is damaging to our potential, so we need to remove the fear of expending too much energy by giving ourselves a well-earned rest in between periods of high-intensity output. It's much easier to work productively when we know a break is round the corner, not just at the end of a long day. A marathon runner that tries to push on without any let up can easily 'zone out' and lose focus long before the finish line, whereas competing with a balanced sprint–rest ratio guarantees that we'll be challenged, energised and inspired all the way.

GETTING INTO OUR ENERGY GROOVE

Our personal energy is a measure of how strong, invigorated and driven we feel at any given moment.[2] When it's high, we produce great work; when it's low our productivity plummets. So far, so simple. But what's not so simple is learning to stay tuned in to our fuel gauge so that we can take action *before* it starts pointing towards empty.

First off, how can we recognise when our bodies are at their peak energy levels? Many of us simply use our own judgement – we can tell when we're feeling tired or when we're feeling pumped up and ready to go, even if we don't know the reasons why. The problem is that we tend to ignore these signals, and carry on working as normal regardless of our bodies' rhythms. While we like to imagine that we're machines, which operate in a *linear* way, we're actually organisms, which move in a *cyclical* pattern. And we need to

---

[2] Stack, Laura, M. (2005). 'Maintaining the energy you need to be productive'. *Leave the Office Earlier*. The Productivity Pro, December, No. 79. [Online] Available from: http://www.theproductivitypro.com/newsletters/num79December2005.htm

plug into the natural rhythm of our bodies if we want to do our best work. Cue psychophysiologist Peretz Lavie and his 'ultradian rhythms'.[3]

The ultradian rhythm

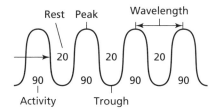

Through a series of experiments, Lavie investigated the patterns of 'sleepiness' that emerge throughout the day and outlined his findings in a 1995 US Army report. He discovered that we tend to get sleepy every *90–120 minutes*, particularly in the mornings. These 90–120 minute cycles are our ultradian rhythms which define when we're naturally at our most alert and productive. We have more focus and motivation, so it's the best time to get things done. After these 90–120 minutes, there's approximately a 20–30 minute stretch during which we hit a trough and our energy sinks. At these times, we feel tired, irritable and groggy, and we lose focus. Then the cycle starts again and we head back up towards another 'high'. Often we try and override the 'down' times by finding artificial ways to pump up our energy, such as caffeine and sugary/fatty foods. But when we try to stay wired past our productive point, our stress hormones (adrenalin and cortisol) kick in to keep us going, so we end up working in 'fight or flight' mode rather than performing at our best. We become reactive and less able to think clearly, creatively or critically because our concentration is shallow. The trick around this is to take advantage of the peak 'high energy' periods in the cycle to tackle our most challenging tasks without distractions, and to wind down, recuperate and replenish our energy levels before they hit rock-bottom – 90 per cent output in 90 minutes is a deal we can hardly afford to miss.

[3] Lavie, Peretz, Zomer, Jacob and Gopher, Daniel (1995). 'Ultradian rhythms in prolonged human performance'. *US Army Research Institute for the Behavioral and Social Sciences*, ARI Research Note 95–30, February. [Online] Available from: http://www.dtic.mil/dtic/tr/fulltext/u2/a296199.pdf

PUTTING THE SCIENCE INTO PRACTICE

Businesses need leadership that recognises the value of 'strategic renewal' and that there are gains to be made in taking care of employees. The number of hours we hunker down at our desks doesn't determine the quality of our output, so we need to create a workplace that nurtures a balanced relationship between intense work and time for personal replenishment. In your new role as a Chief Energy Officer, one of your main responsibilities will be to help others appreciate that humans are designed to operate rhythmically between spending and renewing energy. By listening to the body's natural rhythms, you can learn to adapt your daily routine in a way that allows you to bring more energy and intensity to the hours you work, and to unplug and refuel when you need to. Here are some quick habits you can introduce to boost your performance potential at once:[4]

1. **Split your work into 90-minute blocks.** By arranging your day into ring-fenced sessions of uninterrupted time, you're making a pact with yourself that you'll use that time wisely to fully immerse yourself in an important task. During each 90-minute window, go 'all out' on that task and don't worry about conserving your energy. Oh, and switch off any digital distractions that could break your focus. If your day's going to be full of disjointed tasks (emails, client meetings, idea generation sessions, preparing plans, routine bits and bobs), aim to batch similar types of activities together for a more concentrated approach. Your groupings might include people tasks (training, reviewing, negotiating); brainstorming and creative work; reading and researching; planning and reporting; meetings; thinking and decision making; administration; personal projects; emails and phone calls. Another tip for added drive and motivation is to give yourself a small goal to achieve at the end of each work block, so you don't waver as the session progresses.

2. **Plan your breaks – and take them.** After each 90-minute session, take a break for 15–20 minutes to rest and rejuvenate. Plan in advance what you're going to do in your 'pit stops' so you can optimise this time. It's unfortunate that we spend so much time planning our work,

---

[4] Ciotti, Gregory (2012). 'The science behind why better energy management is the key to peak productivity'. *iDoneThis Blog*, 9 October. [Online] Available from: http://blog.idonethis.com/science-of-better-energy-management/

but we rarely ever get around to planning our downtime. As important as it is to be fully engaged in your task during your high-energy periods, it's just as crucial to actively disengage yourself during your breaks – to completely 'unfocus'. Finnish consultant and blogger Sami Paju recommends changing your channel of activity when you're taking your scheduled break.[5] We humans have three channels of activity – cognitive, physical and emotional. If you've been doing a lot of thinking and brainwork, then you need to switch off from the cognitive channel, for instance, by taking a stroll, doing some colouring-in (buy an adult colouring book), reading something light or lowbrow, getting a snack or simply shutting your eyes for a few minutes. A great way to engage the emotional channel is to listen to music or play with your kids, or you could get your physical channel going instead by doing something active that will keep you fit as well. Also, it goes without saying that having a proper lunch break (away from your desk) is highly advised, however tempting it may be to juggle eating with working. This idea of taking breaks is a lot harder than it sounds, especially if you take pride in being a workhorse. Through practice, you'll learn to listen to your body so you know when you're reaching a low-energy period. When you start feeling drowsy or your mind starts to wander, it's a sure sign you're heading for a dip in energy levels and that you need to stop what you're doing. Grab a drink, text a friend, have a gab with colleagues at the water cooler, watch funny YouTube videos or sit outside for a bit. In a short while, you'll be able to regain your focus and get back to work with full zeal.

3. **Try power napping or an alternative.** I know this can be a tough one to implement, especially if you work in a loud, open plan office – but at least give it a go. Try and fit in a short nap of 20–30 minutes at a time of day when your natural alertness often begins to flag (usually around three or four in the afternoon). Find a nice quiet place with a comfy couch or seat and let yourself nod off. If you've ever seen the TV show *Mad Men*, you'll know that advertising executive Don Draper would often nap in his office and wake up full of creative fire. The character might be fake, but the benefits are real. If the idea of napping doesn't do it for you, try a relaxation or meditation exercise instead.

[5] Paju, Sami (2010). 'Supercharge your productivity with ultradian rhythms'. *Lateral Action*. [Online] Available from: http://lateralaction.com/articles/productivity-ultradian-rhythms/

Quality over quantity

Considering the amount of time we devote to our work, being told that we aren't performing at our best can be a hard pill to swallow. This is because we think in terms of quantity rather than quality, but as we've seen, 'more, bigger, faster' doesn't always generate the best value. Good self-leadership is about using *quality energy* to keep our heads clear and our concentration high, without falling foul of burnout and illness. It's one thing to be keeping busy, but when you're always on the move, you're not taking the time to plan what your next action will be and why you're doing it – you're relying on *habits and routines* to see you through. Scientists reckon that our brains try to make as many of our behaviours as possible automatic, so that we have more mental energy to devote to other things. The meals we eat, the newspapers we read, the way we exercise, how we organise our workload and what we do when we get home are all habits. One study by a Duke University researcher in 2006 found that as many as 45 per cent of the activities we perform each day are automatic, rather than due to well-considered decision making – so we're actually on autopilot a lot of the time.[6] The problem is that the auto-habits we become accustomed to in our work life can sometimes trip us up and prevent us from taking the best course of action. They cause us to be *reactive*, rather than *proactive*. When we're constantly reacting to what's around us and taking mental shortcuts, we aren't giving ourselves the chance to create the outcome we really want.

MANAGING THE CHIMP

In his acclaimed book *The Chimp Paradox*, Professor Steve Peters explores the ways in which much of the behaviour and decision making of human beings is governed by the emotional and instinctive part of their mind. He refers to this as the *Chimp*, as opposed to the other (more rational) part that is the *Human*, which is essentially you and your unique personality.[7] Driven by

---

[6] Neal, David T., Wood, Wendy and Quinn, Jeffrey M. (2006). 'Habits – a repeat performance'. *Current Directions in Psychological Science, 15*(4), pp. 198–202.
[7] Peters, Steve (2012). *The Chimp Paradox: The Mind Management Programme for Confidence, Success and Happiness*. First edition. London: Vermilion.

survival, the Chimp can be paranoid and jump to conclusions, and will act irrationally and destructively at times. The Human, however, is driven by self-fulfilment; it will use balanced judgement to analyse facts and establish the truth, with a view to finding satisfaction in life and helping others. Dr Peters' argument is that these two parts, though they can work together, will frequently come into conflict and struggle for control of your thinking, and the Chimp (which operates five times faster than the Human) will often emerge victorious. That's great if you're under threat, because the Chimp's function is to keep you alive and out of danger. But it's not so great when you're under mounting work or emotional pressure, as it's likely to be the irrational Chimp part of you that reacts first instead of the more thoughtful Human side, with actions that you might later come to regret and consequences that you don't want.

How the brain receives information

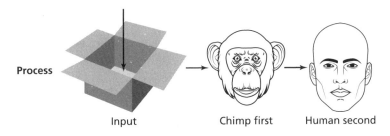

Imagine you have an important meeting to attend and you find yourself stuck in traffic, facing the prospect of being late (again!). What are your immediate thoughts and feelings to the situation? Are you frustrated? Irritated? Stressed? Cursing your luck? Maybe a combination of all of these? This would be a normal and natural response: one which most people would have under the circumstances. However, Dr Peters would say that this is your Chimp at work, acting on high alert and taking charge of your mind in an emotional, instinctive and ultimately unhelpful way. After all, what good does it do to have your Chimp acting like it's in the jungle when you're trapped in a car? It doesn't change the external circumstances (the traffic won't budge on account of you screaming and shouting); it doesn't make you feel any better (actually it makes you feel worse); and it's also a complete waste of time and energy that could be spent thinking about other things. It's monkey madness!

Now consider how you wish you *could* respond to a situation like this. Personally, I would want to stay calm first of all, taming the Chimp's immediate fearful response. That way I could logically reflect on what might happen if I'm late to the meeting. Is it really the worst thing that could happen? Some clear thinking would help me see that being late isn't the disaster my Chimp would have me believe it is. Finally, in a less anxious and more constructive frame of mind, I'd be better able to plan what I might do in the event of being late, so that I'm completely prepared. I imagine this is how most of us would *like* to behave when these kinds of disruptions crop up. The point is that you *can* respond this way, by encouraging the Human in you to override the Chimp and take back control of your mind.

Exercise 8.1: How do you react?

One method for assessing how you react to potentially stressful events is to reflect on a frustrating experience you've had recently, whether in the home or workplace. Think about how you responded at the time and answer these questions:

- How did you think, feel and behave during this experience?
- Did your reaction benefit you in any way? How?
- Did your reaction affect you negatively in any way? How?
- How would you like to have reacted to this experience (consider thoughts, emotions and behaviour)?
- With hindsight, do you feel you *could* have reacted in this way?

Try this exercise with other examples. You may be surprised to see how often you allow the instinctive and irrational part of your brain to take the reins in certain situations, when the power to respond more helpfully (read: rationally and logically) lies within your grasp.

Tip: In future, a simple way to check if the Chimp is in control is to ask yourself, 'Do I want to behave in this way?' If the answer's 'No' then it's clear the Chimp is acting on your behalf. Take a deep breath and pause to give the Chimp time to calm down, and then reassure him with facts and logic.

REACTIVE VS PROACTIVE THINKING

Being able to 'manage the Chimp' is not just useful in situations that are directly and transparently stressful (as in the 'late for a meeting' example above); it can also help us perform better in general and even foresee or avoid potential problems in the future. Take the following scenario:

'An opportunity to expand your company into new territory lands on your desk. Fabulous, you think. Aware that your competitors will soon get hold of this information and act on it themselves, you quickly put a team together to work on the venture with a really tight deadline, using a go-to plan that's worked for you on several occasions in the past. During the course of the project, several unexpected complications spring up on the scene, and you soon realise that you've underestimated the time and effort it will take to get it all done. On top of that, you have to deal with loads of silly mistakes that have been made because your team has been so stretched. Rather than reorganise the plan, you push the deadline back and pull in more people who've been working on other important assignments. Soon a backlog of urgent work builds up across different departments because you've left them high and dry in favour of wrapping up this crucial project. Waaaghh!'

This is a good illustration of how quick-speed *reactive* thinking can lead you to make pressure-fuelled snap judgements that ultimately slow down your productivity, instead of increasing it as you'd hope. The fastest and easiest choice isn't always the right one. The alternative to reactive thinking is to respond to situations in a more controlled manner – looking to the future, analysing the outcomes and exerting self-discipline – rather than allowing instincts and habit to take over. This is what we call being *proactive*. Instead of letting events set the agenda, you take a moment to look at the wider picture and base your response on what you see there. As a leader, your best insights and biggest, most impactful decisions can only really come about when you give yourself the luxury to think! In the example above, the delays and complications could have been side-stepped by simply taking a bit of time at the beginning of the project to proactively prepare, rather than impulsively rushing in and throwing all your resources at it. With a bit of clear thinking and foresight, you could have anticipated potential obstacles and put contingency plans and back-up processes in place to deal with them. In the end, pushing back the deadline and bringing in more manpower could have been avoided, along with all those vein-bursting moments of stress.

Take a look at the two leader types in the table below.

Reactive vs proactive leadership

REACTIVE LEADER	PROACTIVE LEADER
• Behaviour is influenced by initial feelings and intuition.	• Behaviour is the result of reflection and rational thought.
• Reacts to change in an automatic and habitual way.	• Foresees change and takes steps to make the best of it.
• Focuses on finding and fixing problems.	• Focuses on achieving performance goals and outcomes.
• Responds to problems as and when they arise.	• Is prepared for problems and makes plans to deal with them in advance.
• Makes decisions without input from team and uses own solutions.	• Involves team in making decisions and finding solutions.
• Focuses on the immediate, short-term issues.	• Focuses on the bigger picture and plans ahead.
• Pushes people for quick results.	• Shares a compelling vision that inspires people to achieve results.
• Teaches team to expect instruction – a 'telling' approach.	• Teaches team to be self-reliant – a 'coaching' approach.
• Shifts blame onto things that are beyond his/her control.	• Takes responsibility for his/her situation and acts accordingly.
• Relies on tried-and-tested methods to get speedy but conventional results.	• Takes the time to consider innovative methods in order to create new opportunities.
• Quick to punish or lay blame for errors.	• Helps team to learn from mistakes.

Clearly, the ability to be proactive gives you a clear advantage in the workplace and helps you lead yourself and others better. A proactive leader is more visionary because they can look at the big picture and foresee change, and they tap into the strengths of their team to help them achieve business outcomes. Such leaders take control of situations – they realise they have the freedom to choose their behaviour, and will use their energy wisely to contemplate what their immediate and future actions will be.[8] By contrast, the reactive leader is short-sighted and often acts like a 'lone ranger', making decisions and fixing problems by themselves, without input from their team.

[8] Covey, Stephen R. (2004). *The 7 Habits of Highly Effective People: Powerful Lessons in Personal Change*. Second edition. London: Simon & Schuster.

Reactive leaders don't plan ahead for what's around corner and are often thrown into crisis mode by issues that seem to arise 'out of the blue'. This constant firefighting is a waste of energy and leaves them exhausted and overwhelmed, as well as always having to play catch-up. If you're weighing heavy on the reactive side, don't be too concerned as you can learn to adopt a more proactive approach with a bit of dedication and practice. The key thing is to manage your energy, as when you're tired (either physically or mentally) it's harder for your proactive Human side to exert control over the reactive Chimp. With that in mind, here are three helpful steps:

Step 1: Review past habits

The first step to shaking off reactive thinking is to figure out when you've been doing it. Spend some time analysing your past behaviour to identify situations where you've reacted instead of responded. How did these situations turn out? With the power of hindsight, think about how you could have been more proactive in your approach, and consider the effect this might have had on the outcomes. Be mindful of your trigger situations and come up with strategies to avoid one-step thinking in future.

Step 2: Hit the pause button

When you're faced with a new task, problem or challenge and are about to sprint into action – stop! Use self-control and take a step back. Challenge 'here-and-now' thinking by asking yourself if the course you're about to take is really the only option. It's likely that you're in reactive mode. If you can manage to stop yourself, then this is the perfect opportunity to practise going down the proactive route by being more flexible, incisive and considered in your thinking.

Step 3: Predict, plan, perform

Being proactive means you must first develop foresight so you can anticipate events, problems and future outcomes (*predict*). Get a handle on how things work – understand the patterns, routines, daily practices and cycles that exist in your business as this will prime you to make the best possible decisions.[9] And keep a watchful eye on your work environment and its changing landscape. Avoid using your past to predict how the future will unfold and instead enlist your creativity to imagine multiple possibilities. Consider the issues that have the potential to cause disruption in your business and find viable ways to prevent

---

[9] Scivicque, Chrissy (2010). 'How to be proactive at work: My 5 step system'. *Eat Your Career*. [Online] Available from: http://www.eatyourcareer.com/2010/08/how-be-proactive-at-work-step-system/

them so that they don't become concrete roadblocks, e.g. a delay in a bulk order or the loss of key employees or suppliers. Contingency planning will allow you to move quickly to recover from a setback before it turns into a major disaster, for instance, by using freelancers or a temp agency to cope with any HR shortfall.[10]

Strategise for the future by setting short- and long-term goals in as many areas as possible (*plan*). Like a chess player, learn to plan your moves three steps ahead, not just one at a time. Make the effort to organise 'thinking time' for yourself and others to focus on innovation and planning, while always having your vision in sight. When you know where you are and which direction you're going in, it will be easier to spot if you veer off track and to make course corrections as needed.

Understand that, as a leader, you're only as good as your team and you need their full cooperation if you're going to be able to take effective action when it's needed (*perform*). Engage with your team members; allow them to make a contribution and recognise their input. For instance, if you're running a huge promotional campaign and need to pull out all the stops to deal with the expected demand, empower your team to be proactive in handling any unforeseen snags or hiccups, without fearing a backlash should they make a mistake. If you've chosen your path well, you can stand confidently behind your decisions.

Digital distractions

Technology is everywhere. There's no turning our backs on it. We live and work in a world where we're constantly connected to multiple devices and communication vehicles – email, smartphones, tablets, the web, social media, and even good old TVs. Technology is a major godsend in our working lives – it provides easy access to huge volumes of information; it helps us analyse data to get to the core of a problem; it allows us to forge stronger relationships and connections globally; and it offers a fertile breeding ground for new ideas and innovation. Technology is simply awesome! But there's no doubt that it comes with some 'side-effects'. For many of us, it's difficult to keep a clear head and focus on what we're doing amidst the relentless buzz of digital noise:

---

[10] McQuerrey, Lisa. 'How to become proactive rather than reactive'. *azcentral.com*. [Online] Available from: http://yourbusiness.azcentral.com/become-proactive-rather-reactive-10908.html

the alerts, beeps, notifications and vibrations. And the distractions are oh so tempting – 'Just one more YouTube video', 'I wonder how many Likes I've had on my Facebook post', 'Ooh that news story looks interesting'. Think about your own experiences: how often do you break away from a task you're working on to read your messages or search for something on the internet?

A 2005 study for computing firm Hewlett Packard assisted by Glenn Wilson, a psychologist at King's College, London, looked at the effect of technology on people's productivity.[11] Based on findings from over 1000 participants, the researchers concluded that when you're distracted from an activity by incoming email or phone calls, your IQ drops by 10 points, which, bizarrely, is more than double the drop you would get if you were smoking marijuana (4 points). I mentioned these statistics in a presentation I gave at a university, and the students later wrote in their newsletter that I claimed it was better to smoke marijuana than respond to emails! Hopefully that was down to misinterpretation rather than wishful thinking.

At an extreme level, a hyper-connected environment destroys your attention span and mental equilibrium, and sees your productivity nosedive. Being 'plugged in' all the time leads to information overload, a dilution of focus, attention deficit hyperactivity disorder (ADHD) and digital dementia (where overuse of technology dulls cognitive abilities). In 2014, a global Human Capital Trends study by Deloitte University uncovered the following:[12]

Deloitte University Study Results (2014)

As a result of information overload and an always-connected 24/7 environment, the 'overwhelmed employee' has become commonplace in today's workplace, with 65 per cent of business leaders citing it as an 'urgent' or 'important' concern.

57 per cent of the respondents believe that their organisations are 'weak' when it comes to helping leaders manage difficult tasks and helping employees manage information flow.

▶

---

[11] Wilson, Glenn. 'The "infomania" study'. *Dr Glenn Wilson*. [Online] Available from: http://www.drglennwilson.com/Infomania_experiment_for_HP.doc
[12] Hodson, Tom, Schwartz, Jeff, van Berkel, Ardie and Otten, Ian Winstrom (2014). 'The overwhelmed employee: Simplify the work environment'. *Deloitte University Press,* 7 March. [Online] Available from: http://dupress.com/articles/hc-trends-2014-overwhelmed-employee/#end-notes

> Despite rating employee overwhelm as a serious issue, 44 per cent of those surveyed said that they were 'not ready' to deal with it yet, i.e. leaders just don't know what to do.

Deloitte's findings are supported by a horde of other recent studies which demonstrate the productivity-draining impact of technology. According to a 2013 Internet Trends report by venture capital firm Kleiner Perkins Caufield & Byers, mobile device users check their phones a whopping 150 times a day (wow!).[13] And 57 per cent of work interruptions are caused by collaboration and social tools such as email, messaging and social networks, or by switching windows amongst disparate stand-alone applications.[14] More disturbingly, research by the neurologist Larry Rosen in 2014 suggests that the average office worker can only focus for *seven minutes at a time* before either switching windows or checking Facebook and similar networks.[15]

INFOMANIA

The gadgets and gizmos of modern work life make dizzying amounts of information available to us at the click of a button. Jonathan Spira, author of *Overload*, has delved deep into the hazardous impact of too much information. His concern is that 'there is little time for thought and reflection in the course of a typical day. Instead, information – often in the form of email messages, reports, news, websites, RSS feeds, blogs, wikis, instant messages, text messages, Twitter, and video conferencing calls – bombards and dulls our senses'. The statistics that Spira presents are more than enough to get our attention:[16]

[13] Meeker, Mary and Wu, Liang (2013). '2013 internet trends'. *KPCB*, 29 May. [Online] Available from: http://www.kpcb.com/blog/2013-internet-trends

[14] Harmon.ie. (2011). 'I can't get my work done! How collaboration & social tools drain productivity'. 1 May. [Online] Available from: https://harmon.ie/blog/i-cant-get-my-work-done-how-collaboration-social-tools-drain-productivity

[15] Rosen, Larry (2014). 'Technology and the brain, the latest research and findings'. Wisdom 2.0 Conference 2014, 2 March. [Online] Available from: https://www.youtube.com/watch?v=n0OqA0pmAag#t=84

[16] Spira, Jonathan B. (2011). *Overload! How Too Much Information is Hazardous to Your Organization*. Hoboken, NJ: John Wiley & Sons.

Information overload – facts and figures

- Information overload cost the US economy almost $1 trillion in 2010.
- 94 per cent of people surveyed have at some point felt overwhelmed by information to the point of incapacitation.
- 66 per cent of knowledge workers feel they don't have enough time to get all their work done.
- 58 per cent of government workers spend half the workday filing, deleting or sorting information, at a cost of almost $31 billion.
- Reading and processing just 100 emails can occupy over half of a worker's day.
- Many email exchanges that go on for days and weeks can be resolved with a five-minute phone call.
- For every 100 people who are unnecessarily copied in an email, eight hours are lost.
- After a 30-second interruption, it can take up to five minutes to re-focus on the task you were working on.
- Knowledge workers spend only 5 per cent of the day engaged in thought and reflection. Information overload decreases the ability to manage thoughts and ideas, or to be creative and innovative.

Source: Spira, J., *Overload* (John Wiley & Sons, 2011).

Too much information and too many interruptions without time for thinking and reflection can seriously choke our productivity, energy and engagement levels. The high-tech props that surround us become a hindrance rather than a help, interrupting our 'flow' when we're working and cutting into our concentration for the important tasks we're doing. What's more, wading through torrents of data takes up most of our mind space so we have little left for thinking creatively and proactively. Instead of using our mental faculties wisely to brainstorm ideas, evaluate options, manage our thoughts and plan ahead, we feel pressure to act on new information instantly so we can 'get it out of the way'. We *react* to it. The problem with this short-term reactive approach is that we end up making mistakes or wrong decisions because we haven't taken the time to think about the data rationally and objectively.

THE MULTITASKING MYTH

Modern devices and software are designed to help you multitask. Why do just one thing when you can do four or five things at once? But multitasking is not something that we humans – not even women – are much good at. It's OK if we're only working on bitty, fragmented tasks that don't need that much attention, but not for those that require us to be creative, think in abstract ways, absorb learning or really dig into a topic. That's because what we think of as multitasking is really 'multiswitching', bouncing from one task to another, and there's evidence to show that it actually wastes our time and concentration.

In 2006, neuropsychologists at Vanderbilt University in Nashville discovered that a 'response selection bottleneck' occurs in the brain when it's forced to respond to more than one task simultaneously.[17] Subjects who were given two simple tasks to perform at the same time experienced a significant slow-down in brain activity. They took up to 30 per cent longer and made twice as many errors as those who completed the same tasks in sequence. Task switching causes time delays and energy loss as the brain decides which task to perform. On making its choice, it has to turn off the cognitive rules for the old task, and then turn on the rules for the new one. All this forced shifting of gears comes at a heavy price. Your mental clarity suffers as the brain frantically switches its attention to and fro, such as when you try to write an email while talking on the phone while also reading a text. And the more tasks you add, the more challenging it gets as each job competes for finite resources in the brain, leaving you feeling drained and no doubt irritated afterwards.

I don't know about you, but I sometimes find it hard to stay cool and collected when I'm trying to focus on too many things at once. It's not so much the high-tech juggling that bothers me, but the jarring feeling that occurs when I'm interrupted in the middle of something heavy. It takes a while for me to find my groove again. A 2007 study by Microsoft Research and the University of Illinois found that it took employees up to 15 minutes to effectively resume a challenging task when interrupted by something as simple as the ding of an email, whether they responded to it or not.[18] The harder the interrupted task,

[17] Dux, Paul E., Ivanoff, J., Asplund, Christopher L. and Marois, René (2006). 'Isolation of a central bottleneck of information processing with time-resolved fMRI'. *Neuron*, **52**(6), pp. 1109–1120.
[18] Iqbal, Shamsi, T. and Horvitz, Eric (2007). 'Disruption and recovery of computing tasks: Field study, analysis, and directions'. Paper presented at the Proceedings of the SIGCHI Conference on Human Factors in Computing Systems, San Jose, California, 28 April to 3 May, pp. 677–686.

the harder it is to get back on track. Tot up the number of brain-scrambling interruptions you get in your average day, and it becomes obvious why you might struggle to keep your train of thought.

The fact is, people are far more productive if they *singletask* and only do one thing at a time. That's not to say you shouldn't ever multitask. Sometimes urgent activities crop up which must be done right now and involve a bit of hopping around. Sometimes you have to wait for other actions to happen before you can finish what you're doing. These make multitasking a necessary evil on occasion. By all means do it when you need to, but don't make it your default method of working. And always bring 100 per cent of your attention and mental resources to bear on high-priority tasks.

It takes some willpower to control the impulse to multitask when you know it's not in your best interests or when you're hijacked by outside stimuli. So when you really need to work on that strategic plan, steel yourself against the temptation to check your messages, log into Twitter or type a quick email reply. What's great is that not all technology leads to toxic multitasking. There are loads of useful tools and apps out there designed to keep you from multitasking and distractions, so you aren't jumping between tabs or drawn to your Facebook page while in the middle of something (see box below).

Exercise 8.2: Focus, filter, forget

There are plenty of methods you can use to protect yourself from the distractions caused by technology and info overload. I'm a fan of the *Focus, Filter, Forget* approach for helping me get back down to business:

1. FOCUS

- **Block out 'thinking time'.** Set periods of time in your day when you determine that you won't allow yourself to be distracted. You can decide for yourself how long this needs to be – it might be as little as half an hour or as long as two hours, depending on your needs. Choose a time that fits with your natural energy and work patterns. For instance, if you find you think better in the early afternoon, then block out an hour of 'thinking time' after lunch.

- **Shut it all down.** Brief your team so they know when you're going to be in a focused work session. Switch off your smartphones and tablets, making sure to store them out of reach. If they're not there, then they can't bug you. Shut down email and close web browsers so you can singletask to your heart's content.

- **Master your emails.** If an email is only going to take two minutes or less to respond to, then answer it straight away. For emails that will take longer or require further action, mark them with a flag or unread so you can tackle them in batches later on. Send an 'I'll get back to you' response if you need to. Delete all irrelevant emails immediately so they don't clog up your inbox and forward those that can be better handled by someone else. Make a point of refusing to answer to emails on which you've been copied in and set up your program to automatically filter these emails into a special folder that you can look at when you have extra time. Finally, instruct your team and other people around you about what kinds of emails you're happy to receive and are deserving of your attention.

2. FILTER

- **Adopt the 80/20 rule.** Filter your media sources to engage with the information that really matters. Make a list of the 20 per cent best websites/blogs/Twitter feeds/magazines/news sites/discussion boards that send you 80 per cent of the most interesting and relevant content. These are the ones you should continue following. The rest can be trashed.

- **Clear the junk.** Block spam and ditch any unnecessary mailing list subscriptions so they're not adding to the 'digital noise' around you. If a media source hasn't provided you with anything of value in the last six months then it's overdue for cancellation. Try signing up to a free service like unroll.me. This scans your inbox for subscription emails then allows you to either unsubscribe from them with one click or roll them into a single, daily email.

- **Tidy up.** Set up carefully labelled folders on your computer and organise your internet bookmarks to make it easier to find, share and archive information. Build up a regular filing habit so distractions don't 'pile up'. Try and file daily if possible.

- **Get tech-wise.** Use apps or software tools to keep distractions off your radar:

  - Anti-social: A social network-blocking software.
  - Nanny: Blocks specific websites from your browser.
  - Controlled multi-tab browsing: Limits the number of tabs you can have open in a single window on Google Chrome.
  - Freedom: Blocks the internet from your computer for a pre-set period of time (great for when you're working on a task that doesn't require the web).
  - Time out: A Mac app that reminds you to take a ten-minute break every 50 minutes, and a ten-second 'micro-break' every ten minutes.

3. FORGET

- **Switch off alerts.** Reconfigure your settings on your phone or computer so you're not alerted immediately to messages or notifications. Schedule specific times in the day to check them.

- **Take a cyber-break.** If it gets to the point where you feel overloaded, consider unplugging from technology for a set part of the day, or even a whole day if you can hack it. Drag yourself away from your computer and do tech-free tasks. For instance, talk to your colleague instead of emailing them; write a letter instead of typing it up on the PC.

Energising and engaging others

Energy and engagement go hand in hand. They are the two main drivers that dictate your potential, enthusiasm and commitment to doing your best work. Being low on energy can have a drastic influence on how engaged and productive you are, and this quickly filters down to the individuals under your leadership. Research by Gallup in 2015 discovered that only *35 per cent* of US managers are engaged in their job, a strikingly low percentage. What's worrying about this is that disengaged managers create disengaged teams.[19]

---

[19] Adkins, Amy (2015). 'Only 35 per cent of US managers are engaged in their jobs'. *Gallup*, 2 April. [Online] Available from: http://www.gallup.com/businessjournal/182228/managers-engaged-jobs.aspx

There is generally a 'cascade effect' where leaders' lack of engagement trickles down to their managers, and in turn, their employees. When added up, this can have huge consequences for your organisation.

It's long been observed that you can take a sample of people with similar skills and capabilities but their levels of performance can vary dramatically. Much of this is down to the magnitude of their *enthusiasm*. Enthusiasm is a combination of energy and inspiration:

Enthusiasm = Energy + Inspiration (EI)

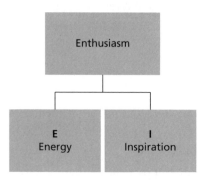

Notice what E in Energy and I in Inspiration stand for? *Emotional intelligence.*

E + I = Emotional Intelligence

Emotionally intelligent leaders know that if they make an effort to look after their people, inspire them to find meaning in their work, and create positive workplace energy, they'll benefit from a team that has more profit-making potential, is more committed to the organisation's goals, is more innovative and is less likely to change jobs or be off sick. By contrast, teams who are unhealthy or disengaged can prove to be a risk to employers as individuals show signs of absenteeism, sickness, presenteeism, arriving late, deliberately elusive behaviour and animosity towards the leadership.

Process-wise, if you follow the advice on energy management we've looked at so far (and practise the tips and tools in Chapter 9), then there's no question you'll succeed in being a positive influence on your team. But there are other – more direct – ways of elevating people's energy levels and enthusiasm at work. Take a look at the guidelines below. Soon you'll be adding *Chief Enthusiasm Officer* to your growing list of titles too!

1. TALK OPENLY ABOUT ENERGY AND WELLBEING

Leaders should send a clear message that employee wellbeing matters. If you want to build a team culture where people are encouraged to unplug and renew, you need to send the right signals. Applaud people who work sensible hours, take full lunch breaks, use their annual leave and who rest and recuperate after busy periods, and slap the wrists of those who don't. Colleagues take their cue from how leaders behave, so remove the stigma surrounding stress, burnout and depression. You want people engaged and stretched, but not to the level where they overwork and their health goes down the toilet. That does no one any good. Raise awareness about energy management and promote open dialogue so that people feel comfortable to share their experiences, rather than repressing them and contributing to a harmful team culture. Make the most of internal communication channels to provide information and embed positive attitudes – blogs, factsheets, advice for managers, useful websites and FAQs. Use posters, pamphlets, notice boards, company newsletters or even the intranet to get the message out. Impart some of the wisdom you've gained from reading this book, or maybe discuss the ways you take care of yourself. Invite an outside speaker to come in and talk to your team about the value of maintaining their wellbeing and the small changes they can make to improve their health. The more people are enlightened about the significance of energy management, the more likely they are to take measures to increase their own energy and to look out for others on their team.

2. TAKE REGULAR 'PULSE CHECKS'

Although they may work as a team, it's important to monitor your people as individuals where energy management is concerned, just as you would in regard to their work performance. Have regular one-to-ones with team members to check how they're doing and to reflect on what might be affecting their morale or causing them stress. Plot their energy on the *Mood Meter*, a tool created by psychologists at the Yale Center for Emotional Intelligence.[20] This is based on the Affect Grid developed by James Russell and colleagues in 1989.[21] The mood meter is a chart for mapping the overall mood state of

---

[20] Caruso, David R. and Salovey, Peter (2004). *The Emotionally Intelligent Manager: How to Develop and Use the Four Key Emotional Skills of Leadership*. San Francisco: Jossey-Bass.
[21] Russell, James A., Weiss, Anna and Mendelsohn, Gerald A. (1989). 'Affect grid: A single-item scale of pleasure and arousal'. *Journal of Personality and Social Psychology*, *57*(3), pp. 493–502.

individuals or teams using the relationship between feeling (on the x-axis) and levels of energy (on the y-axis). Energy levels can be high or low, while feelings can be pleasant or unpleasant.

The Mood Meter

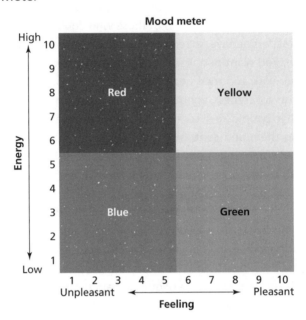

Ask each individual in your team the following questions:

- How are you feeling on a scale from 1 to 10, with 1 being unpleasant and 10 being pleasant? Plot the number on the mood meter.
- How energetic are you feeling right now? 1 means you have low energy and 10 means you have high levels of energy. Now plot the second number on the mood meter.

Using the mood meter can help you become more mindful of what your colleagues are going through and gives each individual a tool for self-regulation of their energy and emotions. Depending on what quadrant their mood falls in, they're more likely to be inclined to certain activities:

- **High energy/low feeling = RED.** The emotions most associated with this state are anger, frustration and anxiety, so the employee is more prone to attack. This mood can, however, be usefully harnessed for debating a serious topic, defending a cause or highlighting safety protocols.

- **Low energy/low feeling = BLUE.** The person in this state is literally 'feeling blue' as this quadrant is characterised by boredom, sadness and despair. This can be an ideal time to carry out more solemn tasks such as those requiring critical evaluation of their own or another's work, or error checking and forensic-type activities.

- **Low energy/high feeling = GREEN.** This quadrant is associated with emotions like tranquillity, serenity and satisfaction. It's a good mood for studying, reading or reflective activities. In group conditions, people in this state are usually calm and more likely to reach consensus.

- **High energy/high feeling = YELLOW.** This combination creates joy and excitement. These emotions are conducive to brainstorming and thinking about creative solutions. At a team level, it indicates healthy cooperation and is a great time to get started on a new project or bounce ideas around together.

Once the assessment is complete, offer tailored advice according to whether the individual is under a positive or unproductive mood/energy influence. If necessary, use coaching techniques to shift the mood meter into the appropriate quadrant depending on what kind of the work your teammate has coming up. The key with energy pulse checking is to pay attention and look for changes over a period of time. It's not a good sign if they have major 'mood swings'. Could it be that they're overloaded with work? Or have they fallen into bad habits such as overusing technology, constant multitasking or reactive thinking? Remember that being busy-busy all the time doesn't mean they are energised and engaged. Are they working on 'quality' tasks that are important and challenge them to do their best work as opposed to just getting lots of little things done and dusted ('quantity')? People often report being very busy working on activities that are de-energising them. That's your cue to help align them with tasks that will re-energise them.

You can also use this tool as a fun way to 'read' the collective mood of the entire team. Add a standing item to team meetings where people can talk about their wellbeing and energy as a group and include this activity as part of it. Give them permission to raise issues and to discuss personal as well as work matters if they want to. Building pulse checks into your team culture is a great way to make energy management a priority and to maintain good working relationships.

3. BE CANDID IF YOU'RE SUFFERING

In many workplaces, mental health is the elephant in the room. Any hint of stress, burnout or depression is treated as taboo: 'We don't talk about that around here'. Too often, team members are scared to talk to their bosses about what they're going through and problems can spiral. I know from my own experience that openness and honesty in this situation is the best policy. When a leader speaks out about problems they've had, it can have a huge impact. I discovered that for myself after recovering from my bout of depression. When I went back to the office, I was straight with everyone about my experience. I didn't completely shut the door on it or go around pretending like it never happened. After all, I'm as human as the next person. Being a leader didn't give me special powers of immunity over such things. By talking about stress, depression or other sensitive issues candidly, you can help to normalise conversations about them and prevent others falling into the same trap.

4. PROMOTE 'WELLNESS' ACTIVITIES

Leaders can demonstrate the organisation's commitment to wellbeing by implementing a variety of wellness initiatives. Even simple actions such as supporting a campaign to encourage people to take lunch breaks and work healthy hours will help. However, merely having a wellness scheme in place offers no guarantee of improving employees' wellbeing. People have to be aware that it exists and actually *want* to use it. According to Gallup, only 60 per cent of US employees are aware that their company offers a wellness programme, and only 40 per cent of those who are aware of the programme actually participate in it.[22] It could be that some people see it as the leadership's 'flavour of the month' which will soon be forgotten about. You need to show that your efforts towards wellness are genuine and that they are an expression of the value you place in your employees.

For wellness to work, you need to enthusiastically promote participation by as many people as possible – ideally aiming for a participation rate of at least 80 per cent. Ensure wellness activities are free and convenient for your team. Offer coaching and health screenings onsite during work hours so people aren't

[22] Witters, Dan and Agrawal, Sangeeta (2014). 'What your wellness programs are missing'. *Gallup*, 7 July. [Online] Available from: http://www.gallup.com/businessjournal/172106/workplace-wellness-programs-missing.aspx

forced to give up breaks, lunch or paid time off. Even so, you'll find that many people *still* won't participate despite everything being free and accessible, so take it one step further and offer incentives such as memberships for local health clubs, sports leagues or programmes. Or set up fun contests and give prizes to those who make the most progress towards health goals. There are lots of small, low-cost activities that you can implement quickly; and taken as a package they will provide fantastic opportunities for employees to maximise their fitness, health and overall wellbeing. For instance, at Microsoft we used to organise family Olympic Games, where employees could invite their families for a fun day of sports events. This did wonders for building engagement and social support, as well as motivating people to get fit. It can also help to hold regular training and instruction on the benefits of being involved in the company wellness programme, and to set up a wellness library in a designated area stocked with videos, books and leaflets to inform people. Include information on mental, emotional and spiritual health, as well as physical. Why not also go ahead and appoint a 'wellness champion' to inspire people to manage their energy better, to promote key programmes at all levels and to answer any questions people may have? A supportive and 'inclusive' culture really does make an impression and will encourage participation.

5. CREATE A POSITIVE PHYSICAL ENVIRONMENT

You'll be surprised by how much our physical surroundings – noise levels, space, equipment, temperature and light – affect us on a mental and emotional level. One of the biggest drains on our energy and enthusiasm is *clutter*. British trend-forecaster James Wallman has highlighted how an excess of clutter and possessions distracts us from the things which are most important, depleting our energy and resources. He's termed this condition *stuffocation*, and it permeates our workplaces as well as our personal lives.[23] A 2011 study by the Princeton University Neuroscience Institute found that a cluttered environment has a negative impact on people's ability to focus and to process information.[24] We can all relate to this to some degree – disorderly surroundings have a way of making us feel disorderly in our heads. Clutter also collects dust and makes it time consuming to find things. Look around

[23] Wallman, James (2015). *Stuffocation: Living More With Less.* Second edition. London: Penguin.
[24] McMains, Stephanie; Kastner, Sabine (2011). 'Interactions of top-down and bottom-up mechanisms in human visual cortex'. *The Journal of Neuroscience,* 31(2), pp. 587–597. [Online] Available from: http://www.jneurosci.org/content/31/2/587.long

your work environment. Are there filing cabinets bursting with irrelevant paperwork? Are people's desks completely chaotic? Do you have things that are broken still sitting around, waiting to be fixed? Are there tangled computer and equipment cables in full view? Bookcases and drawers crammed with items you don't need? Piles of paper just placed on random surfaces? Then it's time to 'de-stuffocate'! Have a space-clearing ceremony with your team to cleanse and purify your office space. This probably sounds like a very New-Agey thing to do, but making an occasion of it signals respect for your business and brings in fresh, positive energy. There is something enormously cathartic about throwing away things that are long past their usefulness and organising the important stuff. Once you and your team are done, you will all breathe better, gain new perspective and feel more energetic.

As well as de-cluttering, there are a number of other ergonomic and environmental features you can utilise to create a physical space that's less energy-draining and more conducive to clear thinking. The following come highly recommended:

- **Green plants.** Introducing greenery to sparse workplaces can lift your spirits and increase output by 15 per cent. Houseplants like ivy and chrysanthemum do a great job of cleansing the air of toxins. Other plants that thrive in an office environment include aloe, spider plants, cactus, rubber plant and peace lily.

- **Quality lighting.** The more it imitates natural light, the better. Poor lighting can cause eyestrain, blurred vision and headaches. Replace fluorescent tubes with full-spectrum tubes as this is the closest you can get to sunlight indoors. If your office lighting isn't suitable, bring additional desk lamps into the office or fit diffusers on overhead lights to create more comfortable conditions, especially for reading and working with print.

- **Colours.** Use colour consciously in the workplace to benefit people's health and productivity. For instance, orange is an optimistic colour that stimulates creativity; yellow promotes intellectual activity and heightens motivation; red invokes energy and passion; blue is calming and fights tension, helping workers focus on tasks; while green is restful and has a healing effect on the body.

- **Music.** Music improves mood and can help boost creativity and output. Pipe soft, uplifting music without lyrics around the office to create an ambient background.

- **Aromatherapy.** Essential oils can be used to counteract mental fatigue, irritability, tension and stress in the office. For instance, lavender is said to calm the mind and reduce computer errors by at least 25 per cent. Geranium or mandarin can help balance moods, while rosemary or peppermint can be used to enhance focus and concentration.

- **Personal touches.** Encourage your team to customise their work area by adding personal items, such as photographs, scented candles, inspiring pictures or decorative accessories.

- **Chairs.** Padded and comfortable, with adjustable height and armrests. They should be able to rotate and have a backrest of 50cms to provide adequate support. Feet should touch the ground or a footrest. When sitting straight your arms should be at a 90-degree angle for typing on the computer.

- **Desks.** Lots of surface area. Minimum 76cm deep. Ideally this should be at elbow height (adjust chair to suit if the desk doesn't have adjustable height settings). Space dividers can be used between different desks to help manage noise levels and offer privacy. An L-shaped desk works best if you perform a number of different tasks.

- **Computers.** The bigger the better in terms of screen size. Monitors should be placed at least 50cm from the eyes. The normal recommendation is for the top of the monitor to be at eye level, so you look slightly down.

- **Layout.** The art of Feng Shui has been proven to be effective in offices. Make the entrance to your office attractive and eye-catching. Arrange your desk so you can see who is entering the office or place a small mirror where you can see the entrance if it's behind you. Hang pictures on the walls depicting motion. Provide a dedicated space for people to unwind and disconnect from work for a short while.

- **Temperature.** Too hot and productivity drops as people are more distracted. Too cold and you increase the number of errors made and likelihood of people getting ill. The temperature for optimum work effectiveness is 21–22°C.

There are no fixed rules – experiment and see what works best for you and your team.

A four-way strategy for managing energy

'The key to success is to keep growing in all areas of life – mental, emotional, spiritual, as well as physical.'
JULIUS ERVING, AMERICAN ATHLETE

Energy is power, whichever way you look at it. Just as a light bulb relies on electrical power to stay switched on, high-performance leaders need tonnes of power to see them through each day, and that can only come through preserving their energy sources and keeping in tip-top condition. While machines can run on one source of energy, we humans have *four* core energy needs – physical, emotional, mental and spiritual. By managing how we spend and renew our energy, and getting fit on all four of these core levels, we can guarantee a better quality of life for ourselves and model healthy behaviours and choices for those around us. Much of leadership is essentially an energy-balancing act.

Getting the balance right between the things that zap people's energy and those that boost it will do your team the world of good, helping them bring more of their potential to work every day. The better people's needs are met, the happier they'll become, and happy teams create successful organisations.

Energy management in the workplace

Full engagement at work involves satisfying four human needs:

- **Physical:** to spend energy productively and periodically rest and renew (engage the body).
- **Emotional:** to enjoy pleasant moments and feel cared for, valued and connected (engage the heart).
- **Mental:** to be empowered to set boundaries and focus in an absorbed way (engage the mind).
- **Spiritual:** to find a sense of meaning and purpose in what we do beyond our immediate self-interest (engage the spirit).

In 2014, The Energy Project, in partnership with the *Harvard Business Review*, studied the effects that employers' ability to meet the four core needs (physical, emotional, mental and spiritual) had on their workers' performance. The results from over 20,000 employees are very telling:[1]

The effect of meeting employees' core needs

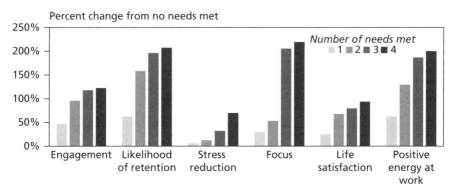

Source: Schwartz, T. and Porath, C.,'The power of meeting your employee's needs' (https://hbr.org/2014/06/the-power-of-meeting-your-employees-needs). Reproduced courtesy of Harvard Business Publishing.

[1] The Energy Project and Harvard Business Review (2014). 'The human era @ work: Findings from The Energy Project and Harvard Business Review'. White paper. [Online] Available from: http://documents.kenyon.edu/humanresources/Whitepaper_Human_Era_at_Work.pdf

As these statistics show, the greater the number of core needs met, the greater the increase in several variables of employees' performance and wellbeing. Meeting three of their core needs, for instance, can more than double their positive energy at work and improves their focus by roughly 200 per cent!

I'm glad these figures have got your attention because all improvements in 'human sustainability' begin with you – the leader. Enhancing your energy in all four of the dimensions will see your satisfaction and productivity go through the roof – and because energy is contagious your entire team will follow suit.

Effective energy management involves two key principles:

- **Energy renewal:** Unlike machines, human beings are designed to pulse rhythmically between work and rest. After a period of activity, we need to replenish our energy reserves to regain the energy we've spent. This is especially important for the mental and emotional domains, as most of us are over-trained in these areas.

- **Building capacity:** We can increase our capacity to store energy by stretching ourselves and pushing past our current limits, then allowing for a period of intensive recovery. This is how we develop bigger 'muscles' to better cope with the tasks ahead. The majority of us are under-trained physically and spiritually, and would benefit greatly by building our strength in these dimensions.

With this in mind, I've compiled the following four-way strategy to get you off to a good start on sustaining and maximising your available energy. Many of the tips overlap and help to renew more than one energy source at a time, so you're likely to see results very quickly.

Physical strategy

If you're not an athlete or your role isn't very active, you might be tempted to discount the physical element. After all, the skills relevant to your work – thinking, planning, creativity and the like – come from the brain, as do your feelings of engagement and happiness, so wouldn't focusing on the other three elements be more useful? Well, no. Physical energy is our primary and most fundamental source of fuel, even when our jobs are predominantly sedentary.[2] It serves as the base of all our other energy sources as we tap into it for everything we do. Making sure we give ourselves proper rest and nourishment positively impacts on our mental and emotional performance by helping us focus and manage our dispositions better. And physical exercise can boost our cognition and clarity of thought, and gives us the vitality to maintain commitment on whatever mission we are on. When our physical systems are out of whack, everything else goes out of balance too. That's why to perform and feel at our best, a good physical foundation is essential. Our physical energy is regulated by four everyday factors, which are all important for creating better physical health, strength and endurance: diet and nutrition, exercise and fitness, daytime rest and sleep.

DIET AND NUTRITION

On hearing the word *diet*, our reaction is to automatically think 'losing weight'. The two have become almost synonymous in modern culture, which breeds a seemingly endless slew of diet fads for its weight-conscious audience. But what we eat and how we eat impacts on more than just our weight – it can dramatically alter our concentration, productivity and performance throughout the day. A study of 20,000 employees by Brigham Young University in 2012 revealed that those with unhealthy diets were 66 per cent more likely to report a loss in productivity in comparison to healthy eaters.[3] This research also found that the employees who rarely ate fruit, vegetables and other low-fat foods at work were 93 per cent more likely to have a higher loss in productivity. The cost that poor diet and nutrition can have on the success of a business is therefore potentially huge. That's why as a leader who expects to reach his/her full potential and play a supportive role in employee wellbeing, you need to get to grips with the basics of good nutrition.

1. **Fill up with the right fuel.** Everything you eat is converted by your body into glucose (sugar), which enters the blood stream and 'feeds' the brain, helping it stay alert. If you go for a long period of time without eating, your body starts to shut down to conserve energy and your glucose levels drop, as does your metabolism. At this point, most

---

[2] Loehr, Jim and Schwartz, Tony (2003). *The Power of Full Engagement: Managing Energy, Not Time, Is the Key to High Performance and Personal Renewal*. New York: Simon & Schuster.

[3] Hollingshead, Todd (2012). 'Poor employee health means slacking on the job, business losses'. *BYU News*, 19 August. [Online] Available from: https://news.byu.edu/news/poor-employee-health-means-slacking-job-business-losses

of us will find our attention starts to drift and we have a tough time staying focused. Often we react by devouring anything within reach to get an immediate surge of energy – we'll grab a quick doughnut mid-morning if we skipped breakfast or a fast food lunch while on the run. Sugary foods like cakes and sweets, or starchy, processed foods like white bread and French fries, release glucose quickly, giving you a brief burst of energy. This prompts your body to secrete insulin to stop your blood sugar levels getting too high. While you might enjoy a 20-minute spurt of alertness, the insulin release will cause your blood sugar levels to crash, leaving you weak, edgy, ill-tempered and hungry again. Like a junkie on a comedown, you feel the need for another quick fix and reach for a sugary or starchy snack to raise your energy levels back up, starting the whole blood sugar/insulin cycle off again. Here is a typical graph of our blood glucose levels, showing the difference when we eat more sugar-rich and starch-rich foods:

The blood sugar rollercoaster

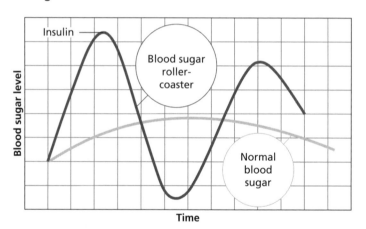

The key to smart eating is to recognise what gives you a sustained level of energy, as opposed to a sharp – but short – spike. To avoid alternating between energy peaks and plummets, it's imperative to introduce more 'slow-releasing' foods into your diet, such as oats, wholegrains, brown rice or pasta, and non-starchy fruits and vegetables like berries, apples, leafy greens and peppers. For proteins, look to chicken, fish, cottage cheese, eggs or tofu, and consume healthy fats from nuts, seeds, olive oil and avocado. These foods release energy slowly but steadily over the course of the day, so you can maintain a high level of concentration during those stretches between meals. For a better idea of what types of foods should be on or off the menu, I'd recommend referring to the *glycaemic index (GI)*, which can be found on numerous websites online. Many simple carbohydrates such as cakes, bagels, white rice and white pasta are high on the GI index. The low GI foods are the ones you should be looking to add to your diet.

2. **Eat smaller meals, more often.** Many of us are in the habit of only eating two or three meals a day, often going hungry in between and then stuffing ourselves when it's time to eat, leaving us feeling bloated and sluggish. However, most nutritionists would agree that eating smaller, balanced meals at regular intervals throughout the day is a more effective way of prolonging energy. Firstly, it means you'll have a continuous supply of glucose to the brain for the entire day, as well as the right kind of nutrients to keep it healthy. Secondly, smaller meals means your digestive system doesn't have to work as hard and you feel less groggy when you return to work, helping you slip into focus much quicker. And thirdly, it removes the temptation for unhealthy snacking, offering an easy way to improve your existing diet. Start out with a solid breakfast (porridge with fruit is a great option) and aim to eat a total of five–six meals throughout the day. Space your meals out evenly to keep blood sugar levels steady, and try to stick to a routine if you can. Been overeating lately? Then try to eat only at fixed times while sitting down at a table. If you've lost your appetite, push yourself to eat at mealtimes – though you might not feel hungry, your body (and your mind) still needs fuel to run at full capacity.

Although this style of eating might seem impractical in the middle of a busy workday, it doesn't have to be if you plan well and/or prepare your meals in advance. In a *Harvard Business Review* article, health and productivity expert Ron Friedman gives a very good piece of advice: 'Make your eating decisions *before* you get hungry'.[4] By choosing what you're going to eat for your meals in advance, you're less likely to fall into the trap of picking the cheaper, faster, processed options. Here are some tips:

- *Waste not, want not.* Bring in leftovers from the previous evening's meal to the office whenever possible, to save you having to run out and buy something when you're starving.

---

[4] Friedman, Ron (2014). 'What you eat affects your productivity'. *Harvard Business Review*, 17 October. [Online] Available from: https://hbr.org/2014/10/what-you-eat-affects-your-productivity

- *Nice and simple.* Stock up on foods that are easy to prepare but still nutritious, such as stir fry vegetables.
- *Fill up the freezer.* Cook large batches of healthy dishes at a time, split them into small portions and put them in the freezer or refrigerator ready for the week ahead. Defrost and/or reheat as and when needed.
- *Plan ahead for eating out.* If you're going out to lunch, choose where you're eating in the morning, don't wait until you're heading out the door to decide. By pre-committing instead of acting on impulse, you'll be better able to resist the allure of unhealthy grub.
- *Snack away.* Make sure you have some healthy nibbles to hand for grazing on whenever you get the munchies – raw veggies, fresh or dried fruit, nuts and protein bars, rather than cakes and chocolate bars. Bring your stash of healthy snacks into the office on Mondays and place them by your computer, so you have them available throughout the week.
- *Mix a protein shake.* If there's no time to grab something to eat, protein shakes are a handy way to replace your meal rather than skip it completely. And they're much better for you than downing another coffee or soft drink.

3. **Establish healthy habits.** Diet is usually one of the first things to suffer if you're feeling overwhelmed, anxious or irritable. If you haven't been taking great care of your eating habits lately, or you're going through a low-energy period in your life, perk yourself back up with these helpful hints.

- *Drink plenty of water.* Nearly two-thirds of your body is made up of the stuff, so drinking more water is one of the most critical things you can do to up your energy and purify your system. Not drinking enough water decreases your body's efficiency and can cause headaches and general lethargy. The European recommended intake is 1.6 litres of fluid per day for women and 2 litres of fluid per day for men. 'Fluid' can include other drinks that give you water such as fruit juices, milk, soft drinks, tea and coffee, but water is by far the best source. I recommend carrying a bottle of water around with you and swigging it throughout the day, re-filling it at a water cooler as and when you need to. If you don't like the taste of plain water, try sparkling water or add a slice of lemon or lime for a bit of flavour.

- *Limit or replace caffeine.* Too much caffeine can shift your body into a state of heightened agitation and restlessness, which triggers an anxiety response even when you're not really stressed. The European Food Safety Agency guidelines state that up to 400 milligrams of caffeine a day appears to be safe for most healthy adults – roughly the amount of caffeine in four cups of instant coffee, eight cups of tea, ten cans of cola or two energy shot drinks. Stay within these limits and don't consume caffeine late in the evening as it disrupts sleep. Try replacing coffee, tea and cola with decaffeinated tea or coffee, or better yet, green tea or other herbal drinks. Green tea has enough caffeine to wake you up, but not so much as to give you the jitters. At night try chamomile tea as it contains natural chemicals that are soothing to the brain.

- *Take your vitamins.* It's a good idea to take a multivitamin each day to ensure you're getting all the vitamins and minerals your body needs. Even marginal vitamin deficiencies can negatively affect your energy. For instance, deficiencies in B vitamins such as folic acid, B6 and B12 can trigger depression or low mood as these vitamins are vital for making and processing neurotransmitters in the body. Up your daily intake with a B-complex supplement. Vitamin C is a great antioxidant and all-round energy booster. Try downing a Vitamin C drink if you need a big shot of energy before an important meeting or speech.

- *Get your good fats.* Omega oils 3, 6 and 9 are essential fatty acids, which we need for healthy brain function. Most of us get enough of the omega 6 and 9 varieties, but fall short on the omega 3s. The best sources are cold-water fish (mackerel, salmon, cod, sardines and tuna) and fish oil supplements. If you're not crazy about fish, however, try flaxseed, walnuts, omega-3 fortified eggs, and dark green leafy vegetables.

- *Avoid the bad stuff.* Many people under pressure use alcohol, cigarettes and/or drugs as a 'quick fix' to help them feel better. In the long run, these substances actually interfere with your motivation and wear down your physical and emotional energy. For instance, alcohol is a depressant and causes mood swings. It's also full of empty calories. A pint of lager is 200 calories, similar to a sugar-coated doughnut, so drinking heavily can cause you to gain weight, just as you would if you were eating one doughnut after another all evening. Choose to respect your body and mind by radically reducing your intake or cutting them out altogether.

- *Make it a team effort.* Support your teammates to make improvements in their diet by introducing programmes that encourage healthy eating in the workplace. Joining an organised initiative or club (such as Weight Watchers, Slimming World or Rosemary Conley) as a team is a great way to socialise the process and keep everyone motivated.

EXERCISE AND FITNESS

Newsflash: exercise is good for us. But we knew that already. We're all familiar with the obvious benefits of regular exercise – shedding unwanted weight, improving our appearance, and making us less susceptible to aches and pains. Less well known is the fact that it can be paramount to our success, bringing:

- lower stress
- better concentration
- sharper memory
- greater mental stamina
- enhanced creativity
- faster learning
- improved mood (great for those we collaborate with!).

A robust body of research has proven the link between exercise and mental capacity time and time again. For instance, a joint study by the University of Bristol and Leeds Metropolitan University presents evidence that exercising during work hours can boost your performance during the very same day. The researchers in this study looked at the impact that using the company gym had on over 200 employees at various corporations. The results show that on the days when the employees visited the gym, the subjects reported a higher level of productivity and were able to manage their time more effectively than on non-gym days. They also saw an improvement in their communication with colleagues and tended to feel more satisfied at the end of the day.[5]

---

[5] Coulson, Jo C., McKenna, Jim and Field, Matthew (2008). 'Exercising at work and self-reported work performance'. *International Journal of Workplace Health Management, 1*(3), pp. 176–197.

If you want to begin feeling these benefits yourself, then it's time to dust off your old sweatpants and get exercising. Don't even think of coming out with the old 'I just don't have enough time' excuse. I'm not advising you to adopt a gruelling five days a week bodybuilding workout here. The time for exercise *is* there – the trick is to manage your energy wisely to use it to your best advantage. You can see a difference in fitness after only a few weeks of beginning an exercise regime, so you won't have to wait long for results. The typical recommended exercise protocol is 20–30 minutes of continuous exercise, three to five days a week. While this is a good formula to follow, it's not set in stone and the key is to find a routine that works well for you. Here are a few suggestions that won't have you feeling exhausted before you've even begun:

1. **Mix it up.** In order to be motivated to get up and go, you need to look for a combination of physical activities that you actually enjoy doing. Doing the same thing week in week out is tedious. It's much better to mix things up so you're not bored into giving up. Just as your mind needs variety to keep it stimulated, so does your body. I recommend alternating between different types of exercise – cardiovascular, strength training and flexibility/posture training. All three types are important for improving your physical fitness and building your energy capacity:

   - *Cardiovascular ('cardio')*: This is an energetic, rhythmic type of exercise that increases your heart rate and forces you to breathe harder to get more oxygen into your lungs. Activities include brisk walking, running/jogging, swimming, dancing, hiking, cycling and sports like football, squash or tennis – basically anything that gets your pulse rate up.

   - *Strength training*: This exercise involves short, powerful bursts of activity that build strength, resilience and muscle mass, while also boosting your metabolic rate. Activities include things like weight lifting, squatting, using a resistance band, toning or using your own body weight to pull or push. Gardening and building work also fall under the scope of this exercise.

   - *Flexibility/posture training*: This type of exercise stretches your muscles and helps your body stay limber and in shape. It's like 'physical housekeeping', ensuring that your body is being used properly and your posture is kept in line. Some examples include yoga, tai chi, Pilates, Alexander Technique, martial arts and various stretching exercises.

2. **Fit exercise into your lifestyle.** Again, this is about selecting what's right for you. Some people prefer to get their exercise out of the way first thing in the morning, taking a brisk walk or jog before having their breakfast. Others prefer to wait until they've finished working for the day before heading out to the gym or a spinning class. Examine your lifestyle and decide when you can best slot in some exercise. If you enjoy shopping on Saturday mornings, then it's probably not a good idea to plan your gym sessions for afterwards because you might be too tired and won't be able to stick to a routine for long. Try to exercise on your most sedentary days instead, even if it's just a walk round the block with the dog after work or a game of football with your kids in the park on Sunday. When planning your exercise sessions, don't just think outside of work hours, think of regular exercise as part of your job. Given the improvements in cognitive performance you get directly after moderate exercise, it's well worth trying to fit in at least 20–30 minutes of physical activity in the workday, perhaps during one of your breaks. Or schedule a prolonged fitness session during your lunch hour. This sets a great example for your team to follow. Let them know you're all for them getting themselves into shape during work hours.

3. **Invest in your progress.** Show your commitment to exercise by focusing on mastering an activity rather than just 'getting a bit fitter'. Set staged goals that enable you to push for new levels of fitness or competence and monitor your progress. For instance, if you run or swim, time how long it takes you to complete a certain distance and check again at monthly intervals. Hire a personal trainer or enrol in a class to improve your performance, and buy yourself the right clothing or equipment to show you mean business. Establish a plan that you will work your way up to doing – say, one hour of exercise three to four times a week. Enter your exercise sessions into your calendar or to-do list and tick them off as you do them. Notice how good you feel afterwards.

4. **Gang up.** Exercising with other people is a good way to inject more fun into your fitness schedule, which improves your chances of sticking at it. Also, you'll be less likely to back out of classes or sessions for the fear of letting others down. Team activities are especially great. Try volleyball, football, doubles tennis or any sport where your efforts can contribute to the team's success. Consider setting up sports clubs, walking groups or team fitness activities in your workplace where co-workers can motivate each other.

5. **Move about at work.** Sitting for prolonged periods of time can have a damaging impact on our overall health and ruins posture. Office workers are particularly at risk. Break up long stretches of sitting with exercises:

- Small movements every 35–40 minutes, e.g. stretch in your chair (roll your neck and shoulders, stretch your arms high, flex your feet).
- Large movements every 90–120 minutes, e.g. get up and walk around for a few minutes, or do some jumping jacks.

Some activity is always better than none, so look for everyday moments that can be made more active at work. For instance, take the stairs instead of the lift or walk/cycle to a meeting instead of getting a taxi.

DAYTIME REST

In **Chapter 8**, I explained how the human body moves from higher to lower alertness in 90–120 minute ultradian cycles throughout the day – accounting for the ebb and flow of our energy. To work optimally, we need to allow for those moments when our energy drops and take time to rest to fill our tank back up. If we try to override these cycles, our body shifts into 'fight or flight' mode, flooding itself with stress hormones. This is when some people reach for a double-shot coffee, cigarette or junk food to relieve the immediate symptoms of stress, but in doing so they add to the underlying problems. Long periods of energy expenditure without sufficient recovery eventually lead to burnout and breakdown. In a Formula One Grand Prix, even the fastest high-performance racing car couldn't win the race without at least one or two pit stops. People are no different in this respect. If we want to keep racing ahead at top speed, we need to build regular 'pit stops' into our days to refuel and repair. Otherwise, we might find ourselves with a blown engine before the race is even over. The 2014 Quality of Life @ Work Study found that employees who take a brief break every 90 minutes report:[6]

- 28 per cent better level of focus
- 40 per cent greater capacity to think creatively
- 30 per cent higher level of health and wellbeing.

[6] The Energy Project and Harvard Business Review (2014). 'The human era @ work: Findings from The Energy Project and Harvard Business Review'. White paper. [Online] Available from: http://documents. kenyon.edu/humanresources/Whitepaper_Human_Era_at_Work.pdf

If you're fed up of traipsing home like a zombie at the end of the day or feeling shattered to the core by the end of the week, make a point to take a break every 90–120 minutes during the workday. Catch up with some reading, listen to music, surf the web, call a friend, get some exercise or simply gaze out of the window. If you use public transport for commuting to and from work, don't look at your emails or pull your work files out, do something to help you switch off instead. Socialise with other passengers or try a ten-minute 'body scan' meditation. Anything will do as long as it helps you chill out and replenish.

A BETTER NIGHT'S SLEEP

We all feel the difference when we've had a night of sound slumber. Sleep well and you wake refreshed and ready to face the day ahead, whatever it brings. Sleep badly, and there's a high chance you'll struggle to concentrate, be low on energy and have difficulty getting things done all day. In a 2015 study of 21,000 employees undertaken by Rand Europe and the University of Cambridge, those who slept six hours or less were found to be significantly less productive than their counterparts who slept for seven or eight hours.[7]

The vast majority of us need between *seven and nine hours of sleep* to function at our best, but there is a wide variation. The older we get, the less sleep we tend to need and the lighter it becomes. For the most part, we can cope well enough with getting up at the same time each morning – our alarm clocks see to that – but getting to bed at a decent hour each night is somewhat trickier. Being bombarded with work worries or distractions long after we leave the office means that we often delay going to bed, and then when we do, we find it hard to drop off and enjoy a deep, trouble-free sleep because our minds are still whirring. It's not unusual for busy leaders to wake up in the small hours, anxiously playing over recent events or fretting about what they have to do the following day. But the more stressful our lives are, the more important it is to sleep well. The following 'smart sleep' guidelines should help you achieve more restful and peaceful nights:

1. **Keep a consistent sleep schedule.** Going to bed and waking up at the same time each day regulates your body's 'internal clock', as it becomes accustomed to a particular pattern of sleep and natural

[7] Hafner, Marco, van Stolk, Christian, Saunders, Catherine, Krapels, Joachim and Baruch, Ben (2015). 'Health, wellbeing and productivity in the workplace'. *Rand Europe*. [Online] Available from: http://www.rand.org/content/dam/rand/pubs/research_reports/RR1000/RR1084/RAND_RR1084.pdf

rhythm. The advantage of this is that you function better in the day and get better quality sleep at night. If you have your alarm set for 6:30am, then aim to be in bed by roughly 11pm every night. I know it's tempting to lie in at the weekends, but try to stick to the same schedule every day of the week to avoid a Monday morning sleep hangover. If you're struggling to fall asleep the odd night, it can be frustrating. Don't force yourself or keep looking at the clock as this can actually increase the stress you feel. If you're not asleep after around 20 minutes, get out of bed and do something restful, like reading or listening to music – preferably in another room. Climb back into bed when you feel sleepy.

2. **Dim the lights and get comfortable.** To promote sleep, it helps if your bedroom environment is set up right. Quiet, dark surroundings are best for most people. First of all, make sure you have the practicalities covered with a comfortable bed and mattress. If your mattress is seven years or older and it's showing signs of wear (sagging, tears, holes, stains) then replace it pronto. Clean sheets and pillowcases will help too. Darkness is a powerful cue to tell your body it's time to sleep. Use heavy curtains or blackout blinds to block out light, or try an eye mask. The temperature of your bedroom should be fairly cool (ideally between 16 and 18° C) and the room should be well ventilated. Peace and quiet is a must! Turn the TV off and lower the volume of noise outside (traffic, loud neighbours) or inside (snoring, ticking clocks) with earplugs or a 'white noise' appliance.

3. **Power down before bedtime.** If you're the kind of person who likes to check emails, go on social media, send texts or do a last bit of work on your laptop before going to bed . . . stop! Create a cut-off time for all work-related activity – perhaps 7 or 8pm, so that you can wind down properly. In addition, try to avoid looking at lit screens within an hour of going to bed, or 30 minutes at a push. Scientists have found that the blue light emitted from electronics (computers, mobiles and TVs) has the potential to disrupt sleep because it delays the release of the sleep hormone melatonin and sends alerting signals to the brain. However, if you're unwilling to detach yourself from your devices no matter what, limit your exposure to blue light using:

- *Amber/orange glasses*: The tinted lenses on these glasses are highly effective at blocking the blue light spectrum that disrupts melatonin production.

- **f.lux**: An app that adapts the colour settings of your device's screen depending on the time of day. After dark, the colour temperature on your screen will automatically become warmer and less bright, reducing the amount of blue light emitted.

4. **Follow a relaxing bedtime routine.** The more relaxed you are by the time you get into bed, the better you'll sleep. Use the hour before you go to bed to unwind and put yourself at ease by doing things you find both enjoyable and soothing (but try to avoid anything that involves looking at a screen, including watching TV – see above). Following a similar routine nightly will make it easier to fall asleep promptly because your brain creates the association that it's sleep time. Here are some good examples of bedtime 'rituals':

- Take a warm bath.
- Listen to some relaxing music.
- Read a book.
- Write in a personal journal (this is good for dumping your worries).
- Practise relaxation or meditative exercises.
- Reflect on the successes of the day and things you're grateful for.
- Do some gentle yoga.

Emotional strategy

Emotional energy is your ability to control and maintain your emotions. People with high levels of emotional energy will feel positive, enthusiastic and happy. Those with low amounts of this energy are more prone to feeling agitated, angry or anxious. During times of stress and vulnerability, when your physical reserves run low and you fail to give yourself sufficient time for recovery, you can become emotionally out of balance and negative. From an energy perspective, negative emotions are costly and inefficient as they zap your energy stores at a rapid rate. Over the long term these feelings of frustration, worry or despair can be highly destructive, tipping you into depression. Managing your emotional energy well benefits your performance in a key way – it develops your *endurance* to play at a high level for longer without tiring. The more you fill your emotional reserves, the more resilient you become and the more capable of performing effectively while under great strain.

For leaders and managers, it's extra-important to recognise and manage your emotions during intense, high-pressure situations. Your emotional energy is linked to your ability to influence others. We all know at least one smart exec with lots of intelligence and physical drive who clearly struggles to control their emotions and have positive social interactions. This person might be great at lots of things but they would no doubt make a poor leader due to their limited ability to influence and inspire people. Negative emotions are infectious and they prompt fear, anger and defensiveness in others, undermining people's ability to perform at their best. Your skill in managing emotions represents your level of *emotional intelligence*, which is a high predictor of your ability to achieve greater fulfilment and wellbeing for yourself and others, not to mention strong business results.

As a positive leader, you have the power to take control of how you feel, adopting strategies to counter negative emotions after an upset and regain your emotional equilibrium. At the same time, you should also do things that breed positive emotions, like blocking time for activities purely because you find them enjoyable and fulfilling, as these are great sources of emotional renewal and recovery. The following are methods that I recommend to cope with the highs and lows and bring you back into balance.

BREATHING AND RELAXATION

Focused breathing is one of the quickest and most effective ways to deal with everyday negative emotions. If at any point you find yourself getting wound up, irritated or excessively upset, then taking as little as two minutes to focus on your breathing can work wonders in calming you down and alleviating your anxiety. Though breathing is obviously something we do non-stop, what's remarkable is that very few of us actually do it *properly*. We tend to go through each day breathing in a shallow way: what we might call 'breathing from our chest'. And the more stressed we get, the more shallow, rapid and irregular our breathing becomes. This is because the body's first reaction to feeling threatened is to increase the heart and breathing rate. When we panic, we 'over-breathe', which lowers the carbon dioxide level in the blood, reducing the blood flow to other organs. In other words, it stops all but the basic survival mechanisms in the brain from working properly and prevents us making rational decisions. By contrast, when we're asleep our breathing is slow, deep and steady, and occurs in the diaphragm rather than the chest.[8] This is the

[8] Mind Gym (2005). *The Mind Gym: Wake Your Mind Up*. London: Sphere.

ideal way to breathe, as it lowers our heart rate, removes muscle tension and restores the balance of carbon dioxide in our blood to a normal level, keeping our mood under control. *Focused breathing* is when you make a conscious attempt to breathe in this manner, to calm your body and calm your emotions. The next time you're feeling emotionally out of sorts, take a couple of minutes to do the following exercise:

Exercise 9.1: Deep-breathing technique

- Lie down or sit in a relaxed posture, without crossing your arms and legs. (If necessary this can also be done standing.)
- Close your eyes and keep your face relaxed.
- Pay attention to your breathing. Put your hands on your abdomen and chest, if it helps.
- Keep your mouth closed and breathe through your nose.
- Breathe gently but deeply from your abdomen, so that your diaphragm rises as you inhale and falls as you exhale. As you breathe in, think 'in' silently to yourself, and as you breathe out, think 'out'. Imagine you're blowing away your stresses on the out breath.
- It's important not to hold your breath as you perform this exercise: keep your breathing natural. Don't worry if you struggle at first – as you become more relaxed, so will your breathing. As a guideline, try counting to four as you breathe in and up to seven as you breathe out.
- As you observe and feel each breath, notice how it becomes easier to detach from your emotions and worries. Rather than being automatic reactions, you can turn them into conscious choices through your control.
- Do this for a couple of minutes, or as long as you want, making sure to keep your breathing gentle and steady.

This focused breathing technique can also be expanded into a *progressive muscle relaxation* exercise, which gives you a more thorough emotional lift. Visit http://positiveleaderbook.com/musclerelaxationexercise for instructions on how to do this. The activity will require more time – at least 10–30 minutes is the recommended length – so you'll have to make sure you have a free block of uninterrupted time to do it.

MAKE TIME TO ENJOY YOURSELF

This sounds like an obvious one, and in many ways it is. But how often do we really take the time out of our busy schedule to do the things we love? During my coaching sessions with others, I'm appalled at how few hours a week executives will allow themselves to spend on activities that they find enjoyable and emotionally renewing. The fact is 'pleasure' is treated as a luxury rather than something that we should be doing regularly to banish emotional negativity. This seems to be supported by a Direct Line Insurance study from 2013, which surveyed 2000 people on their ideal free time outside of work and compared it to their actual free time. The results found that six hours and 59 minutes was the desired amount of leisure time we need to feel happy and relaxed, but in reality people only tended to get an average of 4 hours 14 minutes as a consequence of being constantly on the go.[9] As far as energy management is concerned our leisure and work activities are inextricably linked, and getting the right work–life balance is essential to our productivity. Quality Leisure time is vital for revitalising ourselves emotionally and re-igniting our passions, both of which boost the enthusiasm and energy we bring to our work.

It's important to give yourself something to look forward to and which you can enjoy doing during your time outside of work. Going on the occasional holiday or weekend break can be a wonderful experience, but these can be few and far between, so think about some other activities or hobbies you'd like to pursue more frequently. Don't just consider pleasurable activities that are immediately gratifying and passive, such as watching television, surfing the web, a visit to the fairground or going shopping; also look for activities that you have to put some effort into, such as gardening, reading non-fiction, cookery classes, playing sport, learning a musical instrument or searching for valuable antiques to add to your collection. The depth or quality of emotional renewal is important, and delayed gratification can often bring stronger feelings of positivity in the longer term for more sustained happiness. Combining both 'pleasure' and 'flow' activities will give you the best of both worlds. Depending on your interests, here are some things you can try:

- music – listening to music, singing or playing an instrument
- gardening

---

[9] Bell, Poorna (2013). 'The official amount of free time you need to be happy'. *The Huffington Post*, 7 June. [Online] Available from: http://www.huffingtonpost.co.uk/2013/06/07/seven-hours-work-life-balance_n_3401624.html

- arts and crafts – drawing, painting, pottery, drama
- reading – fiction and non-fiction books, newspapers or magazines
- cinema, concerts or theatre
- days out – visiting museums, theme parks, art galleries or boat trips
- cooking – trying new recipes, baking or cake decorating
- animals – keeping a pet or visiting farms
- making love
- needlework – knitting, patchwork, embroidery or tapestry
- sport – watching or playing
- classes – dance, yoga or even language learning
- puzzles and games – charades, board games, crosswords, card games, Sudoku or computer games
- friendships – talking, hanging out or doing stuff with friends
- photography – taking photos, editing images or visiting exhibitions
- writing – blogs, stories, letters or poetry.

Exercise 9.2: Haves, shoulds and loves

The busiest amongst you might need to actually stop and think about what it is you'd love to do, as you may have barely given it any thought before. A useful way of identifying this is to draw up a table, distinguishing what you *have* to do in your time outside of work, what you *should* do, and also what you'd *love* to do.

I HAVE TO . . .	I SHOULD . . .	I'D LOVE TO . . .
Go food shopping	Pay a visit to my aunt who I've not seen in ages	Play fun games with my kids one evening
Find a babysitter for next week		Catch up with old friends
Go through my finances and then stop by the bank	Fix that leak in the kitchen	Read that book I've been meaning to
Take the kids to the dentist	Take the car to the garage for a check-up	Watch that TV show everyone's talking about
Take my laptop to be repaired as soon as possible	Buy a new suit and a pair of shoes	Have dinner at that new restaurant that's just opened
	Mow the lawn and tidy up the garden	

Filling in a table like the one above should give you a clearer understanding of what you're doing too much of and what you're not doing enough of. Ideally, there would be some sort of balance between your duties and your pleasurable activities. Are you spending too much of your time and energy in the first two columns and neglecting the last? Well, now that you know exactly what it is you'd enjoy doing, it's time you got into the practice of actually *doing* it. The key is to make these activities a priority and view the time you spend on them as an investment in your emotional wellbeing. Timetable personal events and activities, such as booking an evening to cook a meal for friends or work on a hobby. If it's in the diary, it's more likely to happen. Aim to introduce an enjoyable and emotionally nourishing activity into each day, even if it's as small as watching your favourite TV show with your partner, with no distractions.

MEASURE YOUR MOODS

Every leader has heard this classic business rule: 'If you can't measure it, you can't manage it.' In some ways, this holds true for your emotions as well. If you don't measure how you feel on a regular basis, you won't have the data you need to take better control of your emotional energy. Without data to raise your awareness, you'll be less empowered to balance your emotions and adapt your mood in ways that positively influence your life and performance. Using a *mood chart* can be extremely valuable in tracking your up and down moments, as well as clarifying the things in your life that emotionally energise or de-energise you. A mood is effectively 'how you feel', and by recording how you feel on a regular basis, you can determine when and whether you need to change it. Over time, you can use your mood chart to read the warning signs and predict an oncoming period of stress. That way you can then step in with intervention strategies to prevent yourself losing your emotional equilibrium.

Exercise 9.3: Mood chart

Create your own self-reflection mood chart using the example below as a guideline.[10] Fill the left-hand column with the activities that are most important in determining your emotional wellbeing. Feel free to add as

---

[10] Adapted from the 'peace of mind' chart featured in: Owen, Jo (2012). *How to Manage: The Art of Making Things Happen*. Third edition. Harlow: Pearson.

many rows as you deem suitable. For instance, in addition to the items given below, you could include physical environment or working conditions as another area of relevance, or big events such as a merger, project or promotion at work. Score yourself against each item in terms of how good or bad you feel about it. Use a rating scale of 0–10, with 10 being extremely positive/good, 5 being moderate and 0 being extremely negative/bad. I recommend doing this in weekly intervals, as daily assessments can get a bit heavy.

Mood chart

ACTIVITY	RATING							
	WEEK 1	WEEK 2	WEEK 3	WEEK 4	WEEK 5	WEEK 6	WEEK 7	WEEK 8
Eating and drinking	8	9	4	2	4	7	8	9
Exercise	8	8	3	0	3	6	9	7
Amount of sleep	7	8	4	2	3	6	9	8
Progress at work	8	9	7	2	4	5	7	8
Relationships at work	8	6	2	4	3	5	6	8
Relationships at home	7	7	4	3	9	6	9	7
Leisure and hobbies	7	4	2	1	5	7	8	8
Friendships/ social life	6	7	2	2	8	8	7	8
Skill development/ education	7	5	3	4	6	7	5	8
Overall	66	63	31	20	45	57	68	71

Each time you complete your mood chart, you're effectively giving yourself an emotional check-up. Become your own observer over the course of three months and see what your moods have to tell you. If you're a bit of a technophile, mood tracking apps like MoodPanda.com can also help you with this process.

As in the example above, you might notice that when you're struggling with heavy challenges and stressors at work, relationships with your bosses or colleagues may come into conflict, and even your personal life feels the strain. It's easy to let your physical sources of energy go to pot when this happens, but these are precisely the times when you need to take better care of yourself and reach for family or social support. Or you might find it works the other way around. For example, you may detect that eating a poor diet and getting less than four hours' sleep for a few nights on the trot gives you a tendency to become extremely irritable and this proves to be an early sign of issues spiralling at work.

It's helpful to remember that a negative feeling is just your mood talking, and that you can change the message when you take steps to manage your emotions.[11] Spending a minute or two thinking about the things you're grateful for can serve to lift your mood considerably. Gratitude puts moments of negativity into perspective. The issues or problems that lower our mood pale into insignificance against the many blessings that fill our lives and give us reason to be content. Gratitude isn't the only answer, however. You have the power to change your mood in whichever way works for you. You might find that breathing and relaxation techniques do the trick of chilling you out or that hobbies and friendships help to shift your mood. It could be that a simple programme of regular exercise, healthy eating and getting enough sleep is enough to stabilise you, or that a more fundamental reorganisation of your life is necessary. Keeping a comprehensive mood diary, positive affirmations, meditation or the advice of a coach or mentor are other great options for your personal advancement. Anything goes, as long as it works to improve your emotional health.

Mental strategy

As you can probably guess, mental energy relates to your mind and intellectual focus – your ability to concentrate, analyse, learn and be creative. Thinking consumes a great deal of energy. The brain represents just 2 per cent of the body's weight, but accounts for 20 per cent of the body's oxygen consumption

[11] Miller, Liz (2009). *Mood Mapping: Plot Your Way to Emotional Health and Happiness*. London: Pan Macmillan.

and 25 per cent of its glucose utilisation.[12] Activities like planning, brainstorming, report writing and problem solving can wear our minds out rapidly. Yet despite this, we seldom take the time to mentally recharge ourselves. Concentration is like a muscle – it needs to rest for a while after periods of high stress (exertion), or else it becomes weak. The consequences of not getting enough mental downtime include increased mistakes, bad judgement, poor decision making, lower creativity and inefficient consolidation of information.

The one major thing that trips us up on a mental level is a lack of prioritisation. To perform at our best, we need to *focus, focus and focus* some more. Certain mental practices, such as good organisation/planning and mindfulness, help to build our 'mental muscles' so we can direct our energy more productively. And by removing distractions and saying 'no' to extra unnecessary demands, we can avoid overloading our minds to the point of destruction. Here are some simple, powerful strategies that will help you tune out energy-draining disruptions and inject a sharper focus to your work.

MINDFULNESS AND MEDITATION

When you're combating work overload, your ability to be present in the moment and control your thinking is diminished. Mindfulness and meditation practices help you take back that ability, and to better appreciate and enjoy your experiences as they occur. *Mindfulness* simply means to be present.[13] It's the ability to be aware of what's going on both inside you and around you. The idea with mindfulness is to become fully engaged in the moment – to really 'live' the experience without analysing it, mulling over the past or worrying about the future. After all, you can only influence the here and now. You can't do anything about the past and the future is still out of your hands. Most of us are so caught up with the jumble of thoughts, worries, agendas, judgements and arguments that crowd our minds that we fail to notice things around us or savour what we are doing. For instance, while you've been reading this book, has your mind wandered off elsewhere? To thinking about what's for dinner or the state of your latest project, for example? At work, we 'mindlessly' go through the motions rather than really connecting with our

[12] Magistretti, Pierre J., Pellerin, Luc and Martin, Jean-Luc (1995). 'Brain energy metabolism: An integrated cellular perspective'. In: Floyd E. Bloom and David J. Kupfer (Eds). *Psychopharmacology: The Fourth Generation of Progress*. New York: Raven Press, pp. 657–670.
[13] Puddicome, Andy (2011). *Get Some Headspace: 10 Minutes Can Make All the Difference*. London: Hodder & Stoughton.

actions and the sensations we are feeling. Mindfulness teaches us how to step back and quieten the mind, freeing it from its usual chaos of chattering thoughts. We can then direct our attention wherever we choose, responding thoughtfully rather than reactively to what's going on around us.

While you should aim to become more mindful in everyday situations, introducing short pockets of time in your schedule to practise mindfulness can be incredibly beneficial in making it a habit. That's where meditation comes in. Meditation is the oldest technique known to man (and woman!) for producing a state of inner calm and relaxation, and provides you with the optimum conditions for practising mindfulness. It's a way of focusing the mind (on breathing, on an object, a mantra or what is happening in the moment) and stopping it from chasing anxious or unhelpful thoughts. Major companies like Microsoft, Aetna, Intel and General Mills have introduced widespread programmes to foster mindfulness and meditation amongst their workers. Those that have incorporated mindfulness as a leadership practice, such as Intel, are seeing some very positive outcomes. A survey of the Intel employees who participated in the programme found that average stress levels had decreased, while general happiness had increased. Moreover, the respondents reported that it had a positive effect on their mental capabilities, such as their ability to focus, creativity, innovation and level of engagement.[14] With these kinds of results, it's no surprise that mindfulness is one of the hottest topics in the world of business right now.

How can we practise mindfulness?

Many people find it useful to practise mindfulness in combination with meditation or relaxation exercises because of the inner stillness they generate. Putting your body at ease and focusing on your breathing is a useful starting-point for becoming aware of the present moment. However, it's by no means the only way. You can be mindful when you're sitting down in a peaceful place, going for a walk in a park or a quiet street, having a soothing hot bath, eating lunch, driving or when stroking a pet. It helps to find an environment that's tranquil, and in which you're not likely to be disturbed (which means keeping phones at bay). Clear your head of intrusive thoughts and allow your senses to stimulate you – focus on what you can see, feel, smell, hear and taste.

[14] Schaufenbuel, Kimberly (2014). 'Bringing mindfulness to the workplace'. *UNC Kenan-Flagler Business School*. [Online] Available from: http://www.kenan-flagler.unc.edu/~/media/Files/documents/executive-development/unc-white-paper-bringing-mindfulness-to-the-workplace_final.pdf

Once you're in this heightened state of awareness, try thinking about possible solutions for work-related problems or ideas you could develop. You'll be pleasantly surprised by the creativity and insightfulness you can gain from tuning out in this way.

Exercise 9.4: Daily mindfulness

To become more mindful in your everyday life, choose to do one simple activity mindfully each day. Pick something mundane and uncomplicated from your morning routine such as getting dressed or brushing your teeth. Or opt to be more mindful while doing a domestic chore like washing the dishes, making the bed or ironing clothes. Focus all your attention on the task and register how you're feeling and what you're experiencing as you do it. Use all your senses to really appreciate the moment and make it richer and more engaging. If distracting thoughts or worries pop into your mind, don't hold onto them. Simply imagine them floating away into the distance like helium balloons and turn your awareness back to the task.

Write down some mindfulness exercises to practise over the course of the week:

- During my morning routine, I will practise mindfulness of (e.g. shaving, cleaning teeth, making the bed).
- During the week, I will practise mindfulness of the following chore/s (e.g. ironing clothes, vacuuming).
- During the week, I will practise mindfulness of the following pleasurable activity (e.g. walking in nature, taking a hot bath, eating lunch with friends, cuddling with a loved one).

FOCUS ON THE IMPORTANT

Too much of our time and effort is spent on seemingly 'urgent' activities that aren't very important in the big scheme of things – reacting to phone calls, random email requests, routine chores or people turning up at our door. These deplete our energy, meaning that we have less available to invest in our highest priorities and the vital tasks that will help to advance our mission, such as long-range planning and creative brainstorming. A great way to help you re-think what's most important and prioritise the demands on your to-do list is to use a matrix such as the FranklinCovey Time Matrix, below, and also found in Dr Stephen Covey's *The 7 Habits of Highly Effective People*.[15]

Urgent/Important matrix

	Urgent	**Not urgent**
Important	**Quadrant I** Urgent and important	**Quadrant II** Not urgent and important
Not important	**Quadrant III** Urgent and not important	**Quadrant IV** Not urgent and not important

Source: Covey, S., *The 7 Habits of Highly Effective People* (Simon & Schuster, 2004). Reproduced courtesy of FranklinCovey.

The table above shows the four quadrants that our usual tasks can fall into:

- **Quadrant 1: Urgent and important.** Crises; deadlines; pressing problems; 'firefighting'; some meetings.
- **Quadrant 2: Important and not urgent.** Preparation/planning; relationship building; active recreation; creativity/innovation; personal development.
- **Quadrant 3: Not important and urgent.** Interruptions; low-value phone calls and emails; low-value meetings and reports.
- **Quadrant 4: Not important and not urgent.** Trivia; busy work; timewasters; internet-surfing; junk mail.

Spending too much time on the left side of the table – constantly dealing with urgent tasks, moving from one to the next with barely a pause for breath – can be majorly overwhelming. Some mental stress can be a positive thing, but too

[15] Covey, Stephen R. (2004). *The 7 Habits of Highly Effective People: Powerful Lessons in Personal Change*. London: Simon & Schuster.

much and you'll feel out of control and struggle to perform well on the things that really matter. That's not to say that you should overlook the tasks in Quadrant 1. Items that are important and urgent are clearly the ones that require your most immediate attention, as there could be serious consequences if you don't attend to them. However, the secret to successful mental energy management is to spend the bulk of your time in Quadrant 2, doing your most important 'high-grade' work, even when it's not time-sensitive. Devoting more of your energy to thinking creatively and planning for the future will put you in a better position to achieve excellence. Without adequate attention, you'll find that high-value projects can suddenly end up in Quadrant 1 when a deadline looms or if problems arise due to insufficient planning and preparation. So take steps to avoid that happening by being proactive.

The tasks in Quadrants 3 and 4 are those you should really be looking to cut down or leave off your to-do list. If it's not important then you have to ask yourself whether it's really worth doing. To activities like this, you can apply what I call the *Three Ds*, which are *Delay, Delegate* and *Dismiss*. If a task carries next to no significance, then dismiss it altogether – there should be no room for pointless busy work or excessive web-surfing/game playing in your schedule as these activities steal your concentration. If you like to check social media or browse the internet to let off steam, save it for when you're on a timetabled break. As for those tasks that are urgent but aren't important, you need to get out of the habit of feeling as if you *have* to respond to them immediately. They might appear to be emergencies, but most of the time they're not; they're merely distractions or interruptions. If a task can be done in two minutes or less, then you may as well do it. If not, delay or delegate it instead. Scheduled meetings can be postponed if they interfere with your more important work; those reports that are due in soon can be passed on to someone else; and some interruptions might not be worth your time at all.

Spiritual strategy

Overlook this one at your peril! Spiritual energy is the most powerful of all the four sources of energy and is the force for action in every area of our lives. It drives our motivation, direction, passion and commitment as we journey through life. In describing the spiritual energy domain, we don't define it in a purely religious or metaphysical sense. Instead, it represents our connection to a strong sense of *purpose* and system of *values*, which are necessary ingredients for living an authentic life regardless of our religious beliefs. At a practical level, it's the personal mission that inspires us, brings out our enthusiasm and enables us to achieve full engagement. To maintain our spiritual energy, we must draw upon the things that give us meaning and align with our true conscience and character. Sometimes this means using our strengths and virtues in service of something other than ourselves, subordinating our own needs to raise children, help others or aid a cause. By doing what we believe is right and reconnecting with the values we find most uplifting and profound, we can get huge gains in our energy.

So, balancing and building your spiritual energy involves two major things:

- finding your life purpose and directing your actions towards it
- knowing what your deepest values are and being true to them.

A clear sense of purpose and a healthy value system is a great source of strength, comfort and guidance, especially in times of difficulty or hardship. Indeed, it's possible to find meaning in anguish and trauma, and a strong spiritual energy creates a stable centre in our lives that can make up for a huge lack in our physical, mental and emotional energy reserves. The psychiatrist and holocaust survivor Viktor Frankl talks about how a deep sense of meaning in our lives can get us through even the most horrific of challenges. I highly recommend you read his classic book, *Man's Search for Meaning,* based on his heart-rending experiences in several concentration camps during World War II.[16]

To be vital and completely energised you need to have a spiritual life. Use the following activities to help you reconnect with your goals and dreams for the future, and to assess how well you're living by your values.

VISUALISE YOUR LIFE PURPOSE

A key way to build spiritual 'muscle' is to pursue aims and ambitions that give you a sense of purpose and enjoyment in life. Having dreams, quests or goals about what you want to achieve, who you want to be and how you want to live is what will galvanise you to leap out of bed in the morning. They're a reminder that everything you're doing is worthwhile and has a *reason* – a grander intent – behind it. Clarifying what gives you purpose takes time; it's not

---

[16] Frankl, Viktor E. (1985). *Man's Search for Meaning.* New York: Washington Square Press.

something you can easily skim over. It involves examining your strengths, values and passions in depth and choosing a path that is genuinely important to you.

To put your purpose into action, however, you need to create a vision for how you intend to commit your energy to manifest the life you want. Ideally, this vision needs to be a balanced picture. In other words, it needs to contain the right mix of energy elements – physical, emotional, mental and spiritual – to bring you total engagement and success, not just the financial or material aspects that most people tend to overvalue. The technique of *visualisation* can be advantageous here. There is vast anecdotal and scientific evidence to prove that even the simple act of imagining something can make it more likely to happen. Visualisation is a handy way to envisage the lifestyle you crave unfolding before you. It keeps you on track with your purpose and serves as a source of renewal when you find yourself wandering off course. Famous celebrities such as Arnold Schwarzenegger, Oprah Winfrey, Will Smith and Jim Carrey have all cited visualisation as key to their success.[17]

Visualisation involves using your mental ability to 'envision' or create future happenings or events in your mind. It might sound a bit like daydreaming, and in some ways it is – but it's *purposeful daydreaming*. What you imagine in your head is completely focused, both in the sense that you determine beforehand what you're going to be thinking about and in the fact that you can create the images with remarkably vivid detail. For instance, you could imagine:

- What you are wearing and how you look.
- Your surroundings – what you can see, hear, feel, smell and taste.
- How you are feeling. Are you confident? Comfortable? In your element?
- How you are behaving. Charismatic? Magnetic? Sociable?
- The effect you're having. What's your performance like? Are your goals being achieved?
- How you feel on successful completion of the task/event. What are you most proud of?

The scope of visualisation as a technique for manifesting your dreams and goals is huge. You can use it to 'see' into your future and imagine yourself taking great

---

[17] Williams, Anna (2015). '8 successful people who use the power of visualisation'. *mindbodygreen*, 8 July. [Online] Available from: http://www.mindbodygreen.com/0-20630/8-successful-people-who-use-the-power-of-visualization.html

strides in satisfying your life's purpose. For example, you can visualise achieving big goals in your career – becoming one of the most successful CEOs in the world; launching your brainchild; teaching people; learning medicine; running your own company; gaining a kick-ass promotion; revolutionising your field of work. Or in your personal life – living in a beautiful home; raising a large family; becoming a bestselling author; travelling the world without any financial worries. On a smaller scale, you can use visualisation to accomplish more short-term, specific goals such as ordering your meal in fluent French, completing a half marathon or giving a successful presentation. It's also a great way to create your ideal day. But you must be able to commit to visualising regularly for it to work. As with any new skill, repetition is key. Trying it once or twice then giving up isn't going to get you anywhere. Commit to doing a visualisation exercise for five or ten minutes a day for three months and see what happens.

Exercise 9.5: Visualisation technique

- Prepare for the exercise by deciding what you want to visualise about. Which goal are you looking to achieve? What changes are you hoping to create? What are the precise criteria for your success? How do you want to be feeling in the scenario? Knowing these details beforehand helps to bring focus to your image, so your thoughts are less likely to stray from the purpose of the exercise.

- Find somewhere you can relax and put yourself in a comfortable position, preferably sitting in a padded chair or lying down on your bed. Close your eyes and begin to concentrate on your breathing. Breathe gently but deeply from your abdomen, so that your diaphragm rises as you inhale and falls as you exhale. Continue doing this until you feel completely relaxed, dismissing any other thoughts that might intrude into your head (especially negative ones!). Focus only on your breathing.

- Now you're ready to begin visualising. Project yourself into the future, either to a specific event or timeframe – whether one day from now, a year from now or five years ahead. Where are you? What are you wearing? Who are you with? What's the weather like? What can you see, touch, smell, taste and hear? Create the scene in as much detail as you can, making it real and convincing. View everything from your perspective just as you would in reality – don't be tempted to see yourself from outside, like in a movie.

- Put emotions into it. Think about your mood and how you're feeling – remember, this is how you *want* to feel, and not how you're worried you might feel. So be relaxed, confident, cheerful, or however you want to be.

- Watch the scene unfold. Imagine events occurring positively and that you succeed in accomplishing what you want. See yourself behaving the way you'd like to behave, saying what you'd like to say and having a great effect on the people around you. Try and put as much detail into it as you can, anything from small snippets of conversation you have with others, to your own movements within the scene. Always remain aware of your own feelings and the positive thoughts that enter your head, even to the very last moment. Everything has gone as well as it possibly could. Revel in your success!

- When you've gotten what you need from the exercise and feel spiritually revitalised, it's time to bring it to a close. Slowly count down from five to one as you continue to breathe deeply, and then gently open your eyes. Get up from your position slowly and smoothly. Reflect on your experience, and take a few moments to savour the calmness and contentment that you're feeling. Know that what you want is yours for the taking.

CONNECT TO YOUR VALUES

Your values are your deepest desires for how you want to behave as a human being – towards yourself, other people, the environment and your work. They define what matters to you most in the big picture and give you a code of conduct for living your purpose. There are literally hundreds of values. Some examples would be: respect for others, generosity, fun, wealth, adventure, security, learning, order, excellence. Those that are motivating to you personally will offer a source of spiritual energy that brings integrity, commitment and perseverance to whatever it is you do.

Knowing your values is one thing; living by them is another. To be meaningful and spiritually energising, your values must be reflected in your behaviour and the choices you make every day. Failing to embody your values indicates that you're disconnected from your true purpose and out of alignment with what you stand for. It's vital that you allow yourself to be guided by your values, regardless of whatever external strains or stresses you may be under.

Exercise 9.6: The Bull's Eye – are you living your values?

You can use the 'Bull's Eye' values-clarification exercise, developed by Swedish ACT (Acceptance and Commitment Therapy) therapist Tobias Lundgren, to evaluate how well your energies are aligned with your values. This has been adapted by Dr Russ Harris, a medical practitioner who wrote the bestselling self-help book *The Happiness Trap*.[18]

STEP 1: IDENTIFY YOUR VALUES

First, write down your values in the four primary domains of life – work/education, relationships, personal growth/health and leisure. For each area, ask yourself:

- How do you want to be?
- What's important to you? What do you really care about?
- What personal qualities or strengths/skills do you want to cultivate?
- How do you want to enrich or build on your relationships?
- How would you like to 'grow' or develop through addressing issues or problems?

Note: Think in terms of general life directions, not specific goals. Values are like a compass for your behaviour, they cannot be ticked off a list like a goal. For example, wanting to be a loving, supportive and respectful partner is a value and takes ongoing action, whereas wanting to get married is a goal. Being an involved and caring parent is a value, taking your kids to a sports match or Disney Land is a goal. Also, make sure they are your values, not anyone else's!

1. **Work/education:** Paid work, career, apprenticeships, studying/education, skills development. Includes unpaid work such as volunteering or domestic duties.
2. **Relationships:** Most meaningful relationships and bonds in your life, including your partner, children, parents, relatives, friends, co-workers and other social contacts.
3. **Personal growth/health:** Physical, emotional, psychological or spiritual health and wellbeing.

[18] Harris, Russ (2007). *The Happiness Trap: Stop Struggling, Start Living.* Wollombi, NSW: Exisle Publishing.

4. **Leisure:** How you play and relax, including hobbies, creativity, sport and other activities for recreation and entertainment.

STEP 2: PINPOINT HOW FULLY YOU ARE LIVING YOUR VALUES

Next, draw a dartboard and divide it into four quarters, with several concentric rings, like the one shown below (or print out a template from the web). Mark an X in each quarter to represent where you stand today in that domain. For example, an X in the Bull's Eye (centre of the board) means you are living fully by your values in that area of life. An X far from the Bull's Eye (e.g. in the outer circle) indicates that you're falling way short of living by your values in that domain. Since there are four domains, you should mark a total of four Xs on the dartboard.

The Bull's Eye values dartboard

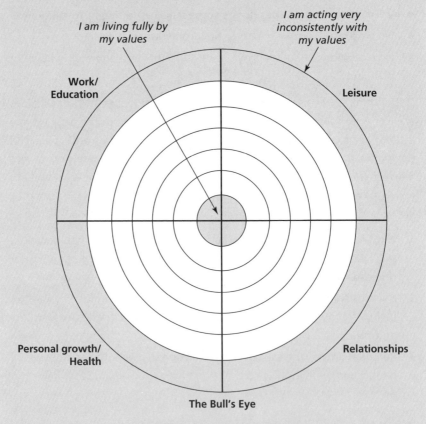

Source: Adapted from Tobias Lundgren's 'Bull's Eye' tool. Sourced by the author from Harris, R., *The Happiness Trap* (Exisle Publishing, 2007).

STEP 3: IDENTIFY BARRIERS AND REASONS FOR NEGLECT

Write down any obstacles that interfere with you being able to live consistently by your values in each of the four domains. What stands in the way of you and the life you want? Which values are you currently neglecting, and why?

STEP 4: MY NEXT STEPS

Think about actions you can take in your daily life that will improve how well you live by your values. What do you want to start or do more of that will help you zero in on the Bull's Eye in each important life area? These actions could relate to behaviours, qualities or skills that you want to develop as a person, or they could be small steps you can take towards a value-based goal. Is there anything you can do to remove obstacles or barriers that you have encountered (from Step 3)? Try to identify at least one or two value-guided actions you are willing to take in each of the four domains.

66-day energy management chart

The suggestions and exercises in this chapter all have the potential to improve your health and wellbeing, but ultimately it's up to you to decide which you'll introduce into your day-to-day life. Even if you can't do all of them, I'd recommend that you make a serious effort in at least one area from each of the four energy strategies. Remember: you're not expected to jump into the deep end straight away. If you're new to a particular endeavour, start off slowly and work on improving it over time. With that in mind, let me introduce the 66-day energy management chart. By recording your daily actions, you can track your progress over a 66-day period, all the while taking concrete steps to use and renew your energy at the right times and in the right ways.

WHY 66 DAYS?

Well, although it's commonly thought that it takes an average of 21–28 days to form a new habit, research by Phillippa Lally and colleagues at University College London indicates that it takes around 66 days for a habit to be truly ingrained into your brain.[19] While this longer statistic might seem discouraging, the good news is that it isn't affected if you slip up on the odd occasion, so it's worth persevering until you get the hang of a habit.

The tables below cover the first seven days of the 66-day period for each strategy and can be downloaded from http://positiveleaderbook.com/energymanagement/ What activities you choose to focus on and how much detail you record in the chart, is entirely up to you – the example provided for each of the four strategies is merely a guideline. Good luck!

Physical strategy

	EXERCISE	DIET (POSITIVES)	DIET (NEGATIVES)	SLEEP RITUAL	AMOUNT OF SLEEP
Example	ten-minute jog; five-minute brisk walk	Brown rice; oatmeal; tuna steak	Chocolate bar; crisps; white bread	Reading; writing in journal	six and a half hours
Day 1					
Day 2					
Day 3					
Day 4					
Day 5					
Day 6					
Day 7					

[19] Lally, Phillipa, van Jaarsfeld, Cornelia H. M., Potts, Henry W. W. and Wardle, Jane (2010). 'How are habits formed: Modelling habit formation in the real world'. *European Journal of Social Psychology*, October, *40*(6), pp. 998–1009.

Emotional strategy

	BREATHING/ RELAXATION	ENJOYABLE ACTIVITY	REFLECT ON CURRENT MOOD
Example	Five minutes of deep breathing	Listened to my favourite music	Anxious about new assignment at work; irritated by colleague's behaviour Positive affirmations: I embrace responsibility and challenge. I am in control of my emotions
Day 1			
Day 2			
Day 3			
Day 4			
Day 5			
Day 6			
Day 7			

Mental strategy

	MINDFULNESS ACTIVITY	IMPORTANT AND URGENT TASKS ACHIEVED	IMPORTANT NOT URGENT TASKS ACHIEVED
Example	Ten minutes in the park during lunch hour	Finished PowerPoint for tomorrow's presentation; re-evaluated project budget	Brainstormed ideas for future project; one-on-one mentoring with six employees
Day 1			
Day 2			
Day 3			
Day 4			
Day 5			
Day 6			
Day 7			

Spiritual strategy

	VISUALISATION ACTIVITY	ACTIONS TOWARDS BIGGEST GOALS	VALUES-BASED BEHAVIOURS
Example	Five minutes in bed after waking up	Wrote two pages of business leadership book; ran for an hour in preparation for charity marathon	Was kind and respectful towards colleagues; had breakfast at home with family; called best friend on the way home
Day 1			
Day 2			
Day 3			
Day 4			
Day 5			
Day 6			
Day 7			

part four

Success vs happiness – positive place (the 'WHERE')

Pursuing the happiness path

'Success is not the key to happiness. Happiness is the key to success. If you love what you are doing, you will be successful.'

ALBERT SCHWEITZER, GERMAN THEOLOGIAN, PHILOSOPHER AND PHYSICIAN

Leaders are lost. In spite of their achievements and material wealth, many top-level CEOs, entrepreneurs and professionals are floundering because they're not having any fun. It's a common trap. All our lives we work hard to reach the pinnacle of success and buy all the flashy material stuff we think will bring us happiness – supposing that by changing the outward picture of our lives, we can change how we feel inside. We're relying on success to make us happy, but our focus is in the wrong *place*. By pursuing the path to success instead of following our hearts, our existence becomes a tiresome treadmill, never stopping, never ending. If happiness is always on the other side of success, then it's fair to say we'll never get there. Positive psychology tells us that there is another path that we might not have considered; one that leads us to a place where success and happiness can live harmoniously in balance.

If we are so rich, why aren't we happy?

Lots of money, lots of joy ... or so we think. The truth is a little different.

Studies have shown that wealth has a surprisingly low correlation with happiness. In most Western countries and in a growing number of developed nations in the East, we are far richer today than we were in previous generations. Real income has risen over the last half century and we have far more material comforts than ever before – bigger homes, more clothes, better cars, longer holidays – and we live in relative peace and security. But we are no happier for it. Indeed, while levels of material prosperity are on the rise, so are levels of anxiety and depression. On the whole, trends from around the world show that happiness and satisfaction do not improve with greater wealth once countries reach 'middle-income' levels. Here's a round-up of the research:

- According to a 2015 large-scale study of 12,000 participants by scholars from Michigan State University and the University of British Columbia, wealth does not make rich people happier in their daily lives.[1] The researchers found 'no trace of a relationship between income and happiness'. That's to say, people who had higher incomes were not necessarily happier, but they *were* less sad than those in the poorest levels of society. This is in part because a certain level of wealth can make people feel more in control of unexpected or negative events.

- Based on data from a massive survey by Gallup and Healthways in 2008 and 2009, psychologist Daniel Kahneman and economist Angus Deaton report that people's happiness rises progressively with their income up to an earnings level of $75,000 (around

[1] Kushlev, Kostadin, Dunn, Elizabeth W. and Lucas, Richard E. (2015). 'Higher income is associated with less daily sadness but not more daily happiness'. *Social Psychological and Personality Science*, 6(5), pp. 483–489.

£50,000) a year. Above that level, however, increased affluence hardly affects happiness.[2] When people have a lot of money, they can buy a lot more pleasures but they tend to savour positive emotional experiences less. Hence a higher income provides little net benefit for happiness.

- British people are less happy than they were in the 1950s, despite being three times richer. According to an opinion poll by Gfk NOP conducted for BBC television, 52 per cent in Britain said that they were 'very happy' in 1957, compared to 36 per cent in 2005.[3]

- A well-known 1985 study demonstrated that the wealthiest Americans – those listed in the *Forbes* 100 and earning more than $10 million annually – reported levels of personal happiness only slightly greater than those of the average office or blue collar worker.[4]

- According to a 2015 study by researchers at Harvard Business School, the University of Mannheim and Yale University, wealthy individuals – whether worth $1 million or $10 million – are not happier as their wealth increases. They always want more! Rich people report that having three or four times as much money would give them a perfect '10' score on happiness, regardless of how much wealth they already have. From these findings, it would appear that chasing wealth is an ineffective means of gaining wellbeing.[5]

- At the end of the 1990s, the wealthiest nations – the US, Switzerland, Denmark and Germany – revealed comparable levels of happiness to those found in New Zealand and Ireland, even though the latter countries had a significantly lower per-capita income level.[6]

[2] Kahneman, Daniel and Deaton, Angus (2010). 'High income improves evaluation of life but not emotional well-being'. *Proceedings of the National Academy of Sciences of the United States of America (PNAS),* *107*(38), pp. 16489–16493. [Online] Available from: http://www.pnas.org/content/107/38/16489.full

[3] Eastern, Mark (2006). 'Britains' happiness in decline'. *BBC News,* 2 May. [Online] Available from: http://news.bbc.co.uk/1/hi/programmes/happiness_formula/4771908.stm

[4] Diener, Ed, Horwitz, Jeff and Emmons Robert A. (1985). 'Happiness of the very wealthy'. *Social Indicators Research,* *16*, pp. 263–274.

[5] Society for Personality and Social Psychology (2015). 'Can money buy happiness? The relationship between money and well-being'. *EurekaAlert!,* 27 February. [Online] Available from: http://www.eurekalert.org/pub_releases/2015-02/sfpa-cmb021815.php

[6] Allard, Gayle (2003). 'GDP and happiness'. *IE Business School,* 22 November. [Online] Available from: http://focus.ie.edu/es/node/2252

- What about the East? Japan was a very poor country in the 1950s but has since transitioned to become one of the richest industrialised countries. Between 1958 and 1987, real per-capita income increased a staggering five-fold, with car ownership soaring and consumer durables such as TVs and washing machines becoming universal. Despite this unprecedented advance in the level of living, reported life satisfaction and wellbeing remained flat.[7]

The grand takeaway from this bundle of research is that money does not directly buy happiness – but it certainly matters. In very poor nations where poverty is rife, the absence of money can cause abject misery while being rich can bring greater wellbeing and improve life satisfaction. In the United States and most wealthy societies, the very poor are lower in happiness, but once a person has enough to meet their basic necessities and comforts, an excess of money brings little or no happiness.

Where money does play a key role, however, is in bringing you the security and freedom to live life the way you want. Just how big a role it plays remains an open question that has much to do with your particular life situation and perspective. Maslow's 'hierarchy of needs' pyramid (discussed in Chapter 5) can shed some light on this.

Maslow's pyramid

[7] Easterlin, Richard A. (1995). 'Will raising the incomes of all increase the happiness of all?' *Journal of Economic Behavior and Organization*, *27*, pp. 35–47.

Money can take care of your lower level needs by buying you physical comfort in the form of better quality clothing, furniture, appliances, healthy food and any other basic requirements. It can buy you security and peace of mind, and reduces your stress levels by helping you pay off debts and make provisions for the future. It also buys better support to help you handle the demands of daily life and solve problems. For instance, it can pay for health care, child care, house cleaning or for additional services like accountants or coaches. In this sense, money provides a critical buffer so that you can have greater control over your life, especially in times of adversity like illness and divorce. These lower levels of the Maslow pyramid represent your *motivational needs*. Lacking a lot of these things can contribute to unhappiness, so you're motivated to go after them – but having them doesn't necessarily make you any happier.

On the other hand, by helping you acquire more conveniences, money can take a weight off your shoulders so you can spend more time focusing on things that *do* make you happy. It gives you more freedom to work on your high-end *inspirational needs* so you can grow and become more fulfilled as a person. For example, you can travel more or upgrade your skills by paying to study for advanced qualifications. You can afford more leisure time to spend on hobbies or with your family and friends, or even leave your nine-to-five job to start a small business. You can improve your self-esteem and confidence through certain luxuries and better cosmetics. You can take on meaningful tasks in your community, show more generosity to others or give more to charity.

Clearly, it's what you do with the freedom that money brings, more than the money itself that influences your happiness. And that comes down to personal choice and circumstance. If spent wisely, money can enhance your happiness; if not, then it can put a major dent in it. You would do well to focus your spending on areas that will bring you lasting pleasure or have the greatest positive impact on your life. If you're in good health and financially well off, but your family life is suffering, spend your money on nurturing your family relationships to increase contentment. Whether you need to reclaim your time, have more fun experiences or find deeper meaning in your life, it's worth spending to get the returns you want.

The 'honeymoon effect'

I'll never forget how overjoyed I was when I first made it big as a General Manager at Microsoft. My elite position came with some great high-level perks to match. Because I was flying so much (200 flights a year), I was allowed to fly business class the majority of the time. I also got to stay in exclusive hotels and cruise around in taxis instead of buses and trains. I felt fantastic and loved the status and prestige I got from my role. But after a few months, I adapted to 'travelling in style' and it no longer provided the happiness boost that it did the first few times. Nearly everyone has experienced something like this, when they've spent months or years pursuing a promotion, sales target, pay rise or any other kind of accomplishment, only to find that the thrill they get from landing it is short-lived. They think, 'Once I become a partner in the firm, I'll be happy' or 'Once I get that facelift, I'll feel great' but the happiness that results from it is fleeting, so after reaching their goal they raise it again. This is called 'hedonic adaptation'. In other words, once you get the goodies, you quickly become accustomed to having them. The brief buzz that accompanies a raise or windfall wears off and you revert to your base level of happiness. So what do you do? You set your sights on something even better. But when you secure the next possession or achievement, soon enough that becomes old hat too and you want something else, and so on. As you accumulate more and more, your aspirations rise in proportion to the gains, leaving you no happier than before.

Hedonic adaptation

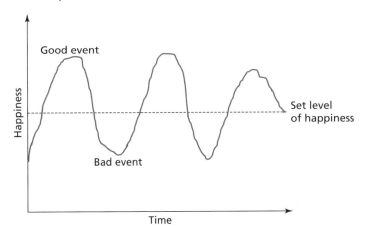

Success vs happiness: which comes first?

Success first, happiness second. Right?

WRONG! Thanks to an abundance of positive psychology research we now know that happiness is a cause of success and achievement, not merely a result. You can have success without being happy, but if you're happy and optimistic to start with, you tend to be more successful in whatever you're doing. In one study, University of California, Berkeley business professor Barry Staw and his colleagues measured the initial level of positive emotions in 272 employees and then followed their job performance over the next 18 months.[8] After controlling for other factors, such as age, gender and intelligence, they found that those who were happier at the outset ended up receiving better performance evaluations, higher pay and more supervisor support later on. Undoubtedly, one of the reasons that happy, satisfied workers are more likely to achieve better job outcomes is that they're more *engaged* and invested in what they're doing.

Our brains are hardwired to function better when we're happy, and so a sunny outlook can give us a chemical edge that helps us come out ahead.[9] To quote happiness expert Shawn Achor, 'Your brain at positive is 31 per cent more productive than your brain at neutral, negative or stressed.' Positive emotions (such as inspiration, awe and gratitude) invigorate our brains by flooding them with dopamine and serotonin. As well as making us feel good, these neurotransmitters help us organise new information, retain it for longer and retrieve it faster later on. As a result, we're geared up for better learning, creativity, analysis and problem solving. Greater flexibility and ingenuity in our mental processing means we can think out-of-the-box and perceive more possibilities, make more accurate judgement calls and find the best solutions to the trickiest problems. In a 2009 University of Toronto study, people were primed to think of positive or negative experiences and then asked to look at a series of pictures.[10] Those who had been put in a negative mood didn't process all the images in the pictures, missing substantial parts of the background, while those put in a good mood saw everything.

---

[8] Staw, Barry M., Sutton, Robert, I. and Pelled, Lisa H. (1994). 'Employee positive emotions and favourable outcomes at the workplace'. *Organization Science*, **5**(1), pp. 51–71.

[9] Achor, Shawn (2010). *The Happiness Advantage: The Seven Principles that Fuel Success and Performance at Work*. New York: Crown Business.

[10] Schmitz, Taylor W., De Rosa, Eve and Anderson, Adam K. (2009) 'Opposing influences of affective state valence on visual cortical encoding'. *The Journal of Neuroscience*, **29**(22), pp. 7199–7207.

We've seen how money, if spent wisely on meaningful goals and activities, can contribute to our happiness, but *happiness also buys money*. Studies suggest that happier people are better at earning more. A 2012 research paper published in the *Proceedings of the National Academy of Sciences of the United States of America (PNAS)* found that adolescents and young adults who report higher life satisfaction or positive affect grow up to earn significantly higher levels of income later in life.[11] Those who experienced a 'very happy' adolescence earned an income about 10 per cent above the average, while those reporting a 'profoundly unhappy' adolescence made about 30 per cent less than the average income. The study also showed that a one-point increase in life satisfaction on a scale of one to five at age 22 translated to $2000 more in later earnings. It's believed that a cheerful, optimistic approach makes people more open to opportunity and new experiences, and they are more willing to take risks and accept challenges, which are predictors of greater earning capability. Having happy people in the workplace also boosts morale and promotes a good working environment, and an employer will want to do all they can to keep such people around, including giving pay rises and promotions.

THE HAPPINESS FORMULA

On becoming president of the American Psychological Association, pioneering professor Martin Seligman turned the attention of psychologists towards exploring happiness instead of human suffering and mental illness. He named this new scientific discipline *positive psychology* and developed a snazzy formula to describe the components that create enduring happiness:

$$H = S + C + V$$

Where:

- H is the degree of happiness we can experience.

This is determined by:

- S – our biological predisposition to be happy, called the 'set point'.
- C – the conditions or circumstances of our lives.
- V – the voluntary actions or choices we make daily (factors under our control).

---

[11] De Neve, Jan-Emmanuel and Oswald, Andrew J. (2012). 'Estimating the influence of life satisfaction and positive affect on later income using sibling fixed effects.' *Proceedings of the National Academy of Sciences of the United States of America (PNAS)*, **109**(49).

If our genetic capacity for happiness – our *set point* – is at a level where it takes very little to make us happy, then we're extremely lucky. Like the genes inherited for intelligence or weight, our set point is coded into our DNA and governs to a large extent how happy we will be over the course of our lives. It explains why some of us struggle with feeling happy, even if we enjoy many positive external conditions (such as money in the bank or a big house) and have lots of freedom of choice.

Our conditions or life circumstances include factors such as whether we're married or divorced, rich or poor, healthy or unhealthy, attractive or plain, well-educated or poorly educated as well as things we cannot change about ourselves like our sex, race and age. They also include aspects such as where we live, our job, political and cultural factors, climate, social network or religious upbringing. Changed circumstances can sometimes contribute to our happiness but play a less important role than most of us believe. For instance, people who become paraplegic and experience a period of depression often return to their previous levels of happiness within months.

Thankfully, our happiness set-up is not just about nature versus nurture, there is a third aspect that's within our ability to control. Our voluntary activities are the internal factors which we have choice or free will over, such as:

- engaging in activities that use our strengths (more situations of 'flow')
- contributing to a higher purpose
- commitment to good character (being authentic)
- having a positive view of the past
- being optimistic about the future
- feeling pleasure in the present.

The 'V' can be influenced. Essentially, you control how you internalise the past, how you anticipate the future, how you interact with the world and what you decide to keep and discard in your daily life.[12] This is terrific news because it means that all of us can be a great deal happier through what we do and how we think.

Sonja Lyubomirsky and her colleagues attached some percentages to this formula showing that roughly 50 per cent of the variance in happiness can be explained by genetics (the 'S' or set point), 10 per cent by the conditions or

---

[12] Hapacus Team (2010). 'The happiness formula: H = S + C + V'. *Hapacus*, 11 March. [Online] Available from: http://hapacus.com/blog/the-happiness-formula-h-s-c-v/

circumstances in our lives (the 'C') and a healthy 40 per cent that's subject to voluntary influence (the 'V').

What determines happiness?

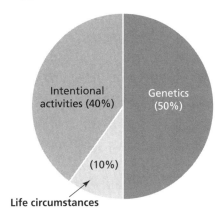

What's interesting is that, even after we take into account our genetic programming (which 'is what it is', as they say), only a teeny tiny 10 per cent of our happiness is influenced by what we face in our lives. Major events such as changing where you live, winning the lottery, becoming disabled, losing a job, getting married/divorced or grieving over the death of a loved one will still only account for 10 per cent of your happiness (or unhappiness). However, your voluntary or intentional activities – what you do and how you think on a daily basis – determine a massive 40 per cent of your happiness. Think about this for a moment – 40 per cent is a big number, and you have control over it.

Before you set out on the happiness path, find out what your starting point is. How happy are you right now?

Exercise 10.1: How happy are you?

The following 'subjective happiness scale' was devised by Sonja Lyubomirsky, a professor of psychology at the University of California, Riverside and widely acclaimed expert on happiness.[13]

---

[13] Lyubomirsky, Sonja (2010). *The How of Happiness: A Practical Guide to Getting the Life You Want.* London: Piatkus.

For each of the following statements and/or questions, please circle the point on the scale that you feel is most appropriate in describing you.

1. In general, I consider myself:

1	2	3	4	5	6	7

Not a very happy person · A very happy person

2. Compared to most of my peers, I consider myself:

1	2	3	4	5	6	7

Less happy · More happy

3. Some people are generally very happy. They enjoy life regardless of what is going on, getting the most out of everything. To what extent does this characterisation describe you?

1	2	3	4	5	6	7

Not at all · A great deal

4. Some people are generally not very happy. Although they are not depressed, they never seem as happy as they might be. To what extent does this characterisation describe you?

1	2	3	4	5	6	7

A great deal · Not at all

HOW TO CALCULATE YOUR HAPPINESS SCORE:

- **Step 1**: Add up your answers for the four questions.
- **Step 2**: Divide the total (from Step 1) by four to get your happiness score.

The average happiness score runs from about 4.5 to 5.5. College students tend to score lower (averaging a bit below 5) than working adults and older, retired people (who both average 5.6). If you're past college age and your happiness score is *lower than 5.6* or so, then you're less happy than the average person. If your score is *greater than 5.6*, then you're happier than the average person. But what's important to remember is that no matter what your general happiness score is, you can become happier.

RUNNING THE RAT RACE

One person who's made leaps and bounds in upgrading our understanding of happiness is Harvard Professor of Positive Psychology Tal Ben-Shahar. In his bestselling book *Happier*, he talks about the *rat race*, which many leaders and professionals in the business world mindlessly participate in – working their socks off in the present for gains they hope will make them happy in the future.[14] The downside of the rat race, as we've seen, is that these gains don't last. However, people seek happiness in different ways and the rat race is just one archetype people can exhibit in the way they live and work. Ben-Shahar created a thought-provoking *Happiness Model* that describes four archetypes in total.

The graph below is divided into four quadrants for the four archetypes: *Rat Race, Hedonism, Nihilism* and *Happiness*. There is also a vertical axis representing *future* benefit or detriment, and a horizontal axis denoting *present* benefit or detriment. Each archetype reflects a different combination of present and future benefit/detriment.

The Happiness Model

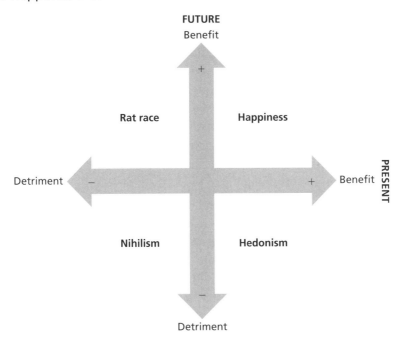

---

[14] Ben-Shahar, Tal (2007). *Happier: Learn the Secrets to Daily Joy and Lasting Fulfillment.* New York: McGraw-Hill.

Looking at the quadrants, the key question to think upon is: *Where do you spend most of your time?*

To help you answer that, let's briefly look at each archetype:

- **Rat Race:** The rat racer lives in the hope of being happy in the future, suffering in the here and now for the purpose of some anticipated gain *(future benefit, present detriment)*. We all know the type. These are the bosses and colleagues who are the first ones in the office and the last to leave, besieged by endless and excessive work. Their eyes are always on the prize, racing towards the next big break or bonus that they think will make them happy, while being unable to enjoy what they're doing in the present. Once they reach their final destination, however, a new venture, project or target almost immediately takes its place, bringing with it added stress and unhappiness. While rat racers may experience brief bursts of satisfaction when they achieve a goal, they rarely allow themselves time to fully enjoy the fruits of their work or appreciate the beauty in each moment. Present happiness is quickly side-lined in order to chase the next goal. This need to feel constantly busy and in control over the future is at the root of much tension and unhappiness in the rat racer's life. You may well have guessed that the reason we see so many rat racers around is that our culture reinforces this belief. If we meet our targets or certain standards on the job, we get a good evaluation at the end of the year and, fingers crossed, a promotion or pay rise. As Ben-Shahar says, 'We are not rewarded for enjoying the journey itself but for the successful *completion* of a journey. Society rewards results, not processes; arrivals, not journeys.' The problem with this is that if we can't get some pleasure out of striving towards our goals, then we're going to be pretty miserable.

- **Hedonism:** At the opposite end of the scale, the hedonist seeks pleasure in the present moment and doesn't give much thought to the potential future consequences of their actions *(present benefit, future detriment)*. It's all about leisure and fun with these guys. They enjoy the good things in life – good wine, good food, good company – and yet they are never truly content or fulfilled in any lasting way. They may flit from job to job or avoid anything remotely like 'hard work' as they lack the direction and forward movement which gives human beings a sense of purpose in life. Although the hedonist's life is fun and easy, filled with joyful distractions, they feel unchallenged and dissatisfied because they never really learn or accomplish anything. We all have a hedonist side that equates effort with pain and doing nothing with pleasure. But genuine happiness is more than just having lots of fun and free time, it involves challenge and the opportunity to learn and grow – through the downs as well as the ups in life.

- **Nihilism:** A Nihilist is someone who has completely lost their lust for life and has given up on ever finding any happiness. Nihilists don't experience any pleasure in the present, nor do they have any sense of purpose or hope for the future *(present detriment, future detriment)*. Under the impression that they aren't in control of their own destiny, they become resigned to the belief that life has no meaning for them and don't expect anything great or enjoyable to happen to them in the future. Stuck in a negative trap of their own making, they feel incapable of doing anything to change their lives for the better. These people are often chained to past disappointments, causing them to lose sight of their goals and give up hope. Positive psychology founder Martin Seligman describes this attachment to past failures as *'learned helplessness'*. If, over the course of your life, you've experienced situations of humiliating defeat, unsatisfying work, loneliness, abuse or loss of control, you gradually learn that there's no escape from the pain and that it's futile even trying to do anything to improve your circumstances. Such thinking leads to despair and helplessness, where people deliberately close their minds to opportunities that could bring potential for happiness. You often see this with older people who resign themselves to their fate, having lost their energy and passion for life. But more and more young people are prone to nihilism due to lack of confidence in themselves and uncertainty about the future.

- **Happiness:** The happy person lives confident in the knowledge that the activities that bring them joy in the here and now will also contribute to a fulfilling future *(present benefit, future benefit)*. They have learned how to set goals that are meaningful, but don't focus exclusively on achieving them at the expense of enjoying today's pleasures at home, at work and in the community. Their job is challenging and rewarding with healthy work hours, so they can still make it home every night for dinner. Not only do they get to work on projects that engage them and bring opportunities to learn new things, they also get a welcome dose of family, fun and leisure time to keep them refreshed while they're on the road to pursuing their dreams. Happiness is therefore a place of balance – where we can enjoy both the end results as well as the process of getting there.

No points for guessing what the ideal archetype is for bringing us closer to happiness (the clue is in the name)! Most modern workplaces reinforce the rat race, and so leaders are often spun dizzy with long office hours, a growing pile of demands, unpaid overtime, stressful commutes, and hardly any free time to spend with friends and loved ones. On and on it goes, so you're unable to really enjoy the benefits of your prosperity and success. Haven't you noticed that there's never a winner in the rat race? Find out if you're stuck on the rat race treadmill with the exercise below.

Exercise 10.2: Are you a 'rat racer'?

As an ambitious or aspiring leader, it can be all too easy to find yourself running the corporate rat race. Look at the questions below and take a good while to reflect on them before giving an honest answer:

- Do you feel a sense of satisfaction with your life at least once a day?
- Do you take time out of the daily grind to chat socially with work colleagues?
- Do you set yourself small targets throughout the week?
- Do you reward yourself for minor successes (by going out for a meal, to the cinema, or socialising with friends, etc.)?
- Do you take time out daily to rest, relax, reflect or meditate?
- Do you engage in pleasurable activities each day (outside of work or maybe even during office hours)?

Ideally, we should be aiming for a lifestyle where we can confidently answer 'yes' to all of these questions. If you answered 'no' to more than one of these, then select the one you think you most need to work on. Try to make a conscious effort over the next week to turn this from a negative into a positive.

DEFINING HAPPINESS

As a former rat racer, my sight was always set on the *destination* (my future success) and I barely noticed all the good things right in front of me and all around me. I wanted to achieve so badly that I was constantly climbing mountain after mountain, and never really took time to enjoy the view. I'm sorry to say I didn't recognise the significance of the *journey* (my present moments of happiness). Future goals are great, but happiness also needs to exist right here, right now – in those moments when you've been inspired by someone, received a kind gesture, got to grips with a niggly task or noticed the beauty of nature.

The hedonist and nihilist archetypes follow a different, but just as faulty, premise as the rat racer. The hedonist believes that only the journey is important, but the nihilist has given up on both the journey and the destination. The thing is, lasting happiness is not a final place or goal (future destination), nor is it one specific mood or single moment in time (present journey); it's both combined. I define *happiness* as:

> *'The overall pleasure you experience while on the path to unlocking your potential.'*

It's important to think of life as an enjoyable journey towards a valuable destination, not a treadmill. How you travel and what you choose to focus on along the way is what makes all the difference in achieving a balance between success and happiness. The path to happiness is easy enough to find if you're willing to get aligned with what makes you unique and gives you meaning – yes, I'm talking about your *personal mission*. It really is time to stop running the rat race and follow your dreams instead.

> *'Happiness is not about making it to the peak of the mountain nor is it about climbing aimlessly around the mountain; happiness is the experience of climbing toward the peak.'*
> Tal Ben-Shahar, Harvard Professor of Positive Psychology

The path to happiness: your personal uniqueness

Do you recall this famous passage from Lewis Carroll's *Alice in Wonderland*?

> *'Would you tell me, please, which way I ought to go from here?'*

> *'That depends a good deal on where you want to get to,' said the Cat.*

'I don't much care where—' said Alice.

'Then it doesn't matter which way you go,' said the Cat.

Like Alice, those of us without a clear purpose can quickly become confused about which path to take in life. Knowing who you are and why you exist drives what you do and where you go. So many people plan their lives or actions without taking time to figure out what their *personal mission* is – what makes them unique and what their ultimate dreams are. Halfway down the path they start to falter because it's obvious that they've gone the wrong way (they're not happy), and it becomes hard to backtrack at that point. Most people keep going and wind up on the rat race, while others take the 'path of least resistance' and focus on the immediate pleasures they can get from the journey. Positive leaders aren't scared to take a different route, to strike out into unmarked territory and make it their own. That's how they find their *happy place*. As prominent positive psychologist Ilona Boniwell remarks, 'To a great extent, wellbeing depends on our ability to choose a direction in life, to form intentions and to make sure we are following a preferred path.'[15]

Purpose is the straightest route to happiness as it fuels your happiness today *and* in the future. Your uniqueness is how you can best make a difference in the world, so it's important to start with that. Engage your strengths, live according to your values and invest in your happiness by doing what you love to do, as well as what you have to do. I believe your *personal mission* is the only true way to find your place in the world (see Chapter 4). Finding the overlap between your strengths, values and passions will help you re-craft your ideas about your life so you can find more meaning in what you do. Guide your co-workers, friends and children to do the same so that you can all live authentically and happily. However, it's unrealistic to expect that you'll enjoy every minute of the process. You might have to study some difficult topics, do unfulfilling work experience, take on unpleasant tasks, or work gruelling hours at times, but if you're aligned to your personal mission you can rest assured that you'll still be on the right track to long-lasting happiness.

SETTING MEANINGFUL GOALS

As we've seen, happiness isn't just about getting to a destination; it's also about enjoying the journey. Goals, of course, are still important, but we need to

---

[15] Boniwell, Ilona (2008). *Positive Psychology in a Nutshell*. Second edition. London: PWBC.

understand that it's not so much the achievement of our goals that makes us happy, but the sense of purpose and direction that they bring to whatever we are doing. If we don't set goals for positive, generative change, we stagnate and stand still – never growing or moving forward. When we know where we're going and that we really want to get there, it's much easier for us to stay on course and remain true to our authentic self. We don't even have to achieve our goals! The mere effort we put into reaching them is enough to strengthen our self-belief and provide a sense of satisfaction. Even if you don't make it into the community orchestra or succeed at the audition for that theatre role, the improvement you'll have made through diligent practice is still something to feel good about. And at least you've enjoyed trying. Anything that's worthwhile in life requires effort and commitment, whether it's learning a profession or raising a child. Setting large, explicit goals can help you make the permanent changes you need to become lastingly happier. Even small goals like reading about a subject that interests you for an hour every day or fitting in 30 minutes of exercise are just as important to wellbeing and happiness. The more our days are filled with activities and experiences that engage our strengths, are congruent with our values and that bring us pleasure, the happier … and more successful, we become. So the upshot of having meaningful goals is that we can make great advancements up 'Success Mountain' while also loving the climb.

When setting goals, remember that you need to keep material/achievement goals in balance with the deeper and more important human goals such as personal growth, meaningful relationships and community involvement. Researchers at the University of Rochester in New York tracked 147 college graduates, evaluating their goals/achievements and level of happiness over a period of two years. The results of the study, published in 2009, showed that the individuals who had attained wealth, fame and image goals (i.e. 'American Dream' goals) were less happy than those who had achieved more intrinsic goals such as helping in the community, personal development and enduring relationships. Why is that? According to one of the students: 'The whole process of being so on the treadmill to wealth, fame and image leaves me feeling like a pawn or puppet in life.' These students missed out on the things that are really important. On the other hand, the students who focused on intrinsic goals 'showed substantial increases in life satisfaction, well-being and happiness areas'. When you focus on what really matters to you and how you can benefit others around you, your life takes on new meaning and everything works out for the best. Forget the 'American Dream' and go after your own personal dream instead, where you can live with purpose instead of feeling like a puppet.

Tips for setting meaningful goals

Here are some positive ways to frame your goals for becoming your best and achieving meaningful success:

- Set positive goals that help you move closer to what you want as opposed to negative goals for avoiding what you don't want. If any of your goals are avoidance goals (doing less of something bad), e.g. 'I don't want to work in an office environment anymore. I'm fed up of designing leaflets on a computer', turn them around into approach goals (doing more of something good), e.g. 'I want to work outdoors more often and utilise my creative photography skills.' Ask yourself: What positive outcome am I seeking for this area of my life (business/career, family and friends, fun and hobbies, health, physical environment, finances, personal growth, spiritual/contribution, etc.)? Conjure up positive images by thinking about all the benefits you hope to gain by achieving this goal (for yourself, your family, your business, your community, society as a whole). How will your life be better?

- Be specific about what you want. Otherwise, how will you know you have achieved it? If you want to do well in your exams, state exactly what you mean by this, e.g. 'My goal is to pass my exams this summer with distinction.' If you want a better job, what would that entail? More fun, more freedom, meeting more people, more money (how much?), more opportunities to learn? Use simple language such as 'My goal is to …' or 'I will …' Or 'I want …'. Make a personal pledge to achieve your goal by a certain date. Research by the Massachusetts Institute of Technology and INSEAD business school in 2002 found that *self-imposed* deadlines can buck us up to get tasks done and are a practical strategy for curbing procrastination.[16] So create a realistic target date for your goal – and stick to it.

- What's in it for me? If you're assigned a goal or task by someone else (your company, boss), look for a 'personal why' in connection to it.[17] Finding a way to link the assigned task to things that matter to you will engage your intrinsic motivation and give the request greater

---

[16] Ariely, Dan and Wertenbroch, Klaus (2002). 'Procrastination, deadlines and performance: Self-control by precommitment'. *Psychological Science*, *13*(3), pp. 219–224.
[17] Webb, Caroline (2016). *How to Have a Good Day: Think Bigger, Feel Better and Transform Your Working Life*. London: Macmillan.

pulling power. Ask yourself: What bigger vision of mine does this task connect to? What would achieving this goal do for me? Will this task help me build my strengths? How does this request support values that are important to me? How would working towards this goal make me a better person?

- Break down ambitious goals into bite-sized chunks. For instance, having 'Write a proposal' as a goal can feel too big for any progress to be made quickly as the specific actions are unclear. But if you break it down into smaller, more doable goals it's much easier to get things done as you focus on scratching each item off your to-do list one by one. For instance, you can split the larger goal of 'Write a proposal' into, 'Gather background research', 'Prepare a rough outline', 'Write introduction', and so on. At each step, ask yourself, 'What's next?' This is how you turn those big goals into the actions that will lead you where you want to be, step by step. Don't forget to add deadlines for each stage to strengthen your commitment.

Exercise 10.3: Goal setting for happiness

Outline each of your big dream goals using the following format, adapted from an approach devised by David Lawrence Preston, author of *365 Ways to Be Your Own Life Coach*.[18] Download a template at Download a template at http://positiveleaderbook.com/goalsettingforhappiness

1. My goal is:
2. Life area:

    (e.g. business/career, health, family and friends, finances, partner/romance, fun and hobbies, personal growth, physical environment, spiritual/contribution, self-image)

3. Target date:
4. Benefits of achieving the goal:

    (e.g. to yourself, your family, your organisation, your community or society as a whole)

[18] Preston, David Lawrence (2009). *365 Ways to Be Your Own Life Coach*. Second edition. Oxford: How To Books.

5. Action steps:

   (What do you need to do in the coming days, weeks or months to work towards your goal? Include regular and one-time activities. Specify dates and deadlines.)

6. Support/resources needed:

   (e.g. Who can help you? What tools, equipment, knowledge or training might come in handy?)

7. How will I know when I have achieved my goal?

   (What does success look like?)

   I confirm that this is a true description of my goal, and that I am committed to achieving it.

Signature...

Today's date.....................................

Date for review..................................

11

In a better place (strategies for day-to-day happiness)

'Keep your face to the sunshine and you will never see the shadow.'

HELEN KELLER, BLIND AND DEAF AUTHOR, POLITICAL ACTIVIST AND EDUCATOR

Self-leadership is vital in creating a happy and successful life. Being happy requires you to be self-aware and 100 per cent willing to put the science of wellbeing into practice. Knowing your *personal mission* and being guided by it is, of course, one of the greatest shifts you can make in embarking on your journey of authentic happiness. However, it's just as important to realise that the small-scale, intentional activities that you inject into your life each day can be equally as powerful in bringing more direct and immediate boosts in your wellbeing. And by definition they are much easier to put into practice. To this end, I'll be giving you a list of seven proven happiness tools and tips you can draw from to feel good on a day-to-day, week-by-week basis. Here's an overview:

1. Count your blessings (gratitude).
2. Learn the ABCs of optimism.
3. Spread a little kindness.
4. Look forward to a treat.
5. Stop comparing yourself to others.
6. Forgive and let go.
7. Give yourself some quick wins.

Lead yourself to a happier place

After years of coaching people to improve their performance and happiness, I've observed that it's those individuals who take time to identify what works for them that are apt to be most successful in creating satisfaction for themselves. The one-size-fits-all approach can often doom our attempts to be happy, leading us on a fruitless mission to implement programmes and strategies that aren't well suited to our interests or lifestyle. Happiness isn't the same for everyone. What works for one person might be totally incongruous for another, and so we can all benefit from a subjective *strategy-fit* to get the most out of the experience. In many ways this is common sense as we all have unique personalities and strengths that influence our preferences. For instance, an extrovert is more likely to enjoy kindness activities that bring her into regular contact with other people (such as volunteering to assist at charity events or lending someone a listening ear), while an introvert can find moments of happiness through quiet time allocated for gratitude journaling or reading for pleasure. A creative person might prefer painting or dance classes as a happiness-boosting treat in the middle of a busy week, whereas a high-achiever might be inclined to opt for the pub quiz or a competitive sport where they can exercise their need to win. Happiness activities also need to be aligned with our home life and work schedule. A stressed out, time-starved CEO might find it easier to choose activities that don't require blocking out huge chunks of time during the day, such as writing a letter of forgiveness while on her train commute.

Your happiness toolkit

Now it's time to gather the kit you need to lead yourself to a happier place. All the tools suggested in this section are validated by scientific research for their contribution to increasing human happiness. I believe most people can use their gut feeling to determine which activities are the best 'fit' for their personality, mission or circumstances. As you read through the strategies, ask yourself if the activity is something that comes naturally to you. Is it something that you enjoy or that you value? Aim to pick *two or three* strategies to focus your energies on throughout the week and create a plan of action around them. There will be the odd item on the list that isn't your cup of tea. But make sure you're not discounting it for the wrong reasons, like thinking it sounds too corny or trite. Most of these activities might seem sentimental or overly simplistic on the surface, but there's nothing hokey about the science that backs them up, so don't be too embarrassed to give them a try.

Once you're happy with your decision, enter the activities into your daily/ weekly planner to formalise them, and, if possible, try to create rituals around them. This arsenal of tools is far from exclusive, so if none of your closest-matching activities have any appeal, then feel free to substitute them for other strategies that can do the job of lifting your spirits. Perhaps exercise, mindfulness or de-cluttering will be more up your street.

1. COUNT YOUR BLESSINGS (GRATITUDE)

Of all the things you can do to increase the happiness in your life, gratitude is top of the list. If you've had a rough day, it's all too easy to get sucked into a purely negative frame of mind, dwelling on where things went wrong and how they could have been different. Sometimes the best way to pull your mind away from the negativity is to reverse tack and reflect on what you're grateful for. Doing this reminds you to highlight the positive things that happen to you each day and to recognise your good fortune. Even small things like beating the rush-hour traffic, a friendly hello from a stranger, being home in time to bath the kids, listening to birdsong or getting new stationary can put a positive spin on your day.

You can express your gratitude in a multitude of ways. You can give thanks in private, through contemplation or a journal, or share your thankfulness with a loved one. Or you can convey your heartfelt appreciation directly to people whom you've never properly thanked. Your gratitude can be applied to the past (being thankful for positive memories, past blessings or elements of your childhood), the present (not taking things for granted) and the future (having an optimistic and hopeful outlook). Here are some methods for showing your appreciation:

- **'Three good things' (daily method):** A simple way to improve your gratitude is to think of three things that you're grateful for each day. In fact, go one better than just thinking of them and make the effort to write them down in a journal or notepad. It doesn't have to be anything fancy – even a Post-it note or scrap of paper will do. The actual act of translating your thoughts into concrete words has been shown to have many advantages over just leaving them to swim around in your head. It helps you integrate your thoughts and put your experiences into context, deepening their emotional impact. If you've got a smartphone, download a journal or diary app and make use of that. You could even take a picture each day to build up a visual record of your blessings, or just type up your thoughts on the computer. There are no hard and fast rules with this.

  You can reflect on your 'three good things' at any time of day that works best for you, although I find that doing it before bed is a great way to reduce stress and clear my head before I nod off. Sometimes I do it just after I wake up too. Before sleep and right after waking are times when you're nicely relaxed and your brain produces alpha waves, so you're in an optimal state to programme your unconscious. Try to be specific in pinning down why something made you feel appreciative – rather than just writing 'my bed', describe the elements of the situation that inspired gratitude and why it felt good, such as the delightful feeling of climbing under fresh, clean sheets. Perhaps it was the sense of awe you experienced while watching a sunset or the feeling of 'flow' you got while working on a particular project that made you feel happy. As well as the day-to-day stuff, try to record the events that were unexpected or surprising, as these tend to prompt stronger levels of gratitude. Like when you laughed so hard it hurt, found a £20 note on the ground or spotted a rainbow. Challenge yourself to find new things to be grateful for each day.

  Don't worry about what makes it on to your list – it can be anything at all, from freshly baked bread, catching up with an old colleague, putting on new socks or an inspiring article you chanced upon. Savour each gift in your imagination and be aware of the depth of your feeling. Keep this up for three weeks and you'll soon find it becomes a habit. After a while, you may find that you don't have to do it every day as you'll start to appreciate the good things more as they happen.

- **'This week I am grateful for' (weekly method):** If journaling once a day sounds a bit much to you, you might prefer to practise the 'attitude of gratitude' just once a week (e.g. on a Sunday evening). Think back over the events of the past week and write down five things that you felt grateful for – anything from the mundane to the sublime. Do this every week for ten weeks in a row and see how much more content and satisfied you are with your life. Ideas to think of include the *material* (food, car, clothes, house, CD collection, books, gadgets, etc.); *yourself* (your health, body, skills/abilities, e.g. listening, dancing, writing, being a good team player or friend); *other people* (your parents, siblings, friends, partner, extended family, pets, boss, colleagues or a random stranger); situations and experiences (a good day at work or college, an interesting conference, a fun party, a vacation).

While you should recall all the good things that happened to you over the week, don't completely overlook the bad stuff. I know it sounds contrary to a lot of what you've heard about positive think-ing, but chewing over the mistakes you've made or how you got through a negative situation can actually bring forth feelings of grati-tude for the valuable lessons learned. Past experiences of struggle or hardship can be blessings in disguise when you see them as testimony to your ability to surmount obstacles and grow as a person.

- **Say 'thank you':** An immensely powerful way to boost your happiness and nurture your relationship with another person is to write them a 'thank you' letter for the positive difference they've made in your life (as a lover, friend, old teacher, co-worker or family member). Express your appreciation of their influence in an in-depth and heartfelt way. What does this person mean to you? How did they help you? What would you like to say to them? What emotions come up as you reflect on this person? How is your life different because of this person? Try and deliver the letter in person rather than sending it, as this conveys just how much this individual means to you, increasing your closeness and connection. Even better, read it out loud to them. I recommend that you make a habit of sending at least one of these 'gratitude letters' a month.

Exercise 11.1: Three good things

To get you started on practising gratitude, fill in the spaces below to describe three good things that happened to you today or yesterday. For each item, try to reflect on *why* you feel good about it or how it came about.

Good thing 1: _____

Good thing 2: _____

Good thing 3: _____

EXAMPLES

- My husband did the vacuuming today without me having to ask. He's so thoughtful at times.

- Lunch with Ellie and Chris. It was great to catch up with old friends again and laugh about our college days. I'm so glad I made that call.

- My colleague complimented my work on the XYZ project today. It made me feel really proud of the effort I've put in.

- Fantastic boxercise class with Liz. I felt so energised afterwards. Good job she suggested it.

2. LEARN THE ABCS OF OPTIMISM

We've already talked about the 40 per cent influence that you have over your happiness (see Chapter 10); well, you may like to know that cultivating optimism is one of the most important choices you can make to create a happier you. Optimism is simply the ability, or tendency, to focus on positive outcomes – on what can go right instead of what can go wrong. It's the attitude of seeing the glass as half full, not half empty, and truly appreciating it. The half empty is still there, it would be silly to pretend otherwise. But we make our lives more difficult when we focus on the negatives of a situation rather than making the best of it. So instead of thinking that your boss is a nasty person who only dumped a load of work on your desk at the last minute on Friday just to ruin your weekend, it's much more productive to think: 'Wow, I must be doing really well for my boss to trust me with this urgent task instead of giving it to someone else. He must have a lot of confidence in me.' See how much better you feel when you don't let the negatives colour your outlook?

Optimists define themselves by their *strengths and successes*, and so they anticipate good things to happen to them. Pessimists, on the other hand, define themselves by their *weaknesses and failures*, and therefore, don't expect good things to happen to them.[1] If you're not an optimistic person by nature, take heart that anyone can learn to be more optimistic regardless of their natural 'set point'. It's a teachable skill, though it may take time for you to change your pessimistic thinking to be more upbeat and cheerful. According to Martin Seligman, who originally defined the idea of *learned optimism*, the key is to first close down your pessimistic thinking patterns before trying to move your thinking from a negative perspective to a positive one. Often, what we say to ourselves when we face a setback can be completely unwarranted. Just because we failed to get the job we wanted doesn't mean we are unemployable or inadequate. These are merely bad habits of thought. Instead of taking them seriously, we should be arguing against them.[2]

Exercise 11.2: The ABCDE model

Use the ABCDE model (adapted from the earlier ABC model developed by psychologist Albert Ellis) to counteract pessimistic thoughts and feelings and find more positive alternatives. In your journal or on a fresh document, work through the following:

- **A is the Adversity:** The event or situation that triggers a negative emotional response, such as stress or worry. It could be a work crisis, a speech to be given, general job dissatisfaction or chronic lack of confidence.

  For example: 'How will I ever get through this week? It's going to be horrendous. There's no way I'm going to meet any of my deadlines and the standard of my work is suffering because I'm so rushed off my feet. It stresses me out thinking that I have to send out work that could be so much better if only I had more time to spend on it. Aaaaghhh!'

- **B is the Belief:** Your interpretation of the event. List your automatic beliefs or initial reactions to the problem. These are often counterproductive beliefs that cloud up your thinking.

---

[1] Rowan, Sophie (2008). *Happy at Work: Ten Steps to Ultimate Job Satisfaction*. Harlow: Pearson.
[2] Seligman, Martin E. P. (2003). *Authentic Happiness: Using the New Positive Psychology to Realize Your Potential for Lasting Fulfillment*. London: Nicholas Brealey Publishing.

For example: 'I can't cope. There aren't enough hours in the day for me to get on top of anything. I'm going to feel stressed and pressured forever, and never make a success of this job. Other people seem to manage their work just fine, so the problem must be me! I mustn't be good at what I do. My boss will be so angry. He probably thinks I'm making a terrible mess of it all.'

- **C is the Consequence:** How you're likely to behave as a result of the self-limiting/defeating beliefs. What impact is this thought having on your life? You may mentally beat yourself up and start panicking, or put the blame on others. Later on, you might avoid similar situations or be seriously worried if you have to do the same thing again.

For example: 'It's no use. I'm going to give up trying. I'll never get it all done, so there's no point. I'll probably lose those clients because I'm so incapable. I might have to leave my job! I may as well hand in my resignation now before I'm fired. No one ever appreciates what I do anyway, and the work wasn't being allocated fairly, otherwise I wouldn't have had so much on my plate in the first place.'

- **D is for Dispute:** Challenge your unfounded beliefs and distorted thoughts about the event. Most negative beliefs are simply overreactions and can be easily shot down. Use facts and logic to make your arguments convincing, or even play devil's advocate if you need to. Take a step back and ask yourself: Is the situation really as bad as I think? Is there another way to look at this? What would I tell my friend or partner if he/she was in the same scenario?

For example: 'Hold on. Perhaps I'm just trying to do too much here. I never ask for help so maybe I could call on my colleague Abbie for some support just this once. And I could delegate some of the routine things on my to-do list to an intern for the time being. That would take away that crushing, overwhelming feeling and help me concentrate on producing the high quality work our clients have come to expect. In the future, I need to take a good hard look at my priorities and find better ways to cope in these situations. I'll speak to my boss about the problems I'm having and I'm sure he'll help me come up with ideas to resolve them. He probably doesn't even realise what a struggle it's been. Maybe I can scale down on some of my non-priority responsibilities and delegate the stuff I'm not so good at to others in the department, or get some training on how to manage my work–life balance. My work is always well received by the client and feedback from my boss has been pretty good lately, so I need to learn to feel happy with what I've achieved instead of stressing about what I didn't have time to do.'

- **E is for Energy:** The positive energy that occurs when you successfully dispute your negative thoughts and beliefs. Describe how you feel now (e.g. lighter, more energised, motivated, empowered, inspired, relieved).

For example: 'I feel so much more motivated and ready to get organised. With guidance and support, I'm confident that I'll get much better at prioritising and streamlining my work procedures. I just need to get into the habit of delegating part of every project so that I don't crack under the pressure. For now, I'll just take it one step at a time and see things through to completion. Asking for help isn't weak; it's the wise thing to do. I probably won't even remember feeling so stressed a month from now.'

Think about your own life and how it would benefit from this approach. During the next five adverse events you face at work, use this exercise to dispute your unproductive beliefs and help you look at the bright side of the situation. Record it on paper or in your journal. After a few goes, the practice should become more habitual and you can simply go through the process in your head. Eventually, you'll train yourself to see the best in life's events and happenstances, bringing happiness into your present day and giving you a better outlook on what the future has in store.

3. SPREAD A LITTLE KINDNESS

One of my favourite activities for boosting happiness is doing acts of kindness. Any good turn we do for someone else – whether it's helping a neighbour, sharing our skills, volunteering or donating goods – produces endorphins in the brain that give us a pleasure boost, known as a 'helper's high'. Acts of kindness can be direct or anonymous, spontaneous or planned, little or big, and their beneficiaries may not even be aware of them. Sometimes the smallest or most random of gestures can make a big difference, such as giving someone a compliment, making your co-worker a cup of coffee or feeding the parking metre for a stranger. Ideally, the good deeds you choose to do should go beyond the kind things you already do on a regular basis. There are two ways you can go about this. Either:

1. Try and do at least one extra kind act each day for a week and see how you feel. By 'extra' I mean something that you don't already do or that's not part of your routine. Mix it up by picking a different one each day, otherwise you might adapt to it too quickly and it will no longer give you the same happiness lift as it did before.

   OR

2. Pick one day a week (say a Wednesday) and make a point of performing five acts of kindness for different people – all five in one day. Make sure you do them deliberately and consciously.

Now, let's look at some ideas for practising kindness in your workplace and beyond. Below is a table of kind gestures you can draw from to get you started. If you can go for the grander options, then please do but don't forget that the little things can mean a lot too.

Kindness activities

AT WORK	ANYWHERE
Help a colleague with a deadline.	Give up your seat on the bus/train.
Offer someone from the office a lift home.	Walk your neighbour's dog.
Make someone new feel welcome by helping them settle in.	Let someone in front of you in the supermarket queue.
Include people in a work group or meeting, particularly those who are reserved or quiet.	Give food to a homeless person and take time to talk with them.
Tell someone if you notice they're doing a good job.	Donate your old things to charity.
Buy cakes, chocolate or fruit for your colleagues.	Babysit for a harried parent.
Make someone a cup of tea or coffee without being asked.	Give someone a sincere compliment.
Organise a social night out for your team.	Let one car in ahead of you on every journey.
Make the effort to chat with someone you don't normally collaborate with.	Offer your change to someone struggling to find the right amount.

AT WORK	ANYWHERE
Be there for someone who is having a tough time in their personal life.	Give directions to someone who looks lost.
Smile and say hello to the people around you.	Look over someone's taxes.
Get your company involved in local community or charity projects.	Volunteer your time at the hospital, library or a charity shop.
Send a card from the office if someone is out on sick leave.	Help someone move house or carry furniture/large items.
Share a new skill or piece of information with a colleague.	Visit a sick friend, relative or neighbour.
Start a mentoring programme to help others.	Have a conversation with a stranger.
Organise a company charity event.	Pick up litter as you walk.
Support a colleague's career progression/advancement.	Tell someone they mean a lot to you.
Give your heartfelt congratulations to a colleague on a promotion/presentation/ good piece of work/award.	Offer to mow your neighbour's lawn, weed their garden or make household repairs.
Introduce 'kindness' initiatives in your team or company, e.g. a 'be kind to your colleagues day'.	Let someone have your parking spot.
Start a social club and get people from different departments involved.	Offer to help with someone's shopping, cleaning or housework.
Leave a small gift on a co-workers' desk, e.g. a mug or snack.	Tutor a child/friend or help them with homework.
Write a thank you email/note/letter to show your appreciation to someone.	Organise a fundraising event for a cause or charity.
Wish a colleague well when they are going on holiday.	Pay for someone's drinks on the next table in the café.
Hold the lift or door open for a colleague.	Pass on a book you've enjoyed.
Wish your colleague well on their birthday or on other special personal days.	Bake something for a neighbour.
Volunteer to go to the shops on a coffee, sandwich or chocolate run.	Help someone with computer/technical/ car problems.

The options for helping others are unlimited. Once you decide to become a kinder, more giving person, you'll know instinctively what you should do. *Keep a record* of all your lovely acts of kindness. Note down what you did, who for and how it went. You can also write down how you felt after each act and whether you found them easy or difficult. Go on, spread a little kindness!

4. LOOK FORWARD TO A TREAT

Feeling good about the future is great for happiness. When you have something to look forward to (a reward or pleasurable activity), it adds a sense of anticipation to your week and brings positive emotions well before the event actually takes place. In fact, sometimes the happiness in anticipation of the reward is just as great or even greater than the happiness experienced in the moment of the actual reward. This is a phenomenon known as 'rosy prospection'. In a 2010 study, Dutch scientists questioned 974 participants before and after they took a holiday trip and found that the most happiness wasn't experienced during or after the vacation, but *beforehand*.[3] Furthermore, a study conducted by researchers at the University of London in 2005 concluded that subjects who looked forward to future positive experiences or events were more likely to measure higher on a scale of subjective wellbeing.[4]

Everyone should be able to pull out their calendar and see at least a few fun activities or rewards scheduled in the coming days, weeks or months. I recently came across the idea of *nexting*, where you plan the positive events you hope to experience in the near future.[5] According to cognitive scientist Daniel Dennett, the human brain is an 'anticipation machine' that loves to imagine its own future. When you plan fun activities like a meal with friends, a night at the theatre or that outing to the zoo you've been meaning to do for ages, your future seems brighter. If you don't prioritise 'fun time' in your life, you can miss out on much needed opportunities for happiness as a parade of mundane tasks or obligations quickly fill up the space. Through *nexting*, you get to forge your own happiness rather than leaving it to chance, giving you a sense of freedom and control over your life.

Even if you're really strapped for time right now, make the effort to put something in your calendar that you can get excited about when you wake up in the morning. The happiness activities you schedule could last anywhere from a few minutes to a few hours to a whole day, or more if you're planning

---

[3] Nawijn, Jeroen, Marchand, Miquelle A., Veenhoven, Ruut and Vingerhoets, Ad J. (2010). 'Vacationers happier, but most not happier after a holiday'. *Applied Research in Quality of Life*, February, **5**(1), pp. 35–47.

[4] McLeod, Andrew K. and Conway, Clare (2005). 'Well-being and the anticipation of future positive experiences: The role of income, social networks, and planning ability'. *Cognition and Emotion*, **19**(3), pp. 357–374.

[5] Lopez, Shane J. (2013). *Making Hope Happen: Create the Future You Want for Yourself and Others*. New York: Simon & Schuster.

a long vacation. View them as the 'treats' that will keep your life sweet and help pull you through all the things you have to do during the upcoming week or month. Here are some tips for planning your treats:

- Plan for *nice, out-of-routine experiences* such as a spa day with the girls, a fancy lunch with a colleague, watching a live football match, a hike up the mountains or a visit to the farm with the kids. A 2014 study by psychologists at San Francisco State University revealed that spending money on life experiences makes us happier than buying material items, because they create great memories.[6]

- Include some *recurring activities*. For example, a romantic date night with your partner every fortnight, a Tuesday evening playing darts with the lads or a night at the flicks with your children every once in a while. If you need more alone time, block out an hour to write in your journal, take photographs, walk in the park, do some gardening or enjoy a long, hot pampering bath.

- Think about *basic stuff* as well as special events. Take a scenic route to work some days or linger over a chocolate cake and cappuccino during your break. Look forward to your favourite TV programme each week or devote a few hours to reading for pleasure or listening to jazz. Anything you love counts.

5. STOP COMPARING YOURSELF TO OTHERS

There's the rival colleague who got the corner office. The friend who travels to the most exotic places. The neighbour with the biggest, most lavish house on the street, and the guy who always seems to charm the pants off everyone. We can't help but compare ourselves to others in order to figure out how 'successful' we are in life. According to social comparison theory, it's in our nature to measure our social and personal worth by looking at how we stack up against others on popularity, home size, looks, income level, job title, athletic prowess, grades, intelligence or any other yardstick we can think of. Social comparison is fine up to a point as it helps us gain a more accurate depiction of ourselves and our standing in the world. It can even serve a positive purpose as we can be inspired by others to better ourselves and our situation. But if it becomes too

[6] Pchelin, Paulina and Howell, Ryan T. (2014). 'The hidden cost of value-seeking: People do not accurately forecast the economic benefits of experiential purchases'. *The Journal of Positive Psychology*, *9*(4), pp. 322–334.

common a habit it does more harm than good, sucking the joy from our lives and feeding into feelings of inferiority, distress and anxiety. The more social comparisons you make, the more likely you are to observe people who seem to have it better than you (who are cleverer, richer, healthier, prettier/handsomer or more charismatic) and so you can't help but make bad judgements about yourself. These are known as 'upward comparisons' and can lead to dangerously low self-esteem and intense envy, because, like it or not, there's always going to be someone out there who can outdo you on some level. On the other hand, the 'downward comparisons' that we make against those who have it worse than us can – shameful as it is to admit – help us feel better about ourselves.

The explosion of social networking and mass media has brought social comparison to a whole new 'virtual' level. We now have so many more opportunities than ever to compare our lives with those of others (including those we know and those we'll never even get to meet). People generally only showcase the best and brightest side of themselves and their loved ones on social media sites like Facebook and Twitter (such as bragging about their amazing new jobs, perfect children or expensive nights out), so it's easy to fall into the upward comparison trap online. When you see lots of updates about the exciting things people are doing or buying, it makes you feel like your own life is dull and unsuccessful in comparison. It can even turn into an unhealthy obsession where you constantly worry over why you're not performing as well as someone else. Here are four tips to loosen the grip of social comparison, both online and off.

- **Remember your uniqueness.** Your happiness in life depends on being true to yourself. No two people are the same. Your strengths, experiences and successes are entirely unique to you, as is your purpose in this world. They can never be accurately compared to anyone else's. When your satisfaction in life is derived from comparing yourself to others, you relinquish your power over your own happiness. But when you're grounded in who you are, grateful for what you have and proud of what you've achieved, you're less likely to be taken in by comparisons. Research by Sonja Lyubomirsky and colleagues into social comparisons reveals that the happier a person is, the less attention they pay to how others around them are doing.[7] Happy people appear to use their own internal standards and

[7] Lyubomirsky, Sonja (2010). *The How of Happiness: A Practical Guide to Getting the Life You Want.* London: Piatkus.

references to judge themselves rather than being influenced by the performance and successes of others. Just because Billy got a pat on the back from the CEO for his great idea doesn't mean that you're mediocre. Indeed, happy people take pleasure in others' successes and wish them well. If you're feeling envy about a friend's success, draw upon your good fortune in other areas to buffer against it. Reframe your thinking to focus on the pluses of what you have, rather than the minuses. Someone in your social circle might have got a promotion but you still have an incredible family unit that adds richness and support to your life. Another cool tip when you catch yourself going into comparison mode is to start running through your past accomplishments to boost your sense of self-worth and good feeling about what you've done. Revel in your own former successes and take heart that, no matter what anyone else has achieved, you've still played your unique part in the world.

- **Take it easy with social media.** Many of us have become far too dependent on Facebook, Twitter, LinkedIn, Instagram and the like for our connection to the outer world we ignore the impact it has on our own inner world. We're so absorbed that we often forget we're only seeing the carefully crafted public version of other people's lives, not the behind-the-scenes unedited version featuring all the troubles, family squabbles and other difficulties. Our self-esteem doesn't stand a chance against all this seeming perfection. While the solution isn't to log off social media sites forever, it will certainly help to limit the time you spend on them and how you use them. Now I love using Facebook and Twitter. It's great to be able to share what I'm up to with my followers and connect with people across the globe on issues that are close to my heart. But you can have too much of a good thing! I can see the value in taking regular breaks from the constant bombardment of everyone's great news and glamorous lives. I find it's not so much social media itself that causes negative self-judgement, but how you use it. When used wisely and in moderation, it can be an awesome tool for enhancing your relationships, networking for business and shaping your public identity.

- **Re-focus on what really matters.** If you only judge yourself on one dimension (e.g. the flashiness of your car or the size of your bank account), you risk exposing yourself to a serious dose of envy if you ever fall short in that area. Instead of paying attention to what society says is important, re-direct your energy towards what really matters to you – love, family, meaningful challenge and accomplishment, spiritual growth, helping others. The greatest successes in life can't always be measured but they should always be treasured. Often, it's a lack of purpose or direction that leads us to compare ourselves to others, so we need to learn to follow our bliss and devote time to the people and activities that align us with our mission. When you're focused on what's true to your heart, comparisons aren't as compelling a distraction. After all, you've got better things to be getting on with.

- **Don't compete with others, compete with yourself.** If you're going to compare yourself to others, do it in a positive not a competitive way. Use comparison as a tool to show you what you want you in life – to motivate you to move forward rather than paralyse you with jealousy. If we look to others as inspiration rather than a benchmark for self-evaluation, we can learn from them to help structure our goals. Admiring their talents and appreciating what they've achieved can help us see new possibilities for ourselves. It's all about growth. Strive to be the best version of yourself as opposed to getting one up on someone else. By focusing on your own goals for self-improvement, you won't feel so much of a need to look at what others are doing, and you'll be more confident about the contribution you can offer the world. Commit to developing yourself a little more each week. Take care of your energy from all four sources (physical, emotional, mental, spiritual) so you can look your best, act your best, feel your best and do your best. Instead of trying to be as good as or better than others, compare yourself to where *you* were in the past and celebrate all the little advancements you make as you go along.

6. FORGIVE AND LET GO

It's not easy to feel content and satisfied with life when we constantly play over how we were wronged, betrayed, insulted or hurt in the past. The good stuff, like empathy and gratitude, gets crowded out in favour of bad feelings and grievances like righteous anger, hate and hostility. These chip away at our happiness and cloud our present moments. While we may have very good reasons for holding a grudge, it can have direct consequences on our health as ruminating over transgressions is a form of chronic stress. It's associated with obsessive compulsive disorder, depression, anxiety and a host of other physical problems too. Seeking revenge or trying to mentally and physically avoid the situations or people that caused us pain are both strategies that will inevitably backfire on us, depleting our strength and damaging our relationships. The only way to reduce the power of bad events to create resentment is to *foster forgiveness*.

Let's get one thing straight. Forgiveness does *not* mean reconciling with the person who harmed you, nor does it mean condoning or excusing the wrongdoer, i.e. 'letting them off the hook'. You're not obliged to kiss and make up or re-establish any form of relationship with them. When you forgive, you don't have to pretend what happened to you was OK or deny the seriousness of the transgression, nor do you have to forget it. And you certainly don't have to waive the right to seek justice or compensation through legal means.

Psychologists generally define forgiveness as a conscious, deliberate decision to release feelings of resentment or vengeance toward a person or group who has harmed you, regardless of whether they actually deserve your forgiveness.[8] It's about taking back your power and creating a shift in your outlook so that you don't stay stuck in anger, self-pity or despair for years down the line. Perhaps you didn't have the childhood, experiences, advantages, education, appreciation, family, career, friendships or love that you felt you deserved in life. Maybe you've been let down, disappointed, betrayed, or worse, bullied, abandoned or violated. Forgiving doesn't remove the bad memory of the offence, but it does help to lessen the sting and transmutes the bitter feelings into neutral or more productive ones. We might think of forgiveness as a noble and generous act extended to someone who wronged us. But in reality, we are the ones that benefit the most because forgiving sets us free to heal and move forward. It brings us peace and closure so we can leave the suffering behind, and makes us a bigger, better, stronger person. Through forgiveness, we can become the hero in the story instead of the victim.

> 'To forgive is to set a prisoner free and discover that the prisoner was you.'
>
> Louis B. Smedes, Christian author, ethicist and theologian

I'm not saying this is an easy thing to do, because it isn't; and it won't happen in an instant either. True forgiveness is a process that takes courage, time and energy to achieve. Start with small things first, like difficult clients, rude drivers or your partner not helping out with the chores, and work your way up to

---

[8] The Greater Good Science Center. 'Forgiveness'. *University of California, Berkeley*. [Online] Available from: http://greatergood.berkeley.edu/topic/forgiveness/definition

forgiving the big wrongs in your life. If you're ready to make the effort, I recommend the *REACH method* created by Everett Worthington, a pioneer clinical psychologist in the field of forgiveness.[9]

Exercise 11.3: The REACH method for forgiveness

- **Step 1: RECALL the hurt.** It's natural to experience fear or anger when we think of a hurt that we find difficult to forgive. The way to overcome the fear or anger is to recall the event as objectively as possible, while in a relaxed state. Visualise the event while taking deep, slow and calming breaths to keep your emotions steady. Avoid judgement in how you think about the other person, don't see them as evil. And don't wallow in self-pity.

- **Step 2. EMPATHISE with the person who hurt you.** Next, try to understand from the transgressor's point of view why they did what they did. What would they say if challenged to explain? Use your imagination to examine their reasons, context, emotions and experiences and create a plausible story that you can live with. This isn't easy, but it's essential. It's worth remembering that we're all capable of behaving unthinkingly at times and that people who lash out at others are usually in a state of fear, worry or hurt themselves. The more you get in touch with your compassionate side, the less you will want to hold onto the hurt.

- **Step 3: ALTRUISTIC gift of forgiveness.** Forgiveness is an altruistic gift that we offer. Remembering a time when you did something wrong, felt guilty and were forgiven can make it easier for you to forgive others. A gift is given to help another person because it's needed. Just as your victim gave you a gift that you were grateful for, you can offer the gift of forgiveness to someone else for their own good. Give the gift freely and not grudgingly, so you can rise above the hurt and get peace of mind in return.

- **Step 4: COMMIT to forgive (ideally publicly).** Make a conscious commitment to forgive publicly so you don't have a chance to back out later. Put your forgiveness into words. You could write a letter of

---

[9] Worthington, Everett (2001). *Five Steps to Forgiveness: The Art and Science of Forgiving*. New York: Crown.

forgiveness to the offender (you don't have to send it), pen a song or poem, write in your journal, or announce your intention to a trusted friend or group you belong to. These are all 'contracts of forgiveness' that help you work towards letting go of resentment.

- **Step 5: HOLD onto that forgiveness.** This is another tough step, because memories of the hurtful event are bound to surface even after you've forgiven the person who wronged you. But having those memories doesn't mean that your forgiveness isn't genuine. When the memories come, be careful not to dwell on a desire for vengeance or wallow in the hurt they bring. Interrupt any negative thoughts by reminding yourself of the commitment you made to forgive, and read back over the documents you've written. Over time, the memories won't be as emotional or disturbing as they were before you chose to forgive.

Use the same formula to formally and willingly forgive yourself too. Freeing yourself from regrets and guilt can make space for more happiness and bring you personal peace. Make a list of all the things you need to forgive yourself for, such as complaining, judging others, getting angry, worrying, hurting someone through thoughtless actions, self-criticism, blaming others for mistakes, feeling jealous. Tackle each area one by one. And remember that your mistakes don't define you, so cut yourself some slack.

7. GIVE YOURSELF SOME QUICK WINS

By now, you're (hopefully!) clear on what your 'meaningful goals' are and have a well-defined view of your overall direction. That's great. So why does it sometimes feel like you're not getting anywhere? As happiness strategies go, one of the best ways to boost positive emotions and job satisfaction is to make progress in meaningful work. If there's something big you need to achieve, it's clear you won't get there in one go. But there are lots of small steps you can take each day or week to move you forward. Most of us choose to keep ourselves on track by writing a to-do list of some sort, with tasks like these:

- Research an idea/venture.
- Fix that annoying software bug.
- Get the report signed off by my manager.
- Set up meetings with potential investors.
- Get in touch with that former client.

- Practise my sales pitch.
- Make a list of my strengths.
- Put money aside for my new pursuit.
- Email Frank to seek advice on which training course to go for.
- Submit my article for review.

This breaking down of our bigger aspirations into smaller tasks is a great recipe for getting things done. Each time we tick one of these items off our list, our brain's reward system lights up with pleasure and we get a rush of fist-pumping hormones like dopamine. This in turn fuels our motivation and confidence to take further steps and get more 'quick wins'. It also explains why we sometimes add an achievement on to our to-do list *after* we've done it, so we can experience the momentary buzz that comes when we cross it off.

It's good to mix up our quick wins to add spice and variety to our day, but it's worth remembering that some wins are better than others. For instance, cleaning out your desk drawer and filing away papers won't be as gratifying as taking a small action towards the major goals that really matter to you (unless a tidy office is high up there on your chart of meaningful goals!). It might seem trivial to focus so much of your attention on making small changes and improvements, but they will net you huge gains over time. You've probably heard of the *power of the 1 per cent* before. Making a conscious effort to improve something by just 1 per cent each day or week, whether it's your relationship with your co-worker (say 'thank you' once in a while), your self-talk and confidence (reframe that negative thought), your knowledge (read that constructive article) or your fitness (book that exercise class), amounts to remarkable progress over time. Rather than being the slow approach, it's more likely to fast-track your success towards your bigger goals, particularly as the thought of making bold changes in one go usually overwhelms people into inaction rather than taking action. With the power of 1 per cent, you make steady progress towards your goals while also injecting small doses of happiness into each day.

So how can you give yourself the best chance of experiencing meaningful progress during the week? Follow these tips to create quick wins that kick-start your success and keep a happy momentum going:

- **Take stock of where you are.** Evaluate where you're up to in meeting your goals for your career, spirituality, family, growth or finances, etc.

Are you happy with your progress as you look at your interests, strengths, knowledge or desires? What do you need to take action on or take more consistent action on? Maybe you need to work on building your confidence before embarking on a certain step, or perhaps you need more support of some kind to improve your approach, e.g. financial advice on how to save more. Clarify what you really want most right now and move forward on that basis.

- **Jot it down.** Whenever a task or idea comes to mind, put it down on paper (literally or digitally) as soon as possible. Don't waste your brain's working memory by trying to hold it in your head. Whether you use a notepad, an app on your phone or your computer, it's important to capture your thoughts as soon as they occur so you have a visual reminder that you can refer back to. Task management apps like DropTask (www.Droptask.com) are great for this, as not only can you store your ideas on the run but you can pare down, prioritise and categorise them in all sorts of fancy ways later on.

- **Create a circle of influence.** Positive psychologist Shawn Achor recommends a technique called the 'The Zorro Circle' to break down a larger project into manageable steps and help you net more quick wins.[10] Like the training of the masked swordsman, Zorro, the idea is that you must first learn to fight within the confines of a small tight circle drawn around you, before progressing to larger circles. First, pick a goal you wish to accomplish. Then determine a circle of influence, or a step towards that goal, at which you know you can be successful. Once you've mastered that area, expand the circle slowly. Keep expanding outward until you've achieved your goal. For example:

My goal is: Pay off my debts.

First, I will: Make a list of my debts and draw a Zorro Circle around the debt with the smallest balance.

Then, I will: Establish a plan to pay off that debt.

Then, I will: Concentrate on that debt until I've completely paid it off.

Then, I will: Draw a Zorro Circle around my next debt.

---

[10] Achor, Shawn (2010). *The Happiness Advantage: The Seven Principles that Fuel Success and Performance at Work*. New York: Crown Business.

The Zorro Circle

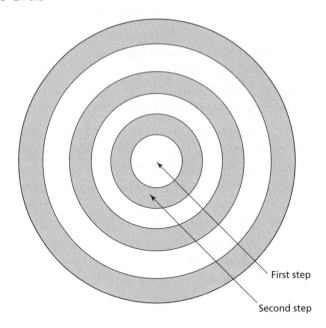

First step

Second step

- **Do it quick – but not too quick.** Allow yourself (and your team) ample time to get stuff done. Progress feels good, but failure doesn't. Consistently setting too-short deadlines will overwhelm the mind, stifle creativity and cause work quality to plunge. Be realistic about what you can do and try to set deadlines that create enough pressure to motivate you, but still allow you the mental freedom to be creative and innovative. If you manage to nail your tasks before deadlines, then the resulting feel-good factor will spur you on to seek out one or two more tasks, fuelling your progress and your happiness.

- **Make it ping.** Make it satisfying to cross off your tasks on your to-do list or workboard, as this motivates you to want to accomplish more and more. Chief Executive of advisory firm Sevenshift Caroline Webb recommends: 'If you're online, give yourself a box to check, and a ping or swoosh to hear. If you're working on paper, give yourself the satisfaction of a big bold line through everything you've done.'[11]

[11] Webb, Caroline (2016). *How to Have a Good Day: Think Bigger, Feel Better and Transform Your Working Life*. London: Macmillan.

Don't you just love that feeling? I consider each item on my list as a small success, even if it's something really simple, like a tweet. This creates a lot of 'high' points in my day that keep me going on to the next task, then the next. You could even set up your own little reward system where you give yourself points for each bit of progress made. As you build up points, you can opt to redeem a certain amount for a short break to relax and bask in how productive you've been.

- **Include 'to-be' tasks as well as 'to-do' ones.** Don't forget to include exercise, rest and other self-care goals alongside the usual work or task-related stuff on your to-do list. By building energy management into your day or week, you're more likely to stay on top of all your heavier tasks and feel better in the process. Block out a bit of 'me-time' to meditate or take a walk so it doesn't get pushed aside in favour of other more pressing demands or routine errands. Or divide your list into two – work and personal. Either way, you'll be making progress in a way that really matters.

- **End on a high note.** Scientists have discovered that remembered happiness has a big impact on our wellbeing. But we don't remember everything that's happened objectively. Instead we're more likely to form biased memories of our experiences. Nobel-prize winning psychologist Daniel Kahneman calls this the 'peak-end rule' whereby we rate an event more by what happens at its *end* than at any prior point.[12] We can use this bias in our favour to boost our overall happiness quotient by engineering peak points at the end of each day/week or when closing a meeting or interaction. For instance, wrap up presentations or discussions by recapping their 'highlights'. This helps to bring the positive stuff back to the front of everyone's mind. At the end of the day or week, take ten minutes or so to review your progress in the work that matters most to you, and honour yourself for each small step. Keep a 'done' list as well as a 'to-do' list and celebrate each little win, even if it's just by giving yourself a mental pat on the back. Software like iDoneThis.com can automate the process by sending you a daily email asking, 'What'd you get done today?' As enlightened playwright Shakespeare says, 'All's well that ends well' – so end on a high note.

---

[12] Kahneman, Daniel (2011). *Thinking, Fast and Slow*. London: Allen Lane.

Your leadership legacy (helping others and social support)

'Being good is good business . . . If you do things well, do them better. Be daring, be first, be different, be just.'
ANITA RODDICK, FOUNDER OF THE BODY SHOP

Being *good* is the bedrock of positive leadership. People want to work for leaders who are, above all, good people. The best leaders understand this and strive to do well by others. They see and approach the world in a way that benefits those around them and focus on conducting themselves in responsible, ethical ways. The 'work all hours, do whatever it takes to get things done' attitude is set to lose its hold as human capital replaces technological efficiency as the primary source of competitive advantage in business. Increasingly, there is a greater call for the kind of leader that demonstrates generosity, contribution, compassion, honesty, appreciation and more; the kind of leader that can be trusted to be of service to his or her organisation, workforce and community. No matter how strong and successful we've become so far, we simply cannot hope to stay great as leaders without doing good. The way I see it, success is based on what we get in life, but true happiness is based on what we give in life. A sense of goodness and contribution helps to build the kind of deep, sustained happiness that inspires us and our followers to do and be our very best.

The 'good' leader: substance, style and service

For the twenty-odd years I've worked in business, I've observed several examples of good and bad leadership approaches. Universally, I've found that a good leader is skilled at three things:

- **Substance:** Doing things they are good at. They are *competent*.
- **Style:** Being a good, authentic person. They have *character*.
- **Service:** Giving for the good of others. They are *caring*.

These three aspects represent three fundamental paths to influence. Most leaders today tend to emphasise their dominance and credentials in the workplace. We all know of leaders who command power through being strong and competent in what they do. These leaders get great results (substance), but they often lack genuine character (style) and disregard the needs of others (service). Some bark out orders, pile on extra tasks or force their already over-strained team to work long hours with scant chance of any recognition or reward. Funnily enough, these leaders tend to be a tad unpopular, eliciting fear rather than trust from their workers. Others isolate themselves in their glittering ivory towers and rarely come out to talk, listen to or simply be around their team. On the other extreme side of the scale, we have those selfless, giving leaders that will do all they can to help others and keep the business on target (service), often to the point of neglecting their own strengths (substance) or coming off 'too soft' with their team (style). Where's the respect in that?

For leaders who want to gain maximum influence with their teams and shine a brighter light of positivity, a balance of all three 'goodness factors' is needed –

substance, style and service. This sounds tricky on the surface, but each of these traits can actually be mutually reinforcing. For instance, knowing and acting on our strengths can help us feel more confident in ourselves and less threatened by others, and consequently we can allow ourselves to be warmer and more open with the people around us. This earns us prestige and helps build stronger connections. Moreover, when we are comfortable in our own skin, we are far more inclined to behave altruistically, sharing of ourselves and our resources to help others feel and be better. Essentially, we become more influential as leaders because others respect *and* like us. Research by leadership consultants Jack Zenger and Joseph Folkman illuminates the value of likeability in leadership. In a study of 51,836 leaders, those who scored high on the Likeability Index were also rated as being highly effective leaders by their direct reports, peers and bosses.[1] Only 27 leaders who were rated in the bottom quartile for likeability were also in the top quartile for overall leadership effectiveness. In other words, there is only a tiny one in 2,000 probability that a leader who is strongly disliked will be considered a good leader. For those opting for a positive approach to leadership, these are likeable odds indeed.

SUBSTANCE (THE DOING OF LEADERSHIP)

At one point or another, every leader has to have something to show for their work. A leader with substance has the ability to get stuff done and get results. They exude competence and strength in whatever they choose to undertake. They have positive action habits, good execution and the tenacity to achieve their goals. The key to having more substance as a leader is to play to your strengths, so the advice to take away here is:

Do more of what you're good at and less of what you're not so good at.

Stop and think about the people in your life that you respect and that have influence over you. How much do they accomplish? Do they have clear strengths? Now compare them to the leaders that you don't admire or that have little sway over you. Do they realise their goals? Are their strengths obvious? Now assess yourself. Do you play to your strengths? Do you set goals for yourself to get better and better at what you do? What you do, how you

---

[1] Zenger, Jack and Folkman, Joseph (2013). 'I'm the boss! Why should I care if you like me?' *Harvard Business Review*, 2 May. [Online] Available from: https://hbr.org/2013/05/im-the-boss-why-should-i-care

do it and what you achieve add to your substance as a leader. If you can spend at least 80 per cent of your time working in your areas of talent and strength, your job will be interesting, fun and fulfilling, and you'll get more things done.

STYLE (THE BEING OF LEADERSHIP)

Those who wish to positively influence others understand that people want to work for someone they believe in, whatever the title on their business card says. Your 'style' as a leader is determined by your character. By this I mean who you are and how you behave, for instance, doing the right thing, being consistent, trusting your team and fessing up to mistakes. Influential leaders not only seek to achieve, they also seek to develop their character and make the most of their gifts as a person to become more authentic. Leaders that lack character might succeed in the short term through sheer authority and performance, but they won't last the long haul unless they make meaningful efforts to be better people. Good creates good – and so leaders who demonstrate positive qualities (such as consistency, integrity, humility, enthusiasm, honesty, vision, confidence, warmth, courage, empathy, optimism, trust, communication and humour) are far more likely to earn the genuine commitment and engagement of their people. Whatever you do, make sure you walk your talk and speak your truth, and you'll be on your way to being the leader you were meant to be.

From enemy to trusted partner

Practical research by bestselling leadership author Jo Owen has shown that *honesty* and *integrity* rank the highest as key criteria in leaders. He reports that a boss who is rated well in these areas, and is there-fore trusted, tends to be rated well on everything else. Bosses who rated poorly on these were damned on all other criteria.[2] Honesty and integrity give birth to TRUST. Before you can have the moral authority to lead others, you have to be able to win their trust. This was a major issue for us at Microsoft with respect to our relationship with the European Union (EU). You could say that after years of legal battles with the European

▶

---

[2] Adapted from: Owen, Jo (2012). *The Leadership Skills Handbook: 50 Essential Skills You Need to Be a Leader*. Second edition. London: Kogan Page.

Commission (EC), our relationship was pretty toxic! Trust was clearly absent as the investigations into our competitive practices dragged on and we appealed to annul the court decision in 2004 and again in 2008 to overturn huge fines. On taking over as Microsoft Chairman of Europe. I knew I had to turn this around in order to inspire cooperation, provide assurance and bring about a mutually agreeable relationship. I set my sights on persuading the leadership team to settle the case rather than continuing to appeal and potentially aggravating the situation. Fortunately, the case was settled to everyone's satisfaction in 2009.

From that moment on, we took steps to build trust with the EU through our different actions, such as investing in data centres in Ireland and the Netherlands, supporting efforts to promote the use of technology and e-skills in education, and even assisting with other non-technology-based projects. Come 2012, I was elected as an advisor for The European Commission High Level Group on Higher Education; notably the only member from the world of business. The turnaround had clearly worked and our relationship with EU institutions was now normalised. We had gone from being an enemy to a trusted and valuable partner.

Remember my 'lessons from tennis' in Chapter 5. It may sound strange, but the philosophies I learned while playing tennis in my youth actually helped me during this period of building a harmonious relationship with the EU. The beauty of these lessons is that they can be applied to life and business in general:

- **Lesson 1:** You are alone in the court as much as you are in your life. Your decisions and reactions are yours completely. Thus, you have freedom of choice in how to respond to the events and happenings in your life.
- **Lesson 2:** You play to the last ball, in tennis and in life. Never give up on your goal.

At Microsoft, we had freedom in how to respond and react to the ongoing legal proceedings. By choosing to settle in 2009 we opened up a more cooperative and productive path for our relationship with the EU. And after that, we didn't give up. Some critics believed that once the case was settled, we wouldn't fulfil our promises. But we did more than keep our word; we used our resources to help the EU with the big issues that were important to them, such as education. We played to the last ball and the relationship went from bad to good, then from good to great.

SERVICE (THE GIVING OF LEADERSHIP)

Last but not least, a good leader sets great store in creating healthy emotional connections with others and making a positive contribution to society. Leaders that prioritise happiness love being of service so they can help others around them become happier too. A leader that's committed to living by values of interpersonal kindness and generosity creates a kind and generous workplace. And a kind and generous workplace is a positive and productive one. It's all about 'being nice' basically. However, being nice only works when you're genuinely concerned about the people who work with you and view them as your equals. Just because you're their 'superior' in rank does not mean they are subordinate to you in value. People are not possessions to be manipulated, boxed, bought and sold. They are beings of unlimited resources and potential and must be treated as such. After all, leaders can only accomplish things through, with, and for others. So it pays to be nice to them. When you really care for others, it shows. Clever gimmicks, tricks or shortcuts can't help you with this one, nor will hiding behind your title. You have to sharpen your empathic powers and unleash your emotional intelligence to full strength.

- Care for and about people. Show interest in who they are and what they do.
- Go out of your way to make a contribution in your local community or the wider world.
- Invest in your team members' physical, mental, emotional and spiritual wellbeing.
- Accept and approve of people – see the good in everyone you come across.
- Become a better citizen by weighing up the consequences of your intended actions or inaction.
- Make heroes of those around you. Appreciate what people do for you and the team.
- Practise giving without recognition. Find a way to contribute to a colleague, client or partner anonymously.
- Maintain responsibility for your teammates.
- Provide support for your team members and offer kindness and compassion when they're struggling.
- Seek win–win arrangements in all dealings and conflicts.

- Build people up. Encourage and help them to accomplish tasks and develop themselves.

- Emphasise the meaningfulness of the work people do.

Researchers at the Rotman School of Management and Duke University, North Carolina, found that kind and congenial people are more likely to be sought out by others in the workplace.[3] When people need help getting a job done, they will opt for 'likeability' over 'ability' in choosing a colleague to assist them, preferring to work with someone who is considerate and cheerful rather than someone who is highly competent but 'not-a-very-nice-person'. Of course, it's important to demonstrate your capability, but if you want to be a leader that people turn to for support, then it helps to show generosity of spirit and be someone who can put people at ease. In other words, you need to give good service as well as have good substance. There's a quote by American novelist Henry James that sums it up nicely: 'Three things in human life are important: The first is to be kind; the second is to be kind; and the third is to be kind.' There you have it.

THE LEADERSHIP APPRAISAL

Exercise 12.1: The leadership appraisal

It's self-assessment time. Being a positive leader means being self-aware, so you need to take a good hard look at how you stand on each of the three core areas of substance, style and service. On a scale of 1–10, how would you rate yourself (the real you) on each of the following statements? The highest possible rating is 10, meaning that you demonstrate that specific quality to a tee. Answer with complete self-honesty. Your scores should reflect the current truth about yourself, i.e. the way you are *now*, not the way you would *like* to be. If you're unsure of your rating, ask those who know you best for their perspective.

---

[3] Casciaro, Tiziana and Lobo, Miguel Sousa (2005). 'Competent jerks, lovable fools, and the formation of social networks'. *Harvard Business Review*, June. [Online] Available from: https://hbr.org/2005/06/competent-jerks-lovable-fools-and-the-formation-of-social-networks

THE LEADERSHIP APPRAISAL	RATING
SUBSTANCE (Doing: Playing to strengths to get things done)	
Determined – a strong will to win, even in challenging times. *I have no difficulty throwing all my energies and strengths into work and sticking to my path.*	
Accomplished – always gets the job done with great results. *I take pride in meeting deadlines and making things happen.*	
Purposeful – sets meaningful goals to drive achievement. *I thrive off big challenges; the greater the vision, the greater the effort.*	
Flexible – excited and enthusiastic when tackling new projects. I take calculated risks and readily adapt to change and the unexpected.	
Growth-seeking – constantly searches out new ways to learn, grow and improve. *I build on my strengths at every opportunity.*	
Total	
STYLE (Being: Demonstrating an upright, authentic character)	
Honest – shows no deceit and takes responsibility for own mistakes. *I tell the full truth, even when it's uncomfortable.*	
Dependable – consistently focuses on doing what's right in any circumstance. *I can be counted on to say what I mean and do what I say.*	
Fair – treats everyone equally, whatever their status, opinions and beliefs. *I strive to be a good person and make fair, considered judgements.*	
Open – receptive to a wide range of ideas and viewpoints. *I listen to feedback and take into account other people's suggestions and input when making decisions.*	
Optimistic – resilient and calm when facing adversity. *I can see beyond temporary setbacks and problems. The glass is always half full, never half empty.*	
Total	
SERVICE (Giving: Looking out for others and making a contribution)	
Altruistic – carries out voluntary work or activities for a good cause. *I make a difference in the community.*	
Social – in touch with the crowd and gets on well with people of all ages and levels equally. *I encourage social connections in the workplace and enjoy getting to know people.*	

THE LEADERSHIP APPRAISAL	RATING
Considerate – shows genuine concern and compassion for others, both inside and outside the organisation. *I care about what people are going through and help others without requiring anything in return.*	
Generous – aware of and sensitive to others' needs and desires. *I make time to learn what people/organisations need from me, and give of my time/energy/resources to help them be successful. Other people benefit from being in my company more than I benefit from being in theirs.*	
Supportive – assists and encourages people instead of pushing and driving them. *I 'coach' rather than 'command'. I make myself available and accessible and give praise and recognition willingly.*	
Total	
TOTAL for all three Ss	

SCORING

- First, add up the five numbers for each section (substance, style and service) and insert your section total in the allocated box on the far right column.

- Then add your three Ss or section totals to get your SSS total and enter it in the final row in the table.

The majority of leaders will score in the mid-range of 70 to 110, with fewer people scoring in the high and low extremes. Where do you fall?

- **Under 70:** It looks like you have a bit of work to do in all three areas in order to achieve a truly positive approach for leading others, especially if you want to influence large groups of people. Do your scores in the three areas indicate a lopsided focus on your part? For instance, are you always getting the job done on time, but running over a lot of people in the process? Concentrate on developing a solid work ethic based on your strengths and explore how you can reveal more of yourself to build a character that's worth following. Become more conscious of your interactions with others to increase your ability to get along with people, and make an effort to help out whenever you can. If you've got a difficult decision to make, aim to think long term and up your 'goodness factor' by opting not to compromise yourself or your business by taking the easy way out.

- **70–110:** It's likely that you're already doing a good job of utilising your strengths to produce results and inspiring others through being respectful, fair and dependable. But are you doing enough? Note which area/s of the appraisal you're strongest at and which area/s might benefit from a bit of extra care and attention. For instance, you might have good character but you won't become great on character alone – emphasise your personality strengths but at the same time work on building quality relationships and task-based skills to produce better results. Lacking in generosity or altruism? Seek out ways to make a difference so that your influence brings about positive change in your workplace and wider community.

- **Over 110:** Very few will ever attain this level of leadership so well done you! As an extraordinarily positive leader with impeccable character, you're capable of large-scale influence, and your kindness is likely to leave a lasting legacy. But even if you have a strong overall score on this test, that doesn't mean you've been taking full advantage of it in the real world. This book gives you all the tools you need to help you grow even further and boost your 'positivity impact', so make the most of it.

Be a giver not a taker

It's time to face the facts. The days of the cold, cunning and performance-obsessed CEO are coming to an end. Reputation and ethics matter more than ever in today's digitally connected world, and people are shunning leaders and organisations that play less than fair in their dealings with workers and customers. In years gone by, leaders were conditioned to leave their human feelings, like kindness and compassion, at the door and be tough as nails in the office so they could win for their organisations. Not anymore. Study after study is proving that leader kindness, generosity and responsible behaviour are strong predictors of team and organisational success. When all's said and done, people want to work for leadership that has a 'soul' and looks out for others. They want their leaders and businesses to contribute value to them while building their empires, not just claim value from them.

No leader is ever neutral. They all 'make a difference' to others, whether positive or negative. I'm sure you can think of bosses in your industry or in other fields who have cut corners or relied on manipulation to get ahead. They may be able to get away with it for a while, but soon enough their immoral behaviour will catch up with them, like the Enron executives whose ethical lapses destroyed the lives and savings of hundreds of thousands of employees and investors. Mud sticks, and those who develop a reputation for underhandedness won't be forgiven easily. Sometimes it's not just about what a leader does, but what they *don't* do. Those leaders who remain unconcerned about others or choose to do nothing are, by their very aloofness or indifference, also making a negative impact on those around them. Positive leaders, on the other hand, focus on leaving a positive legacy behind. They are good citizens who aspire to do the right thing and care about building a better work environment and society for everyone. They give to others and consider the long-term influence of their decisions. Yes, it may take time to build goodwill and trust, but eventually you reap great rewards for your positivity with a reputation that enhances your success. Think about the difference you've made so far with the people in your life and in the wider world. Is it positive or negative?

Being a goody two-shoes is great for business as it sets the tone for the entire organisational culture. Have you ever had a boss or mentor who went out of their way to help you out, even when they had nothing to gain from it? I bet you've remained devoted to that person ever since. Perhaps they even inspired you to help others in the same vein. A fascinating study led by Jonathan Haidt at New York University in 2010 discovered that when leaders were fair and self-sacrificing (i.e. giving of their leisure time, benefits or career for the good of the group), their employees experienced a heightened state of wellbeing called 'elevation'.[4] Consequently, they felt more loyal and committed to their boss and the organisation. Not only that, workers whose leader evoked elation by helping someone were more likely to then do something kind for another team member. So, giving creates a kinder, compassionate environment all around you, where people are inclined to be helpful and friendly towards their co-workers. There's also a performance

[4] Vianello, Michelangelo, Galliani, Elisa Maria and Haidt, Jonathan (2010). 'Elevation at work: The effects of leaders' moral excellence'. *The Journal of Positive Psychology*, September, 5(5), pp. 390–411.

pay-off, as team members who display more citizenship behaviour are more productive and provide improved customer service, both individually and as a group.

Altruistic leaders and teams also enjoy a pretty important benefit themselves – they are happier.

IF YOU WANT TO FEEL GOOD, DO GOOD!

Helping others is not only good for them and a great thing to do; it's fundamental to your own happiness too. Taking the time and trouble to do something altruistic gives you a surge of oxytocin, serotonin and dopamine, all of which spark good feelings within your psychological reward system. A 2015 study by Donald Moynihan and Kohei Enami of the University of Wisconsin-Madison and Thomas DeLeire of Georgetown University found that individuals in their mid-30s who rated helping others in their work as important said they were happier with their life when surveyed again almost 30 years later.[5] Altruism at work can greatly affect the level of meaning in your life, as you have a stronger belief that your work makes a difference. And that gives you something to feel happy about.

The great news is we don't need to make a choice between helping others and helping ourselves. In his studies of what drives people at work, Adam Grant, author of *Give and Take,* has found that self-interest and other-interest are completely independent motivations. You can have both of them at the same time.[6] The happiest and most successful people are actually driven by a hybrid engine of the two. Contributing to other people's happiness brings us meaning and pleasure. However, we shouldn't over-commit ourselves or give up everything for the sake of others. The pursuit of our own happiness should still be a priority. An unhappy person is less likely to feel generous or charitable towards others, and that leads to further unhappiness. Research conducted by Alice Isen and Paula Levin as far back as 1972 reveals that people are more willing to help others and engage in benevolent behaviours when they feel

---

[5] Moynihan, Donald P., DeLeire, Thomas and Enami, Kohei (2015). 'A life worth living: Evidence on the relationship between prosocial values and happiness'. *The American Review of Public Administration,* May, *45*(3), pp. 311–326.

[6] Grant, Adam (2014). *Give and Take: Why Helping Others Drives Our Success.* London: Weidenfield & Nicolson.

good themselves.[7] In a self-reinforcing cycle of virtue and happiness, the more we give, the happier we become, and the happier we become, the more inclined we are to give to others. Giving is clearly a gift that gives back, again and again.

> 'You will discover that you have two hands. One is for helping yourself and the other is for helping others.'
> Audrey Hepburn, iconic British actress and humanitarian

LEAVING A FOOTPRINT

At some point in their careers, most people who serve as leaders will ask themselves, 'How can I make a positive difference?' Often when we reflect on our guiding principles in life and what makes us fulfilled, we find it's not enough to simply take from society; we must contribute something as well.[8] All of us want our lives to be significant in some way and to make the world a better place through our efforts. As leaders, the highest and most enduring gift we can give is the one we leave behind. Positive leadership gives us an opportunity to establish a legacy that we can be proud of and that will never be forgotten. Your legacy will be how much value you added to your organisation and how many lives you improved, at work and beyond.

How can you best make your mark and be a force of good in the world? By liberating your unique strengths and aligning with your personal mission, while also helping others along the way. In doing this, not only will you make the world better for other people, you will make the world better for yourself by boosting your own happiness. Look to Bill Gates for a heartening example of generosity in action. He is super-duper rich, we're talking cosmic proportions, yet he became the happiest he's ever been when he began giving away all his cash. After setting up the Bill & Melinda Gates Foundation with his wife, he began donating the lion's share of his fortune to improving health and education around the globe. In his own words, 'Money has no utility to me beyond a certain point. Its utility is entirely in building an organisation and getting the resources out to the poorest in the world.' Today he is one of the

---

[7] Isen, Alice M. and Levin, Paula F. (1972). Effect of feeling good on helping: Cookies and kindness. *Journal of Personality and Social Psychology*, March, **21**(3), pp. 384–388.

[8] Sanborn, Mark (2006). *You Don't Need a Title to Be a Leader: How Anyone, Anywhere Can Make a Positive Difference*. London: Random House Business Books.

most philanthropic people I know, giving lavishly and selflessly of his time, advice and money to those in real need of it. At the same time, he feeds his own positive energies by pursing a worthy cause he believes in.

At a considerably smaller level, I give of myself in the best way I can too. My calling is to help others unlock their potential and so I offer pro bono advisory services to charities (e.g. PCs Against Barriers) and European government institutions. And I provide opportunities to help give the next generation a great start in life through youth organisations such as AIESEC (international student exchange) and Junior Achievement Young Enterprise Europe. For instance, my speechwriter was always a smart young person from AIESEC, not Microsoft. What I find is that giving – whether in the form of money, ideas or energy – teaches us to look beyond ourselves and reminds us that we are part of a larger community. When we make a contribution that counts, we create stronger connections between people and expand the universe of possibilities, helping to build a better society for everyone.

THREE WAYS TO PLUG INTO PHILANTHROPY

Question: What can you do to help others?

There are many ways to give. Here are some simple charitable ideas for leaders and their teams to put into action:

1. Volunteer

There's a significant correlation between wellbeing and volunteer work. According to a 2012 study by researchers at the National University of Singapore and Duke University, volunteering just *one day* a month can give your life a greater sense of purpose and can make you feel more connected to your community.[9] Dedicating your time as a volunteer helps you broaden your circle of friends and contacts, boosts your self-confidence, makes you healthier, enhances your career skills and provides a fun and easy way to explore your interests and passions – all while doing something good. You might think you're too busy to bother with volunteering right now, but consider this: it's not necessarily the amount of time you give that counts –

---

[9] Son, Joonmo and Wilson, John (2012). 'Volunteer work and hedonic, eudemonic, and social well-being'. *Sociological Forum*, September, *27*(3), pp. 658–681.

what's more important is that you form an *identity* as a volunteer. This means that you have to give back regularly enough to consider the activity part of who you are, which may require only three to four hours of volunteering each month, or perhaps less. Even helping out with the smallest of tasks can make a real difference to the lives of children, adults, animals or organisations in need, and will give you a nice 'warm glow' that keeps your happiness levels topped up.

Where can you find volunteer opportunities?

- Community theatres and arts centres
- Local animal shelters, rescue organisations or wildlife centres
- Libraries and museums
- Elderly care homes and day centres
- Hospitals or health and wellbeing centres
- Children's orphanages or care centres
- Schools and learning centres/tutoring programmes
- Youth organisations, sports teams and after-school programmes
- Historical restorations and national parks
- Service organisations such as Rotary Clubs or Lions Clubs
- Places of worship such as churches, mosques or synagogues
- Environmental or conservation organisations
- The Citizen's Advice Bureau network
- Emergency response organisations, e.g. Police Force, Royal National Lifeboat Institution
- Disabled and Special Needs groups and clubs
- Online databases, e.g. Do-it.org, Reach, TimeBank, Volunteering Matters
- Charity shops/organisations, e.g. customer service, office administration, leaflet distribution, fundraising, driving, public relations and research.

Businesses can and should play a key role in promoting volunteerism; not least because it creates more engaged and fulfilled teams. People who volunteer through their employer are shown to have more positive attitudes towards their organisation and their colleagues. A 2010 study by UnitedHealthcare and VolunteerMatch revealed the following findings:[10]

- 81 per cent of employees say volunteering with their work colleagues strengthens work relationships.
- 76 per cent feel better about their employer because of their involvement in volunteer activities.
- 21 per cent say they would not volunteer if it weren't for the opportunities and direction provided by their employer.

Encourage prosocial behaviour and goodwill in your co-workers by launching a team or company-wide volunteer scheme. Some corporations, such as Unilever and Ben & Jerry's, offer employees paid leave for volunteer work throughout the year as a way to really make it stick. There's plenty of help out there to get you started on your own scheme. Volunteering organisations such as VSO and TimeBank offer a range of options for facilitating employee volunteering, from flexible short-term assignments or personalised long-term programmes to one-off team-building challenges. It's important that you give your teammates a voice in the programme to encourage high participation rates. You could even hold a volunteer fair to raise awareness of what's needed in the local community so they can get a better idea of their options. I recommend designating a lead coordinator to be responsible for spearheading the programme and to act as the main point of contact. This person can take charge of engaging fellow workers and ensuring that company-sponsored volunteering activities are well planned, as well as celebrating the efforts of volunteers to keep spirits high.

2. Spend money on others

One of the easiest ways to give is to donate money. Spending money on other people, called 'prosocial spending', is proven to be a productive means for boosting wellbeing. In one experiment at the University of British Columbia, 46 students were handed an envelope with either $5 or $20 to spend by the end of the day. The ones who were instructed to spend their windfall on others (for instance, by treating a friend to lunch, buying a gift for a family member or donating to charity) were happier at the end of the day than the ones who had been assigned to spend the money on themselves.[11] Another

---

[10] UnitedHealthcare and VolunteerMatch (2010). 'Do Good Live Well Study: Reviewing the benefits of volunteering'. March. [Online] Available from: http://cdn.volunteermatch.org/www/about/UnitedHealthcare_VolunteerMatch_Do_Good_Live_Well_Study.pdf

[11] Dunn, Elizabeth W., Aknin, Lara B. and Norton, Michael I. (2008). 'Spending money on others promotes happiness'. *Science*, March, *319*(5870), pp. 1687–1688.

test tracked how 16 employees spent a profit-sharing bonus of $3,000 to $8,000 at a company based in Boston. The researchers found that those who spent more of their bonus on others registered a higher level of happiness than those who had spent it all on themselves. The size of the bonus itself wasn't a major factor at all. What mattered most was how much of it was spent on others.

Positive leaders can use the power of investing in others to help their team derive more joy at work. Try giving bonuses to your colleagues with one special caveat: they must be spent on prosocial actions towards co-workers or charities. When one team member gives to another, it creates a social connection between them and provides the giving individual with an opportunity for positive self-representation, both of which are great for happiness. Over time, you may find that team interactions improve or that workers opt for gifts that increase shared experiences, maximising the social benefits of a positive and caring work environment. The bonuses don't have to be huge. Google offers a peer bonus plan whereby any employee can nominate another team member to receive a $150 bonus in reward for good work or acts of helping. This might not sound like much given the average salaries at the tech conglomerate, but the mere act of giving the bonus to another rather than spending it personally is what counts in making people feel good.[12] Shopify, IGN and Zappos have similar peer recognition programmes.

Another good way to promote social investment is to set up an internal *employee support programme* where workers can give financial and emotional support to fellow workers in need. Companies like Domino's Pizza and Southwest Airlines offer such programmes, allowing people to donate money to colleagues facing medical or financial emergencies.[13] The act of giving to support programmes strengthens teams' commitment to the organisation and fosters a sense of pride in how they see themselves and the organisation as a whole. People begin to view themselves and their organisation in a more charitable and caring light, which is great news for positive leaders looking to build emotional capital and reinforce the value of giving.

[12] Dunn, Elizabeth and Norton, Michael (2013). 'How money actually buys happiness'. *Harvard Business Review*, 28 June. [Online] Available from: https://hbr.org/2013/06/how-money-actually-buys-happiness/
[13] Grant, Adam, Dutton, Jane E. and Rosso, Brent D. (2008). 'Giving commitment: Employee support programs and the prosocial sensemaking process.' *Academy of Management Journal*, **51**(5), pp. 898–918.

3. Use your strengths and expertise

If you don't have extra money to give, you can always give of your time, expertise or skills. As a leader, opportunities to give will arise pretty much every day and serving in any way you can is admirable. However, you can have a greater impact if you look at the ways you can *best* contribute. Select tasks, charities or committees where you can call on your professional or personal strengths, experience and knowledge to do the most good. List a couple of things that you're good at and translate them into activities you can do for others. For instance, as an experienced and qualified coach, I provide free mentoring services to youth organisations to help young people make the most of their potential. I also draw on my technological background to advise government institutions on how to implement technology in more meaningful ways to benefit society, such as to improve the quality of education and enable more personalised and collaborative learning. What about *your* strengths? If you're a dab hand at graphic design, look into helping non-profit organisations create artwork for their leaflets and publicity materials. Skilled at planning conferences? Then offer your support to organise and coordinate charity fundraising events. If sports is more your thing and you enjoy the company of children, then try coaching at after-school sports clubs.

If time is limited or you can't commit to anything steady, then focus your giving around a simple rule: the *Five-Minute Favour*. All this involves is being willing to do something that will take five minutes or less for *anybody*, without expecting anything in return. Some examples of 'five-minute favours' include:[14]

- using a product and offering honest, constructive criticism
- introducing two people via email, with reference to their mutual interest
- forwarding a link to an article or recommending a book you know an individual would benefit from
- reading a short document and providing helpful and concise feedback
- serving as a reference or writing a testimonial for a person, book, product, or service

[14] Anderson, Kare (2013). 'Pay it forward with the five-minute favor'. *Forbes*, 17 July. [Online] Available from: http://www.forbes.com/sites/kareanderson/2013/07/17/pay-it-forward-with-the-five-minute-favor/#3494ae147733

- sharing, commenting on or retweeting something on Facebook, Twitter, LinkedIn or on other social networks
- posting a note of recommendation/recognition for a person or product on LinkedIn or on other public networks.

Within your organisation, think about starting a *reciprocity ring* where groups of people get together regularly to make meaningful requests and help one another fulfil them.[15] Groups can be any size, although typically they'll be made up of 15–30 members. Each participant in the 'circle' asks for something that will help them in their personal or professional life and group members then make contributions to help meet that request. They can assist by making connections or introductions, using their knowledge, offering resources or giving practical help. By executing the principle of 'pay it forward', new value is created for each individual and for the group as a whole, so in the end, everyone wins. This method was developed by University of Michigan sociologist Wayne Baker and his wife Cheryl at Humax (www.Humaxnetworks. com). Their website contains a suite of tools you can use to deploy the reciprocity ring and cultivate a prosocial environment in your organisation.

Social connections in the workplace

Positive people are social. They want to be around other people and other people want to be around them. Research conducted by Ed Diener and Martin Seligman on 'very happy people' found that being socially connected was the one key characteristic that distinguished them from everyone else. The happiest 10 per cent of the population enjoyed fulfilling romantic relationships, cultivated a rich repertoire of friends (both close and casual) and were involved in group activities.[16] Happy people make great leaders, colleagues, partners and friends because they radiate positive energy, are open to exchanging ideas and show willingness to help others out. Unhappy people, on the other hand, tend to pull away from social situations and contact with others, and they are less willing to contribute ideas in a discussion or offer assistance where needed.

[15] Grant, Adam (2014). *Give and Take: Why Helping Others Drives Our Success*. London: Weidenfield & Nicolson.
[16] Diener, Ed and Seligman, Martin (2002). 'Very happy people'. *Psychological Science*, January, *13*(1), pp. 81–84.

THE POSITIVE IMPACT OF SOCIAL SUPPORT

Social support is crucial for helping us navigate the messy world of work. Many business leaders believe they have to set themselves apart from their team in the workplace and take on the weight of the burden alone. They think that if they rely too much on others, they'll be outdone and lose their hold over the team. But that's not true. No man or woman is an island, and a leader that fails to reach out to others will never be able to hit their full potential. Leadership cannot be a solitary task. Thomas Edison didn't invent the light bulb all on his own, he had a team of 20–30 young assistants helping him. Positive leaders don't see interdependence as a weakness, they see it as a source of strength. When you have a community of companions you can count on at work, you accomplish more because your intellectual, emotional and physical resources are multiplied.

Research shows that the better people feel about their workplace relationships, the better they will perform. For example, a 1996 study of over 350 employees in 60 business units of a financial services company found that the greatest predictor of a team's achievement was how the members felt about one another.[17] This is good news for leaders because, while they may have no control over who is placed on their team in terms of personality, background or aptitude, they can still greatly influence the level of social interaction and rapport within their team. A socially supportive work environment fuels individual engagement and group energy, creativity and focus, motivating people to do their very best. Pret a Manger CEO Clive Schlee puts his company's sales success down to a happy, socially interactive team. In 2013 he revealed that on store visits: 'The first thing I look at is whether staff are touching each other – are they smiling, reacting to each other, happy, engaged? I can almost predict sales on body language alone.'[18]

HOW TO GET SOCIAL AT WORK

Your relationships with others can make your work fun and engaging or they can make it a nightmare. How can you foster more positive and meaningful connections with your boss, your co-workers and amongst your team members?

---

[17] Campion, Michael A., Papper, Ellen M. and Medsker, Gina J. (1996). 'Relations between work team characteristics and effectiveness: A replication and extension'. *Personnel Psychology*, *49*(2), pp. 429–452.
[18] Moore, Peter (2015). 'Pret a Manger – behind the scenes at the "Happy Factory"'. *The Guardian*, 14 April. [Online] Available from: http://www.theguardian.com/small-business-network/2015/apr/14/pret-a-manger-happy-coffee-chain

The SOCIAL model offers a useful approach:

Exercise 12.2: The SOCIAL model

S (SIMILARITIES)

Look for similarities between you and others. In his book *Influence*, Robert Cialdini states that we like people who are similar to us – whether in opinions, personality traits, background or lifestyle.[19] As a leader, you can put people on the path to 'liking' you better using the similarity principle. Start finding ways to connect with those you work with by identifying things you have in common. Did you grow up in the same area or go to the same school? Is there a hobby, interest or sport you both enjoy? Do you like the same kinds of movies or music? Do you share the same ideals? Do you both own dogs? People are remarkably adept at seeing through falseness, so make sure you do this in a genuine way. The more commonalities you identify with your bosses, peers or direct reports, the easier it will be to strengthen your relationships.

O (OPEN APPROACH)

Be open and encourage people to talk to you, especially about any problems they're having. To be a positive leader you must be visible and accessible to your team. People need to feel comfortable approaching you with either good or bad news, and to speak up when they need help. Whether you come across as open or not depends on your everyday behaviour – how you walk into your office each morning, how often you smile, your body language and tone of voice, the number of positive comments you make and your level of enthusiasm. Improve your internal visibility and approachability by keeping your office door open and taking regular strolls around the workplace to check in with the troops, also known as *management by wandering around (MBWA)*. Try and gauge the mood of the physical environment as you look around. Be emotionally alert to how others around you are behaving non-verbally. As you walk about, listen and observe, ask questions, show your gratitude when you see the opportunity, get feedback or ideas, share vital data,

---

[19] Cialdini, Robert B. (2007). *Influence: The Psychology of Persuasion*. New York: Harper Business.

chat about the kids or where you're going on holiday. Have a joke and a laugh. Connect with people. Some leaders are naturally open and have a flair for rapport building. Others have to work at it a bit more. If that's you then start with your self-awareness. In his book, *Before Happiness*, Shawn Achor states that people tend to mirror one another unconsciously, so take a close look at the person you are talking with.[20] Do they seem anxious, disengaged, tired or confused? Then chances are you're not coming across as positive as you should be. Change your own expression, body language and tone of voice and see if the person responds positively to the new script. Demonstrating empathy is a key second step. Show that you can listen to others, consider their perspectives and empathise with them. When you do this, you send a message that there are no barriers between you and open up new avenues for solving problems and working together more closely.

C (COMMUNICATE INTENTIONALLY)

Communication is a core element in all human relationships. It's the glue that holds everything together. Without positive communication, relationships between team members can easily break down. Team development consultant Patrick Lencioni identifies five team dysfunctions that can arise: absence of trust, fear of conflict, lack of commitment, avoidance of accountability and inattention to results.[21] For instance, if people aren't challenging one another in group discussions or having their say about a course or strategy, then it's not a good sign. Dull meetings that lack debate are a strong indicator that people are feeling disengaged or apathetic about the business. Debate is healthy and should be encouraged throughout the team as it can reveal powerful insights to aid your decision making. Sometimes people can become impassioned during debates and this can create conflict, but that's not necessarily a bad thing. Open conflict can actually be productive and critical to team success as it represents an opportunity to examine any underlying issues. It's back-channel conflict that you need to worry about, such as when people reserve their complaints for whispered conversations in the hallway

[20] Achor, Shawn (2013). *Before Happiness: Five Actionable Strategies to Create a Positive Path to Success*. London: Virgin Books.
[21] Lencioni, Patrick (2002). *The Five Dysfunctions of a Team: A Leadership Fable*. San Francisco: Jossey-Bass.

instead of voicing them during meetings. If you want to consistently encourage positive communications within your team and avoid such failures, then it helps to build a process around how you conduct meetings. Follow this systematic approach for more engaged discussions:

1. **Positive priming.** Teams that are positively primed tend to perform better. Start every meeting with a 'positive round-up' to gear your team up for a productive and uplifting discussion. As an idea, ask each participant to share one good thing that happened to them recently at work or in their personal life. What do they have going on at the moment that they are excited about, interested in or proud of? Work around the room, giving each person 30–60 seconds to share their positive update. This process shouldn't take longer than five minutes in total but will generate a burst of positive emotion to get your meeting off to a happy start.

2. **Get clear on purpose.** All meetings should have a stated purpose or agenda. If you're not clear on the type of meeting you should be having, then you probably won't achieve the outcome you want. For instance, are you meeting to solve a problem, make a decision, share information, hear a presentation or brainstorm ideas? Unless everyone understands why they've come together, you could run into obstacles. For instance, with brainstorming sessions the goal is to maximise creativity by producing as many ideas as possible, not to commit to actions or decisions. Team members should stay open-minded and withhold their judgement and analysis of ideas for another discussion. If that doesn't happen, you may find that people are scared to voice their ideas for fear of others shooting them down. Make sure you clearly articulate the purpose of the meeting and outline what you want to achieve during and after it so that it doesn't turn into an aimless social gathering.

3. **Engage the team in dialogue.** During the meeting, encourage full participation by directly soliciting input from each team member. Aim to get all viewpoints and ideas out in the open. Use the 80/20 rule to govern your communication. This dictates that you spend the majority of your time (80 per cent) listening and the minority (20 per cent) of your time talking. Actively listen to others and be attentive to body language. Ask open-ended questions to facilitate a discussion where

team members can feel comfortable to share their ideas or reach the right conclusions and answers for themselves. Make sure you reinforce and acknowledge positive participation so team members feel good about their involvement. This helps to keep the conversation flowing smoothly. If conflict arises, steer people towards the positive by recognising merit in everyone's position.

4. **Get buy-in for action.** Towards the end of your meeting, elicit buy-in and accountability for the decisions made and agree on the action steps that need to take place to move the company or team forward. Summarise an action plan – who will do what and when? Delegate follow-up responsibilities. Identify unfinished agenda items and determine ways to address them.

5. **Wrap it up with a smile.** Summarise what's been accomplished and highlight the positive contributions made by the team. This is your moment to make sure everyone leaves the room feeling good and not like they've wasted their time. Comment on what you liked about the discussion, what you learned and/or why it was successful: 'It was great to get so many different perspectives on the problem. I feel like we've examined every angle thoroughly in making this decision.' Alternatively, ask the team what they think worked well in the meeting or what they found most valuable. This gives people a chance to review what they liked about the way the meeting was handled and the positive things they can take away from it. Remind everyone about the big picture and show enthusiasm for where the company is headed. End the meeting with a genuine smile and thank everyone sincerely for their thoughtful contributions.

I (INTERACTIVE ENVIRONMENT)

Create a fun, interactive work environment for your team to help strengthen social bonds and engagement. Try the following ideas to foster more social connections and add an enjoyable dimension to work:

- **Eat together.** Invite your co-workers to lunch and get to know them as people so you can relate to each other better. Make it easy for co-workers to dine together whenever possible too (e.g. by providing free food or flexible cafeteria opening times). It's a great way for them to get their social needs met and encourage happiness at work.

- **Affinity groups.** Allow employees to set up groups around common interests, such as sports clubs, women's networks, book clubs, walking groups, cooking classes or choirs. These help to build camaraderie and enhance peoples' physical, mental, emotional and/or spiritual wellbeing. Demonstrate your support for these activities by providing funding and facilities, or offer your help in developing a communications strategy to promote the clubs throughout the organisation.

- **Celebrate events.** Small office celebrations for birthdays, graduations, births or team wins are ideal for forging relationships and encouraging a nurturing 'family-like' environment. Inject more fun into a humdrum week by randomly celebrating an unusual occasion such as Bubble Gum Day or Grandparent's Day.

- **Social space.** Give teams space and time so that moments of social connection can develop on their own. Provide a designated area for people to hang out and chat without disturbing other team members. Make it inviting with comfy seats and a coffee machine to indicate that it's OK for people to kick back and socialise for a bit.

- **Make introductions.** One of the easiest and fastest ways to increase social connections in your organisation is to introduce two people from different departments that have never met before. If you think two people would benefit from knowing each other, either in a work or personal capacity, then put them in touch.

- **Fuel team spirit.** Encourage teamwork and spark a sense of community through formal and informal team-building activities. There are lots of ideas for team outings, games and away days out there on the internet to help you connect with your colleagues in or out of the office, e.g. hikes, dinners, bowling. Opt for activities that will appeal to the majority of team members, not a small sub-set, so that everyone can feel comfortable to participate. Encourage greater collaboration amongst project teams or working groups by providing spaces for brainstorming and knowledge sharing. Visual tools such as mind mapping software (e.g. iMindMap from OpenGenius) are handy for helping teams capture and organise information collectively. Use video conferencing software, next-generation chatrooms or enterprise social network technologies like Yammer to build networks and strengthen relationships when people work in different locations.

A (APPRECIATE OTHERS)

Everyone, from the CEO to the office cleaner, wants to feel that they're appreciated for who they are and what they do. If we take time to notice what we value and appreciate about others, we can open the door to great work relationships. This is because when we 'appreciate' something we not only *recognise* its value, we also *increase* its value, just as money in the bank can appreciate. Make a sincere effort to compliment your team or your peers whenever you can. In particular, show your approval of positive behaviours such as honesty, effort, reliability, passion, relationship building and helpfulness. Here are some tips for effective appreciation:

- **Make it a habit:** People feel more motivated and valued when they're given regular positive reinforcement, so compliment small things frequently rather than big things infrequently. Don't wait to give recognition, do it promptly after the event.

- **Public praise:** Show your appreciation in a visible way so others in the organisation can see what's happening. You can mention someone in the company newsletter or praise them at a management meeting or company event in front of their peers.

- **Be specific:** Rather than simply saying 'good job' or 'glad you work with me', offer team mates specific and enthusiastic praise on their work and emphasise how they have contributed to broader business objectives. Make it clear what you want to see more of.

- **Praise the process:** If you only praise outcomes, people will come to believe that only good outcomes matter. Praising the process demonstrates that good working behaviour is important too. For instance, recognise when someone has taken a creative approach, been extra thorough in their reporting, handled their communications well or gone above and beyond the call of duty on a project.

- **Thank you notes:** These could be written on an email, card, Post-it Note or letter. The method is not so important as the meaning behind it.

- **Give a gift:** Be generous and reward a colleague with a small gift such as concert or sports tickets, a plaque, gift voucher, cash award, certificate of achievement, time off work or a thank you lunch.

- **Involve the family:** Treat the person and their whole family with a gift card for lunch, dinner or a show. This is a great reward when someone has worked excessive overtime at the expense of their family. Send a letter of thanks and flowers to their home for even more of a personal touch.

- **Grow their talents:** Offer rewards in the form of education or training to help people develop their strengths and passions, such as a seminar or workshop. Or hire a personal coach for them.

- **Share the love.** Gather your team together and ask all participants to write down two or three things they appreciate about each other on Post-it notes.[22] People should focus on what they are grateful for in their team members – whether their strengths, the things they do or the times they have shared together during their work relationship. Create a table or mind map of the team on a whiteboard/flipchart and post the sticky notes under each person's name. This is a fantastic feel-good activity for establishing a team culture of appreciation.

- **Use the Praise-Question-Polish (PQP) technique.** When you sit down to do a performance appraisal or peer review, follow this formula: First, *praise* the person or team by hunting out as many good things as possible and highlighting what went well. Next, ask *questions* around issues or aspects of performance that you're not sure about. Finally, *polish* off by offering suggestions on how to build on strengths or make a process even better.

L (LEARN)

Increase your social investment and deepen personal connections by getting to know those you work with better. Every month, make it a goal to learn *one new thing* about each member of your team, which you can then reference or discuss in later conversations. This could be something social (non-work goals, pets, hobbies, children's names, favourite foods or holiday spots) or work-related (professional strengths, working style, responsibilities they enjoy, career aspirations). Invite different co-workers to breakfast or lunch and talk about *them*, not work or current issues. Leaders that foster this kind of familiarisation and interest will help people feel more understood, validated and cared for. It's also an excellent

---

[22] Gladis, Steve (2013). *Positive Leadership: The Game Changer at Work*. Annandale: Steve Gladis Leadership Partners.

opportunity to learn ways in which you can help others with the things that really matter to them (and ways that they can help you). If you're new to a team or organisation, adopt a 'learning attitude' from day one. You're probably brimming with new ideas, but don't assume you already know what's what and go about implementing aggressive changes without first getting to know who people are, what they do and how they do it. It's important to learn the ropes fully and gather ideas before you start flexing your leadership muscles, otherwise you risk alienating your team. Instead of believing you have all the answers, assume you still have lots to learn and ask questions to figure out everything you can about the culture, processes, systems and people you're dealing with (especially the people!). This is all-important for earning your team's trust and respect, and for getting their buy-in for big changes. Once you really know your team and their strengths, you'll be ready to lead them to success.

Conclusion: your happiness/success story

'Success is reaching the top; happiness has no ceiling.'
UNKNOWN

Well, you made it to the end of the book. Thanks for reading – I hope that the insights and tools have inspired you to become the best, most authentic leader you can be. We've covered a lot of ground together and I'd like to leave you with some final words of encouragement as you begin your positive leadership journey.

Things have changed dramatically in the last decade or so. The business landscape has gone from hierarchical to flat, multiple processes have been reconfigured or outsourced, there is increased transparency, time constraints are tighter, expectations are higher, and the boundaries between leaders and their teams are breaking down. Though this fluctuating new world offers more ways to innovate and succeed, it offers just as many ways to fail. You simply cannot rely on traditional command-and-control leadership anymore. Focusing on short-term performance to the detriment of long-term team engagement and wellbeing is the loser's route to burnout and disaster. The most up-to-date psychology research is unanimous in telling you that the only way to win as a leader is to be one of the good guys.

The snippets of knowledge shared in this book illustrate the positive principles, skills and behaviours that we can all benefit from to become better leaders in the current age. When you capitalise on positive psychology, you're doing far more than maximising your own wellbeing and productivity. There is a true ripple effect in action – by trying to make yourself happier and more successful, you actually spark the ability to unlock the potential and improve the lives of the people around you. Happiness is literally contagious, bringing benefits to your team, your organisation and society as a whole.

The *4Ps of Positive Leadership* model is your template for happy leading and living. By targeting the four positive dimensions of *People* (strengths and engagement), *Purpose* (mission and vision), *Process* (energy management) and *Place* (the happiness path), it provides you with the framework and tools you need to understand your team better, to guide them in positive directions and nurture them so they remain happy and fulfilled. And it gives you the power to be YOU to your fullest by helping you wake up to who you are and what you really want. Use it as the catalyst to discover your strengths and ultimate purpose, so you can optimise your life and create success in ways that really matter. Allow it to guide you as you venture on your positive leadership journey – a journey where you expertly balance your energy and focus on happiness while pursuing your unique personal mission and aiming high towards your biggest vision.

The positive leadership journey

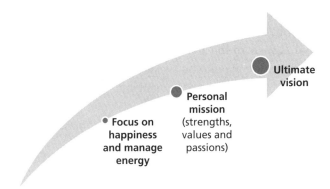

I truly believe this book represents the spirit of the times and offers hope, optimism and possibility for modern leaders. With positive leadership, you're no longer limited to either/or situations and choices – either you're nice or you're tough; either it's quality or quantity; either it's this way or that way; either you win or you lose. The 4Ps approach demonstrates that success doesn't always have to come at a cost and that you can accomplish wins across the board:

- You don't have to be good at everything to be a wildly successful leader.
- You can be 100 per cent yourself and still command respect.
- You can acknowledge people's weaknesses and still build great teams that deliver.
- You can lead with your heart as well as your mind.

- You can serve your team and organisation while still building value for yourself.
- You can do the things you love and still drive superb results.
- You can stop chasing time and build more energy while getting things done.
- You can become a trailblazing, profit-rolling leader and still benefit the wider world.
- You can experience happiness on the way to success, and your team can too!

No matter if you're a boss of 5 people or 500, the leader of a bank, a hospital, school or start-up, you can plug into the power of positivity to inspire your team, get stand-out results and do it in the happiest way possible. Just imagine – if we all choose to play to our strengths, be authentic in our missions and lead with positivity, what might our companies be like? Our communities? The world? I hope that some of the ideas in this book will help you discover a new and meaningful pleasure in how you live and work, and empower you to leave a positive footprint in the history of humankind.

I wish you all the best in creating your very own happiness/success story.

Jan Mühlfeit

What did you think of this book?

We're really keen to hear from you about this book, so that we can make our publishing even better.

Please log on to the following website and leave us your feedback.

It will only take a few minutes and your thoughts are invaluable to us.

www.pearsoned.co.uk/bookfeedback

Next steps

Get hands-on help, training and tools to support your leadership development and unlock your team's potential.

Positive leadership resources and templates

Join us online and gain exclusive access to handy resources and templates from the book at http://positiveleaderbook.com/

- Uncover your strengths and put them into action.
- Find your flow and empower your team with meaningful challenges.
- Effectively manage your energy.
- Set goals for happiness.

Speaking

Jan Mühlfeit is recognised as an engaging and thought-provoking speaker, having lectured to audiences worldwide on topics spanning business, education, personal development and technology. He is the ideal speaker for groups and organisations looking to play to their strengths and create a positive environment in which to grow and succeed.

To book Jan for a speaking event, email jan@muhlfeit.com
Learn more about Jan at http://janmuhlfeit.com/en/

Follow Jan on social media

Twitter: @janmuhlfeit
Facebook: https://www.facebook.com/janmuhlfeit
LinkedIn: https://cz.linkedin.com/in/muhlfeit

OpenGenius leadership training courses

Learn fresh leadership skills and build a positive working culture that will catapult your organisation to new heights of success and happiness. The following UK-based courses are endorsed by Jan Mühlfeit:

- Creative Leadership 5-Day Accredited Course – Cardiff, UK.
- Positive Leadership 1-Day Workshop – Cardiff, UK.
- Bespoke Company Training – OpenGenius in-house training days are tailored to fit the needs of your organisation. Our training experts are passionate about delivering unique and objective-driven courses at your chosen location.

For more information, visit www.OpenGenius.com

Productivity software

Plan, manage and achieve anything, beautifully. A visual task management app that offers a simple and fluid way to get things done. FREE version available. Visit www.DropTask.com

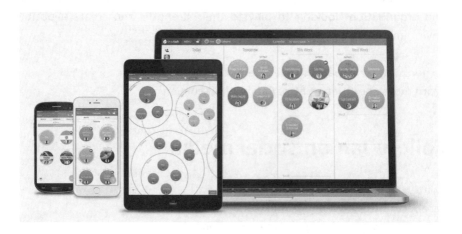

Index

gratitude 253–6
health boost 12
identifying successful strategies for 252
and income 231–5, 237
life circumstances 238
model *241*, 242–3
non-comparison with others 263–6
path to 245–50
personal mission 245, 246
quick wins 269–73
set point (genetic capacity) 238
strategy-fit 252, 253
subjective happiness scale 239–40
versus success xvi, xxiv, 236–45
toolkit 253–73
treats, looking forward to 262–3
and uniqueness 245–50, 264–5
and wealth 231–5
Harris, Russ 223, *224*
Harvard Business Review 193
health
    see also burnout and stress; diet and nutrition
    effect of happiness on 12
    habits 198–200
health screenings 188–9
Hebeler, Peter 109–10
hedonic adaptation 235
hedonist archetype 242–3, 245
Hewlett Packard 177
hierarchy of needs theory (Maslow) 123–6, 127, 233, 234
    see also needs
honesty 277
Human Capital Trends study, Deloitte University (2014) 177–8
human potential, as 'new' competitive advantage xx–xxi
hyperventilation 207

iDoneThis.com 273
important issues, focus on 216–18, 265–6
'Imposter Syndrome' 44–5
incentive theories 123
income, and happiness 231–5, 237
influence, circle of 271
information overload 178–9

inspiration 119–20
    see also motivation; visionaries
    being inspired 104, 105–6
    as being in-Spirit 104
    higher 104–6
    and motivation 122
    needs 125, 234
    providing 104, 105–6, 108
Instagram 265
Institute of Leadership & Management (ILM) xix
insulin 196
integrity 277
Intel 215
interactive environment 297–8
Internet Trends report (2013) 178
interruption, effects of 180–1
intrinsic knowledge 5
introductions, making 298
introversion 21, 56, 252
intuition or sensing 21
IQ (Intelligent Quotient), limitations of 14
Isen, Alice 285–6

James, Henry 280
Japan 233
Jay, Joelle 71–2
Jelinek, Marian 112
job orientation 80, 81, 82
Jobs, Steve 106
Johari Window 27–8
journaling 254, 255
judgement 21, 25
Junior Achievement (youth organisation) 128, 287

Kahneman, Daniel 231, 273
Kami, Mike xiv
Kasser, Tim 127
Keller, Helen 251
Kenexa Research Institute 11
kindness, acts of 259–61
King, Laura xviii, xix
King, Martin Luther 42, 103, 107
Kleiner Perkins Caufield & Byers (venture capital firm) 178
knowledge
    additional, gaining 34, 58
    external versus intrinsic 5

real-world mission statement
    examples 134
team/company strengths 135
values 135–6
work orientations (job versus career
    versus calling) 79–88, 100, 112, 125
working hours 81, 165, 166
work–life balance 34, 147, 209, 259
'Work–Life Questionnaire' (University of
    Pennsylvania) 82
workplace
    energy management 193–4
    social connections in 292–3
    stress in 151–2
    triggering flow in 86–8

Worthington, Everett 268–9
Wright, Frank Lloyd 127
Wrzesniewski, Amu 80

Yale Center for Emotional Intelligence
    185
YouGov (research firm) 146–7
youth organisations 128

Zenger, Jack 35, 276
Zenger, John 18, 105–6
Zes, David 4
'Zorro Circle' 271–2
Zuckerberg, Mark 116